Advance Praise for *I Am the Warrior*

"If you know what a VJ is, Holly Knight's songs are woven into your DNA. She is why you sing at the top of your lungs along with Patty Smyth and Scandal, 'Shooting at the walls of heartache bang bang I am the warrior!' Holly is the reason Pat Benatar grabbed our attention singing 'We are young, heartache to heartache' at the beginning of the epic 'Love Is A Battlefield,' and she is the one who gave Tina Turner the soaring tour de force, 'The Best.' In *I Am the Warrior: My Crazy Life Writing the Hits and Rocking the MTV Eighties*, you'll find out how these and more classics came to be, the path they took to the superstars who sang them, and how they became an integral part of the I Want My MTV years."

—Martha Quinn, MTV VJ

"People who grew up in the eighties tell me that MTV was the soundtrack to their lives...Holly Knight deserves much of the credit. Few songwriters have written such a diverse collection of songs for such a broad range of superstars. You may never have met Holly, but you know her heart from all its journeys through pleasure, pain, obsession, temptation, slow burns, flaws and battlefields. In a decade steeped in the superficial, Holly Knight's songs helped us know love in all its different iterations. Holly Knight is simply the best."

—Alan Hunter, MTV VJ

"Holly Knight is one of the greatest songwriters of our generation. For my money there was no one writing female empowerment anthems and exploring the depths and difficulties of love in the eighties better than Holly. Some of our most legendary music moments on MTV (Tina Turner, Pat Benatar, Patty Smyth) were soundtracked with a Holly Knight song! The eighties...and MTV would not have been the same without her!"

—Mark Goodman, MTV VJ

"I have a profound respect for great songwriters and Holly Knight is just that. One would be hard pressed to turn on the radio or television during MTV's Golden era and NOT hear one of her hits. Tina Turner, Patty Symth, Aerosmith, John Waite are just a few who have recorded her songs. Holly's new memoir takes us behind the scenes of her creative process and her incredible life during those wonderfully heady times. She writes prose as she writes lyrics—straight from the heart, revealing, vulnerable yet strong. Holly Knight is a fierce musical talent and is indeed The Warrior!"

—Nina Blackwood, MTV VJ

"I remember seeing Holly at Record Plant studios in New York while we were recording *Unmasked*. And we had decided we needed a keyboard/synth on one of our songs. I remembered Holly played keys, so I walked into the studio lounge and asked her if she'd like to play on one of our tunes. She jumped up, hurriedly went into the studio and rocked. We loved it. So, we had a quick side conference and then we asked Holly if she'd like to play on the whole album. Big smiles all around. She cancelled whatever she was doing that day, and stayed in the studio with us late into the night. I didn't know it back then, but Holly would soon turn into a songwriter powerhouse. I boast: "Holly Knight? Oh yeah. I know her!""

—Gene Simmons, KISS

"Holly Knight wrote some of the best and toughest songs for female artists. Her songs helped pave the way for women in rock. Not to mention a few dudes. I heard 'The Warrior' once and knew it was a hit. It was a joy to sing. It felt like a perfect match for my voice. Still does. Holly is a badass and always will be."

—Patty Smyth

I AM THE WARRIOR

MY CRAZY LIFE WRITING THE HITS AND ROCKING THE MTV EIGHTIES

HOLLY KNIGHT

PERMUTED
PRESS

A PERMUTED PRESS BOOK
ISBN: 978-1-63758-439-2
ISBN (eBook): 978-1-63758-440-8

I Am the Warrior:
My Crazy Life Writing the Hits and Rocking the MTV Eighties
© 2022 by Holly Knight
All Rights Reserved

Courtesy of Sony Music Archives. Photographer: Ken Nahoum
Cover art by Donna McLeer / Tunnel Vizion Media

PERMUTED
PRESS

Permuted Press, LLC
New York • Nashville
permutedpress.com

Published in the United States of America
1 2 3 4 5 6 7 8 9 10

To anyone who ever had a dream and was told "No."

CONTENTS

Foreword ix

Prologue xi

Chapter One: My Arrival.. 1
    New York City, 1956

Chapter Two: In Film Noir (Spider) 13
    New York City, 1977–1980

Chapter Three: The Demon, the Joker, and the One with
    the Star on His Eye (KISS).. 25
    New York City, 1979

Chapter Four: In Fujicolor (Spider) 48
    Los Angeles, 1980–1982

Chapter Five: I Want My MTV... 68
    New York City, 1981

Chapter Six: Learning to Make Paper Airplanes (Pat Benatar)............. 70
    Beverly Hills, 1983

Chapter Seven: A Night in Heaven ("Obsession")................................81
    Los Angeles, 1983

Chapter Eight: Bang, Bang, I Am the Warrior (Patty Smyth)................87
    Los Angeles, Malibu, 1984

Chapter Nine: "We Fell Out" (Divinyls) 93
    Los Angeles, 1985

Chapter Ten: How I Met the Acid Queen (Tina Turner)...................... 99
    Los Angeles, 1985

Chapter Eleven: Night of the Thirty Toes (Heart) 112
    Los Angeles, 1985

Chapter Twelve: "Well Done, Young Lady!" (Rod Stewart)................. 127
    Los Angeles, 1985

Chapter Thirteen: We Will Be Invincible (Pat Benatar)....................... 147
    Los Angeles, 1986

Chapter Fourteen: 22B3 (Device) 154
    Los Angeles, 1985

Chapter Fifteen: Living In a Haunted House
    (Elvira, Mistress of the Dark)..162
    Los Angeles, 1986

Chapter Sixteen: So You Wanna Be a Cowboy? (Bon Jovi) 167
    Los Angeles, 1986

Chapter Seventeen: I Love a Man Who Takes Charge
    (Don Johnson) 176
    Los Angeles, 1987

Chapter Eighteen: We Got a Soul Love (Hall & Oates)....................... 186
    New York City & Los Angeles 1987

Chapter Nineteen: Why I Put My Dress on Inside Out
    (Steven Tyler) 197
    Los Angeles & Vancouver, 1987

Chapter Twenty: Slow Burn (Ozzy Osbourne).................................... 211
    Los Angeles, 1988

Chapter Twenty-One: Simply the Best (Tina Turner)...........................219
    Los Angeles, 1987–1990

Afterword 235
    New York City, 2013

Songs I Wish I Had Written.. 239

Discography... 246

Song Permissions 253

Acknowledgments... 256

About the Author 258

FOREWORD

*I*t seems a lifetime ago that I first heard "The Best." It's not a song that I've carried—but rather a song that has carried me around the world. The energy it gave me on stage lifted me and the audience, a rare treasure—a universal anthem. Including "The Best," over the years I've counted nine of Holly's songs in my repertoire: "Better Be Good to Me," "Wildest Dreams," "Be Tender with Me Baby," "One of the Living," "Do Something," "Love Thing," "Ask Me How I Feel," and "You Can't Stop Me Loving You."

I felt Holly's words and music often synchronized with what I needed or wanted in that moment.

Those songs have something special—a connection that deeply resonated with people around the globe. Holly has been so graceful and generous to lend me the words and melodies that inspired her.

Holly—I've said it to you before, and I say it now, again, indeed, you are simply the best.

Love,

Tina (Turner)
Zurich, Switzerland

You can't feed me to the wolves,

they come when I call.

PROLOGUE

Back when I started, there were a handful of emerging songwriters who were granted access into the inner sanctums of some pretty big rock bands and solo artists, a sort of "songwriters' elite." I was one of them, although, being a woman, I was the anomaly. I didn't mind being the only one; in fact, I loved it. We were all aware of each other, and sometimes we even wrote together when we weren't busy competing to get cuts on the same albums. I was already a legitimate recording artist, having released two albums and toured with my rock band Spider. I wrote from a place of firsthand experience. It's a different view from the stage than in the audience.

With so few opportunities for women in rock 'n' roll to flourish, we were considered a rare breed, and while it seems that we still are, you'd be surprised how many virtuosos exist—lead guitarists, drummers, bass players, pretty much every instrument. The belief had always been that girls can't rock. What utter crap. From day one, I walked right into the man cave like it was nothing, like I had every right to be there. To say it wasn't without its challenges would be an understatement, and of course, there was plenty of ass-grabbing—on both sides.

An interviewer once asked me, "Why are so many of your songs about fighting?"

"They're not all like that," I responded. "I write about a lot of things."

"But there's this thread of going into battle that runs through some of your biggest songs," he said. "It's not a bad thing, it's very compelling."

I'd never thought about it until that moment, but he'd asked a potent question. When I got home, I went through the titles of some of my biggest songs—"Love Is a Battlefield," "The Warrior," "Invincible," "Better Be Good to Me"—and realized he was right. How had I missed something so vital? After some raw soul-searching, I was able to piece together this much—my songs were more about fighting *for something*, rather than *with someone*. And my weapon of choice was my songs. The "why?" is the question, and a rather hefty one that's taken years of therapy to unravel. I've come to the realization that adversity is not the enemy. It's a gift. If you want something bad enough, you have to show the world that you're not screwing around.

I've been fighting my whole life for the things that mattered to me. It started when I was a child—"I don't like it when you hit me!"—but as I got older, I was able to articulate in a more elegant and creative manner what was most important to me: independence, autonomy, expressing my own voice, anarchy in all its glory, and, essentially, telling people to fuck off in a clever way.

I write songs for a living. I would have done it for free. As it turned out, I didn't have to, which is a good thing because I didn't have a Plan B.

CHAPTER ONE

MY ARRIVAL

New York City, 1956

"Be tender with me baby for always..."
("Be Tender With Me" performed by Tina Turner)

My tiny legs didn't reach the floor when I climbed onto the piano bench, but even at two years of age I knew that music was going to be my first language. I'm a New York City native through and through, born and raised in Manhattan. Being a New Yorker is so embedded in my blood that I have no doubt it has mutated the genetic code of my DNA. No matter where I am, even in California, where I've lived for thirty-eight years, people can tell right away that I'm from New York, even though I have little trace of an accent, except when I get pissed off and say "ga-hed" instead of "go ahead." I proudly, or naively, believe that growing up in the big bad city has given me some cred: yes, I'm a survivor, a (mostly) peaceful warrior. I learned how to take care of myself at a young age, which only served me well throughout my life. My favorite color is black, and I say fuck an awful lot. It's a New York thing.

My family has always been small. My father, Herbert Erlanger, was an only child, as was my mother, so I had no aunts or uncles, and no first cousins. My paternal grandmother Alice was born in Vienna, and my paternal grandfather Gustav and my father were born in Berlin. Both my grandparents were surgeons, and being Jewish, they were extremely fortunate to have patients who warned them of the impending doom: "Get out of Germany while you still can." Heeding their advice, they were forced to leave their robust and prominent medical practice behind, borrowing money from relatives in Switzerland. After crossing the Atlantic on the S.S. *Washington* in 1935 and setting foot on American soil, they set about rebuilding their lives, taking up residence in a prewar building on the Upper West Side of Manhattan, directly across the street from some very large dinosaurs housed in the Museum of Natural History.

Young Herb was just eleven when they arrived, but he adjusted quickly to American life and embraced the culture. After graduating from Columbia University, he continued his education, earning his medical degree from the College of Physicians & Surgeons. He became a resident anesthesiologist at New York Hospital, and on the day I was born, all he had to do was take an elevator up to the nursery to meet me for the first time. He'd made the same journey two years earlier with my brother, Robert.

My mother, Marilyn Shusterman, graduated from Hunter College and worked at the same hospital; she was a hematologist, and that's how my parents met. Her father was from the Ukraine; he was Grandpa Jack to me, and I adored him. My mother's mother, Ethel, was from Boston. When I was four years old, my mother began taking piano lessons from "Uncle" Richard, a German friend of the family who was a concert pianist. To say that he was overqualified to be a piano teacher would be an understatement, but he had agreed to do it as a favor to her. She wasn't very good, but as I listened to her hack away at each piece she tried to learn, I'd pretend to play the piano on any available surface, even my legs. Once she would go in the kitchen to start preparing dinner, I'd creep into the living room, climb on the bench and pick out the music I'd heard Richard play so beautifully. After a few weeks of this, my mother acknowledged that I was the one who had inherited the musical talent in the family.

"Holly, would you like to take piano lessons?"

I yelped with joy and cried out, "Yes!" as I flung my arms around her.

That's when Gordana Lazarevich, a pretty, young woman from Belgrade, Serbia, entered my life. At eighteen, she had immigrated to Canada with her family and, at twenty-one, started teaching me piano while attending Julliard to earn her master's. She would go on to obtain her doctorate from Columbia University. Gordana looked like Julie Andrews, specifically Maria from *The Sound of Music*. I studied with her for seven years. I loved my time with her so much that when she took a summer job as the music counselor at Camp Waseosa on Lake Ontario, Canada, I begged my mother to send me there so I could continue my lessons with her. I was seven when I started camp, and for eight blissful weeks for three consecutive summers, I enjoyed the cool, fresh outdoors, music lessons, and a loving relationship with Gordana, a vast improvement over muggy New York summers and my mother's hot disposition. For those eight summer weeks I felt safe and loved.

When I turned eleven, Gordana broke the sad news to me that she had accepted a teaching position at Barnard College and wouldn't be able to tutor me any longer. I was devastated. I not only adored her, but secretly wished she was my mother.

My real mother got it in her head that she was going to start grooming me as a future concert pianist—if she couldn't play, then she was going to make sure that I did. I didn't mind. It was only when it got in the way of being a kid and having friends, when I would get punished if I didn't do well with both my report card and my piano studies, that it became a drag. She had managed to turn something I loved with my entire being into a chore. After Gordana left, my mother sent me to Mannes School of Music for four years, a more formal school on the upper east side that was a breeding ground for classical performers.

I grew up in a household filled with music, a melting pot of styles and cultures. My mother loved Indian music and took me to Ravi Shankar concerts whenever he was in New York; we listened to African singers like Miriam Makeba; we often went to a place called The Cookery in the West Village to listen to Alberta Hunter sing the blues; and then there were the Broadway musicals that we not only went to, but whose cast records spun on our record player day and night. My favorites were *Gigi*, *Flower Drum Song*, *Lili*, *South Pacific*, and *My Fair Lady*. I loved all the Rogers and Hammerstein and Lerner and Lowe musicals. Once, upon returning from a trip to Jamaica, my mom brought back ska records before anyone in America had ever heard of it. If she went to a Greek restaurant for dinner, she'd come back with a Greek record she'd bought at the cash register. Music was the one place where my mother and I connected. Had it not been for that, we would have had nothing in common. There's no question that she fostered my desire to be a musician, at least until I discovered rock music. She hated rock, with the exception or one or two mellow Beatles songs like "Michelle" and "Yesterday." She thought the rest was noise and that rock musicians were degenerates.

For me, the seas parted once I discovered rock music. I think the first time was on some kid's transistor radio in the school yard, and it really made me sit up and pay attention. I was nine. I ran out and bought a couple of records with some money I'd saved. One was The Beatles' *Rubber Soul* and another one was the Rolling Stones' *December's Children*. The volume I listened at was deafening. I didn't want to just hear the kick drum, I wanted to feel it. Unlike classical music, the songs had words, and the content was either rebellious or romantic. I liked the Stones even more than The Beatles. They were scruffier and more glamorous. Their lyrics spoke to me. I didn't know why yet, they just did. I kept my records a secret from my mother in the beginning, only listening to them when she was out shopping or at work.

Then I discovered the Doors and fell in love with Jim Morrison, just like I had with James Bond, the Sean Connery version. I had fantasies about both in my prepubescent slumber.

Together, they formed my idea of the perfect man, creative and dangerous.

When I first heard Led Zeppelin, I embraced their heaviness and the intense level of sexuality that Robert Plant exuded. I listened to softer artists as well, like Joni Mitchell, the Mamas & the Papas, Crosby, Stills, Nash & Young, and the Carpenters. I sang along to Motown, especially the Supremes, whose songs always lifted my spirits. Black Sabbath came next, then Todd Rundgren and Frank Zappa. I was exposed to a lot of great and diverse music. Still, hands down, my favorite genre was rock.

For my eleventh birthday, my grandmother Alice pooled together what little money she had with my father, and together they took me to the Steinway showroom on 57th Street, directly across from Carnegie Hall. They patiently waited for hours while I played every piano in the showroom, and when I sat down to the very last one, a black satin five-foot-seven grand, I knew it was the one. *Hello, soulmate.* They bought it for me, and the following week it was sitting in our apartment on East 70th Street in the same spot the previous spinet had been. That piano is the centerpiece of my recording studio. I've written many hits on it, including "The Best."

The dysfunctional dynamic between my mother and father was volatile and dramatic. They had this visceral attraction to one another, but they had nothing in common personality-wise and couldn't have been more different. The same year I got the Steinway, they divorced. Music was a place I could escape to that was all mine, far from the hostility around me.

My mother was not a happy person and I never knew why. Even when I was an adult, she would never discuss her childhood or the source of her rage. She certainly had a flair for drama. In contrast to the fantastic birthday present that Herb and Alice had bought for me, there was my mother's present—a haircut. For weeks she had been threatening to take me somewhere to get my hair cut short because I didn't brush it enough. Each time I pleaded with her not to. My long dark hair was the only thing that made me feel remotely pretty.

On the morning of my birthday, at 3:00 a.m., the door to my bedroom flung open and I squinted as the overhead light illuminated the room. She'd decided to cut my hair herself because she knew that I would be too tired and scared to put up a fight at such an ungodly hour. Reaching for the chair beside my desk, she placed it in front of the dresser mirror.

"Sit," she said. I sat down glumly and submitted, too scared to move for fear that she might accidentally cut my face with the scissors. I watched in horror as clumps of my long, chestnut brown hair fell silently in defeat to the floor. When she was finished, she straightened my head, admired her work, and announced, "That's better."

It was short and uneven, one side two inches shorter than the other. I looked awful. I couldn't help muttering under my breath, "Happy now?" I should have kept my mouth shut. I knew her routine by heart, having been through it enough times. She walked over to my closet, and with one grand sweep of her arm, grabbed every piece of clothing I owned and threw it all into the center of the room. Most of it was clothing she had picked out for me, but it was my favorite pin-striped bellbottoms, the ones I'd bought with my own money, that offended her the most. I watched in horror as everything landed on the floor, as if in slow motion. She moved over to my dresser and, one by one, removed each drawer, turning it upside down and emptying the contents onto the floor.

"Mommy please, it's my birthday. Please stop!"

"Look at this goddam mess," she said.

Even the black-and-white TV sitting on top of my dresser didn't escape her wrath as she picked it up and threw it on the floor, crying. Why was she crying? She always cried when she was punishing me, as if it made her miserable too. I think it did. The TV lay upside down on top of the pile with a crack in the screen. She struck me hard on the back, "Don't you ever talk back to me again, do you understand? You're a disgrace. Now clean this mess up!"

My older brother Rob wasn't spared her tirades either, although the lion's share fell on me. I was more defenseless, at least in the beginning. As time went on, it had quite the opposite effect on me, turning me into a fighter. That came later, when I realized I could fight back. For now, if there was a lesson to be gleaned from these violent episodes of hers, it was this: I was a disgrace. She'd said so. She stormed out of the room, slamming the door behind her. Once I heard her bedroom door slam, I started breathing again, welcoming the precious silence. For now, it was over, the storm had moved on. I stood up and looked in the mirror. I didn't recognize the sad little girl staring back at me. No more pretty long hair to hide behind. Silently, I started to pick up my things and put them back where they belonged.

Thinking back on all this craziness, what I find most compelling is how common maternal abuse was amongst creative women back then, so much so that it almost seems cliché, or, at best, a rite of passage. It certainly ignited something fierce in me that said, *I will not be like you. I will be the opposite of you, and I will be special.*

It was the summer of '69. The Beatles' last public performance had taken place earlier in the year on the rooftop of Apple Records, Woodstock had attracted more than 350,000 rock 'n' roll fans, members of a cult led by Charles Manson had murdered five people in Los Angeles, and Apollo 11's Neil Armstrong and Edwin Buzz Aldrin had become the first humans to set foot on the moon.

We lived within walking distance of Central Park on 79th Street and York Avenue, and I would head there to play after school. Often, I'd make my way over to the Metropolitan Museum of Art, which was situated right in the park, and I would find my favorite spot in one of the Egyptian tombs, sit on the cold stones, and do my homework. It was cool and mysterious there, and nobody bothered me. I was on a first name basis with some of the guards. "Okay Miss Holly, closing time." "Thanks Joe. See you tomorrow."

One lazy summer day when I was thirteen, as I was walking through the park, beyond the shrieks and laughter of children playing, I heard music echoing in the distance. I followed it to the source, Bethesda Fountain, the same place where my dad took Rob and me row boating. It had transformed into a hippie mecca for musicians, drug dealers, and kids looking for a place to party. This became my new stomping grounds, and on any given day there would be ten or so musicians jamming on their congas in perfect syncopation, musicians shredding on acoustic guitars, freaks singing and dancing, stoned out of their gourds, and everywhere, the sweet odor of marijuana wafting through the air. Even the dogs were high, and soon enough, so was I.

I befriended a lot of colorful freaks who told me about the Fillmore East, a place they went to see live music. I started sneaking out of the apartment late at night to take the Lexington train downtown to meet my Central Park cronies and head over to the theater on 6th Street. We didn't have much money, so we just talked our way into the back entrance, trading drugs, or simply sneaking in. In years to come, my experience at slipping past the bouncers would come in handy when it came to meeting people and making contacts. The music was so loud you had to shout in someone's ear to say something, and by the end of the night, my voice would be completely trashed. My mother would say, "You know it's just not normal to be so hoarse all the time. You need to go to the doctor."

I saw some truly talented artists play there, ones I had never heard of before who would soon become quite famous if they weren't already: Jimi Hendrix, the Grateful Dead, the Allman Brothers, and Frank Zappa. Hendrix was by far the one that remains indelibly etched in my psyche. His talent was like a superpower. These secret trips down to the Fillmore ignited the first sparks of real passion in my belly, a yearning that merely confirmed what I already suspected every time I put a record on or saw a live performance: I wanted to be a rock star, not because I wanted to become rich and famous, but so I could play the music I wanted to play and fill that empty hole growing inside of me with something other than love. It took a while to figure out, but as an adult I realized that love and creativity contain the same energy. They are one and the same.

When I was fourteen, I got a job at Sam Ash, the legendary music store on 48th Street between 6th and 7th Avenues. It was known as Music Row because of the mecca of music stores that lined the block. Next door to Sam Ash was Manny's, and between those two stores alone, you were just as likely to see a superstar who played Madison Square Garden the night before as a kid in a local band, both buying the same piece of gear. I saw many legends walk through the doors of Sam Ash—Peter Frampton, Ringo Starr, Pete Townshend, and Keith Richards were just a few of them. I liked working in a music store as it put me one step closer to being on the fringe of the music business. But all my coworkers were men, and even at fourteen I had to stave off their stares and advances on more than one occasion. Still, I liked the empowering feeling of earning my own money, something that never changed as I grew older. Self-earned money equaled independence.

I was still attending Mannes School of Music when, at fifteen, I started my freshman year at The High School of Music & Art, sister to the High School of Performing Arts—later named LaGuardia, it was the school depicted in the movie *Fame*. Even though I thought it was cool that Laura Nyro had attended the same high school before me, I hated it there. I was bored by the curriculum and scared every time I took the train up to 135th Street and Convent Avenue.

By this time I'd already had a few boyfriends when Danny Walker, a twenty-year-old drummer with long jet-black hair and emerald-green eyes, entered my life. I'd met him at a farmhouse in New Paltz, a quaint town in upstate New York, when one of my coworkers, Greg, had invited me to go up there with him for the weekend. I'd never have gone, except that he dangled a carrot in front of me by saying there would be a bunch of musicians and everyone was going to jam. I'd never "jammed" with anyone. It was too enticing for me to pass up. Of course, I had to fabricate a story for my mother, but I was getting pretty good at that. I had the best time! I loved playing with the other musicians, it was so easy and natural, and the moment Danny and I laid eyes on each other, we were smitten.

Over the next several months, we continued seeing each other, and, eventually, my mother found out. "You should be focusing on school and your piano studies instead of dating someone twenty years old and acting like a slut!" As a parent now, I can understand her concerns. I *was* very young, but there was nothing normal about my childhood and adolescent years, nothing safe or nurturing, and so, naturally, I went running into the arms of someone who *wanted* to love me.

As the violence at home continued to escalate, I began to think about running away with Danny, although I hadn't seriously considered it enough to form a real plan—not until one day while I was at work when an opportunity miraculously arose. Someone had placed a stack of brochures by the register for a summer program with a newly established institute called The Boston School of Electronic Music. Their curriculum was right on the cutting edge of electronic music, which was beginning to infiltrate the sound of pop music. I was already a devoted fan of Emerson, Lake & Palmer, Kraftwerk, and Walter Carlos (now Wendy Carlos). ELP in particular were one of the first bands to integrate synthesizers into pop rock music. That, combined with Keith Emerson's showmanship and thigh-high boots was all it took to envision myself as the female version of him, one day playing in a band. While Sam Ash had one Arp, and one Minimoog, I wasn't allowed access to them, I was supposed to be working. I wouldn't have known what to do with either anyway, given the chance. I scanned through the brochure and saw a picture of a large room *full* of Arp 2600s and Moog synthesizers. Even Bob Moog was scheduled to come speak. *Holy shit!*

I talked my mother and father into allowing me to go to Boston that summer to attend the school. Those two months forged a strong foundation for me, enabling me to become adept with programming that served me well my entire career. Danny came with me and I was the happiest I had ever been.

One week before I was due to return home, I wrote a gut-wrenching letter to my mother telling her that I wouldn't be coming back. I was too afraid of her. I felt terrible about leaving the rest of my family, my four grandparents, my brother Rob, and even my father whom I was angry with for not intervening and protecting me from her. I said goodbye, not knowing whether I would ever see any of them again. By the time I mailed the letter, we'd made it halfway across the country in Danny's beat-up Ford Econoline van.

We spent the next three years running around the country together, taking odd jobs and collecting unemployment and food stamps everywhere we went, from northern California to Spokane, Washington, then Seattle where we lived for a year. I loved Seattle. It reminded me of Boston. Danny and I talked about putting a band together all the time, but it never fully materialized. We would jam with just drums and keyboards. I was always the more driven one, and I knew it was just a matter of time before I was going to leave him. I just hadn't figured out how, until, on December 17, 1974, I had an epiphany.

We went to see the Beach Boys at Mercer Arena, and I don't know what the hell got into me, but towards the end of the show I went to the front of the crowd and started waving at Mike Love to let me up on stage. There I was, this intent young girl with long, dark hair miming playing a keyboard at his feet. By some miracle, I caught his attention, and in one swift motion, with the help of a few concert-goers, he pulled me up onto the stage eight feet above and led me to a keyboard. As the band launched into "Good Vibrations," he yelled out the chords. "I know the chords!" I yelled back, grinning from ear to ear. I couldn't believe what was happening. I looked out into the audience and knew that this moment was going to shape the rest of my life. Now, I'd been given proof of something I'd always believed in. I'd been given a tiny glimpse of what it was like to be on a big stage in a big theater, playing with a big band. It didn't get any *bigger* than this. The outpouring of adoration from the audience was like a drug that filled up my whole being.

When we got home and went to bed, I looked over at Danny sleeping peacefully. He didn't want or need much, while I wanted it all. It was obvious that I was much more ambitious than him, and I realized that at some point we were going to go our separate ways because he was going to hold me back.

We moved back to Boston, and after two years, there still was no band. Then we reached an all-time low. We couldn't pay the rent on our apartment and ended up squatting in a boarded-up townhouse on Commonwealth Ave. In its heyday it must've been beautiful with all its carved molding and thick Victorian wallpaper. We ran an illegal extension cord into a neighboring garage for electricity and slept on a tattered old mattress on the floor, our roommates the rats that came out at night. One morning I woke up to the acrid smell of fire. At the foot of the mattress, our portable heater had burst into flames. That was it for me. I was homeless, broke, hungry, sick of my boyfriend, and fed up. I had to find a new life for myself because this was utter bullshit. I had to find a way out. Fortunately, the Universe in all its wisdom intervened, aiding and abetting the process.

CHAPTER TWO

IN FILM NOIR (SPIDER)

New York City, 1977–1980

"I fell in love today, never thought I'd feel this way..."
("New Romance" performed by Spider)

I moved back to the film noir city of my youth to find myself. The late 1970s were some of the bleakest years in New York City's history. Bordering on bankruptcy, the mayor cut down the police force, fire, and sanitation departments, and crime flourished. The city was at its edgiest and most dangerous. It was the birth of punk, gonzo journalism, and graffiti. But, considering where I'd been the last four years, with the exception of all the garbage piling up on the sidewalks, I hardly noticed. For me, ping-ponging between jobs, food stamps, and unemployment lines had too long been the norm, so this was a step in the right direction and I was grateful to be back.

I slipped New York City back on like a pair of perfectly broken-in jeans that I hadn't worn in years but still fit me as well as they had before. As soon as my feet hit the pavement, I knew I was home. The electricity and energy felt cathartic, the art and museums, the eternally crowded streets, everything humming on ten all the time. There was familiarity everywhere I went, pockets of the city I knew intimately, and memories that unfolded in my head as I walked through neighborhoods that had witnessed my childhood.

I was back to face my past and take control of my future. I didn't have a single friend I could call, no one I could ring up and say, "Hey, I'm back!" I was utterly alone. I had my family, but there was a lot of healing that needed to take place, if that was even possible, and that was going to take time.

Right before I returned, my grandmother Alice passed away and I was devastated because I hadn't seen her in four years and never had a chance to say goodbye. More than anyone else in my family, she'd inspired me to follow my dreams. Being a doctor takes an inordinate amount of self-determination and diligence. Considering that she became a surgeon in the 1940s—a daring profession for a woman at that time—it was especially admirable. You could be a nurse or a schoolteacher, but a doctor? That took balls. While she had her own anxieties and idiosyncrasies that drove my family nuts, she and I were simpatico. It made sense. I was weird too. Even after her passing, she had somehow managed to rescue me. The lease on her rent-controlled apartment on the Upper West Side of Manhattan was good for another two years. My father decided that I had suffered enough and suggested that I move into her place, offering to pay the rent until I figured things out.

Alice's stylish apartment was in a high-rise building on 70th Street and West End Ave. called Lincoln Towers. The view from the twenty-sixth floor was expansive and stunning. The dark blue ribbon of the Hudson River and the New Jersey Gold Coast lay before me. I hadn't done anything to earn it, but I welcomed the comfort and security with a newfound feeling of hope.

During the four years that I had gone AWOL, I saw my mother once. It was awkward and probably would always be, but for now, there seemed to be some kind of ceasefire as we tiptoed on gilded splinters around each other. We were getting along well enough that I asked her if I could have my Steinway grand. She said, "Yes," and once I had it moved in, I went back to practicing scales and classical music with a renewed fury. One day in the elevator an elegant but sour-looking octogenarian asked me, "Are you the person who lives in 26E?" "Uh, yes, I am," I replied cautiously, bracing for the verbal onslaught she was certainly about to unload on me. Instead, her sourness turned sweet as she said, "You play so beautifully, dear, especially the Beethoven etudes. Do you know any Rachmaninoff?"

I was starting to realize that I could reinvent myself to be what or whomever I wanted to. There was no one to stop me anymore. I was a blank page whose story had yet to be written. This notion was a tiny seed taking hold inside my belly that would germinate over the next several years in the process of asking myself, *Who am I?* It's a question that everyone asks themselves at some point, as if they're describing the protagonist in a book. Are you a villain or a saint, a queen bee or a worker bee, a coward or a warrior?

There were still a number of Alice's possessions in the apartment that I was intending to donate to Goodwill but as I rummaged through it all, I decided to keep most of it. She loved to travel and always brought back treasures from exotic places. Two porcelain lanterns from China, a Grundig radio that picked up stations in India and Japan, French Baccarat martini glasses, and a beautiful set of Viennese china. I kept all the furniture, as it felt comforting to have her lingering presence in the L-shaped studio apartment. I found a coffee-stained black and white photo of her graduation class from medical school and taped it to the refrigerator in the tiny kitchen. She was the only woman among forty men. Amongst all of the dresses and smart suits I gave away, I discovered several little jackets—Chanel, and some other French names that I couldn't pronounce—which I decided to keep. I started to wear them with jeans. I even kept some crazy European hats she had that I found hidden in some round, old fashioned hat boxes on top of a shelf at the back of the dusty closet.

My aspirations hadn't diminished at all. If anything, I was more driven than ever, and was anxious to get out there and start meeting other like-minded musicians. I kept vampire hours, going out every night to clubs and concert halls, catching up on my sleep during the day. "If you need me, I'll be in my coffin," I would joke to my dad. I immersed myself in rock 'n' roll, from the music to the lifestyle, and there was no better place to do this than New York City. It might sound like fun but it was a lonely time for me. I went everywhere on my own. As a result, out of desperation to make friends, I met more people than if I had gone out with an entourage.

Like most urban meccas, the coolest clubs were in the slummiest neighborhoods, and CBGB was the most notorious of them all. The club's name was an acronym for country, bluegrass, and blues, which seemed like a misnomer since the club was famous for showcasing punk bands like Blondie and the Ramones. I ventured downtown whenever there was a local band I wanted to see, hoping to meet people, but the Bowery was a derelict and dangerous neighborhood with homeless people passed out on the sidewalk and crackheads who would wash the windows of the odd car stopped at a red light, the windows always filthier as they drove away. It wasn't the trendy place it is today, where Varvatos, the chic men's clothing store, has taken over the lease. The only thing left to remind anyone that CBGB even existed is its registration as a historical landmark.

I went a lot to Max's Kansas City on Park Avenue and the Bottom Line in the Village, and once they closed for the night, if I was still wide awake, there were always the after-hour clubs and all-night diners. Often, I ended up at the Empire Diner, near the Chelsea Hotel on West 22nd Street, which stayed open until 5:00 a.m., a place where you could keep a cocaine-driven conversation going as the rising sun replaced the candlelight on the tables.

I bought nosebleed seats with what little money I could spare to see the supergroups play Madison Square Garden. Once inside, I would sneak down to the expensive seats close to the stage, and since

I went everywhere solo, it was easy to slip in and out. I'd wait for the bouncer to get distracted by flirting with a few groupies or breaking up a fight, and then sneak past him into the backstage area.

Backstage was an otherworldly place, one where I'd just crossed over to the other side of the looking glass. Unlike the deafening music out front, I could hear it echoing in the distance, along with the soft hush of murmured voices surrounding me. You had to be, or at the very least know, someone of importance to even be there, these royal subjects waiting for an audience with the "royal family." Famous musicians and pop culture celebrities lingered, acting tragically cool and bored with their laminated VIP passes as they waited to be invited into the dressing rooms. Once that happened, those left out would look on in envy as they continued to wait, pretending they were too deep in conversation to notice. Super famous celebs never had to wait, they got ushered in immediately like visiting kings and queens from faraway lands.

I couldn't have been more of an outsider, and I always worried that a roadie was going to come up and ask to see my pass before showing me back out to where the mortals lingered. One night to my surprise, the bass player of the opening act singled me out, inviting me to follow him into a small room. The minute the door shut behind us, he said, "It sure would be nice to get a blow job." He didn't even ask me my name. I ran out of there as fast as my legs could carry me, a feeling of disgust knotting up in my throat.

Overall, I discovered that the best people to hang out with were the rock photographers as they had all-access passes to everything, including the after-parties, and they were the nicest of the lot. Not surprisingly, I noticed they were all men and it occurred to me that the music business wasn't the only place that had a monopoly on hiring men. One night, a photographer I'd been hanging out with said, "Hey, have you been to TRAX? It's this small underground club on 72nd Street and Columbus. A lot of up-and-coming bands play there. I'm going to the after party. Why don't you come with me?"

TRAX was only four blocks from my apartment, and because it was literally underground, there were no windows, which gave it a secret and intimate atmosphere. The black leather banquets lining the walls were in close proximity to one another by design so everyone could hop from one table to the next. It made it pretty easy to make new acquaintances and friends. Almost every night, popular local bands would play a set and every time a supergroup blew through town, they inevitably ended up at TRAX afterwards. I saw many rock stars and wannabes parade through the place over time, the most exciting one being Robert Plant. He was sitting in the booth next to me, and I was too frozen in my spot to do anything but stare at him and his group of friends, wondering what it must be like to be him.

Frequenting these nightclubs was simply the best way to meet people, musicians, and music industry types. Little by little, I met many local musicians. I befriended a group called Riff Raff at one of the Village clubs. They had a cool Stones vibe, and their singer reminded me of Mick Jagger. The guitarist, Ned, owned his own recording studio called Sundragon Recording. He had his shit together for someone so young, which I found inspiring, and we quickly became friends. Right around the corner from his studio on West 20th street was a Gothic Revival church that, in a few years, would be converted into a decadent nightclub—the Limelight, a place where sex, drugs, and loud rock 'n' roll would take place on hallowed ground every night of the week.

On one of my club outings, I met Howie Wyeth, the drummer from Bob Dylan's Rolling Thunder Revue band. Howie was a tall, lanky guy who prided himself in connecting people, always carrying a little black book in his coat pocket. One late evening at Max's Kansas City, he heard me messing around on a keyboard that was still set up on the stage, came over, and introduced himself. "Man, you play really well!" he said, offering his hand. He was such a nice guy and we became fast friends. Call it coincidence or destiny, but one night I ran into him on the street as he was heading down to the West Village to see some friends perform at the Bitter End. Rob Stoner, Dylan's bassist, was playing with his new band Topaz. Howie explained that they had hired a guitarist and drummer to round out the group for some dates until they found more permanent members.

After the gig, we went back to the dressing room and Howie introduced me to the guitarist, Keith Lentin. He had an accent I couldn't place, sort of British, sort of Australian. There was an intense focus about him, like he was going places. But he was quite friendly and he told me how he and the drummer had been playing around town with Link Wray and Robert Gordon. Then he mentioned that they were forming their own band. My ears pricked up.

Howie announced, "Holly plays keyboards. You should get her to join your band. She's really good."

There are always forces at play in the Universe, moments when I somehow know that I'm experiencing a game changer. This was one of those moments. As we talked a little bit longer, Keith mentioned that they wrote their own music. That *really* interested me. We exchanged numbers and promised to connect soon. Then Anton Fig, their drummer, came over and said hello. He had the same strange accent and, before I left, I asked Keith where they were from. "Cape Town, South Africa," he said.

I figured if I didn't hear from Keith in a week, I would call him. I didn't want to seem too anxious, although I was chomping at the bit to talk with him again. The following night, around eleven, I was settling into bed early for a change when the phone rang.

"Hello, is this Holly?"

I recognized Keith's voice immediately. "Yes, it is."

"It's Keith, I met you last night at our gig."

"Of course! I'm glad you called."

"How would you like to come down to our loft in Tribeca? I told Amanda about you and she wants to meet you and play you some of our material."

"I'd love that. What day were you thinking?" I asked.

19

"Now. I could come pick you up in my van."

I looked down at my tank top and underwear. I'd just taken a nice warm bath and was nestled under the covers, starting to fade. *Here's your shot. Get your ass up, you've been waiting for this.* "Sounds great, I'll be waiting for you in the lobby," I answered cheerfully and gave him my address.

This was my shot. I could feel it in my gut. Keith and Anton were already playing with professional recording artists, which would put me closer to that circle, and they were exceptionally good musicians, ready to go with the same amount of enthusiasm and drive that I had.

Keith pulled up and I climbed into the van. As we headed downtown on the west side, the darkened streets rife with potholes, Keith shared more about them. He and Anton had known each other since they were little kids. Like me, they'd become musicians at an early age, and they'd grown up playing in various bands together in Cape Town. Keith met Amanda, the young daughter of a man he worked for, and who, while still a diamond in the rough, was an unusually talented singer with a unique style. When Keith and Anton applied to two different music colleges in America at the same time—Boston's famed Berklee and the New England Conservatory of Music—they were each accepted to their respective schools and moved to the States. By then, Keith and Amanda had fallen in love and gotten married, and they even had a little girl name Chay. Once both men had graduated, the gigs with Topaz brought the three of them down to New York, where they decided to set up camp in the downtown loft.

They lived in a five-flight walkup with no elevator, just creaky, decaying wooden stairs that went straight up with no landings. The building was old and had been built for manufacturing, so the ceilings were high. One flight of stairs seemed like two, and it felt more like a ten-flight walkup. Anton lived there with Amanda, Keith, and Chay. I liked them all right away. Amanda was quite striking with dark brown hair and sea green eyes, and she was outgoing and friendly with me. They played me some rough recordings of ideas they had, and I really liked her voice. She didn't sound like anyone else. Even though she was a rock singer, she had a lot of soul, at times reminding me of Tina Turner and Kate Bush.

The loft was in a nondescript industrial section of town—it hadn't yet become the tony address it is now. It was a raw, trashy space that had a giant room in the back where all their equipment was set up. I listened to their music and thought they were really good, I was anxious to play with them. I jumped right in and said, "Hey, I noticed you have a keyboard back there in the rehearsal room. Can we jam?" "Of course!" Keith replied. We played for hours, losing track of time. It felt as natural as if we'd been playing together for a long time, even without a bass player.

The dirty glass windows turned amber as the sun started peeking through. I could hear the streets coming alive with delivery trucks and people shouting. We were exhausted, and there was no way Keith was going to be able to remain awake long enough to drive me back uptown. Without even asking him, Amanda volunteered, "Holly, you can crash with Anton in his room. I'm sure he won't mind." It's funny how simple things are when you're young and somewhat innocent, and an attraction is just about all it takes to find yourself in bed, making love with someone you've just met.

Later that morning, I awoke to find Anton's side of the bed empty. I could hear cheerful banter coming from the kitchen, so I threw on my clothes and walked in. The three South Africans were sitting at a table drinking coffee.

Keith winked and said, "How'd you sleep?"

"Like a rock, thank you," I replied demurely. Anton and I looked at each other, co-conspirators now, and smiled.

Amanda said, "Have a seat," so I joined them. "We've been discussing it, and we all agree that you should join the band."

"Really? That's fantastic!" I exclaimed. "I accept."

It was such an innocent time, there was no business to discuss then. I'd found my tribe, and I felt confident that there would be no sexism or macho bullshit here, not just because the lead singer was a woman, but because I felt Keith and Anton were emotionally evolved in that respect. They'd recognized something special in me and saw that I was as serious as they were. Clearly, they believed I would bring something special to the band.

The next day, the guys helped me move my Hammond B3, a huge Leslie speaker cabinet, and the rest of my gear into the loft. Doing gigs was going to be a hellacious and ongoing test of our dedication to the cause, as everybody in the band except Amanda had heavy gear. We all knew it was part of paying our dues. We still needed a bass player, and I suggested that we invite Jimmy Lowell from Riff Raff to jam with us. (We were now an "us.") He came, and blew us all away, just as I thought he would. He brought the funk to the band, something we all loved. I wasn't looking forward to telling Ned that I had just pilfered his bass player, but they were having problems anyway and I don't think Jimmy would've left if things had been going well. Fortunately, Ned was cool about the whole thing and our friendship remained intact.

We started to rehearse, and it was always the best part of my day. We shared the same vision: to write original music and get signed to a record deal, make and sell lots of records, and tour. Anything less would be unacceptable. We were so focused that we rehearsed for only a couple weeks before starting to play around town at any dive that would have us, even before we had put together enough music for a full set. We just played each song way longer than necessary until we came up with more material. Even though Anton and I had barely had enough time to get to know one another, we agreed that I should move into his room at the loft. The treks back and forth from Tribeca to the Upper West Side were eating up too much time. It didn't take long before we fell in love, but I always wondered if it was a matter of convenience or the real thing. It worked in the beginning and that's all that mattered. Everybody in the band was broke, but between the four of us, we were able to scrape by just enough to make the rent. Jimmy, who lived with his girlfriend, was the only one who didn't move into the loft with us. I got a part time job working in a frozen yogurt place in Soho, and Keith and Jimmy had day jobs as well, Anton was already getting hired to do sessions, so we would start rehearsals around 6:00 p.m. every day and play until late at night.

The whole thing was DIY. We designated tasks to each member. Whatever needed to be done we did ourselves, printing up fliers, posting them around town. Keith and Anton took all the business meetings and booked the gigs, we moved all the equipment ourselves in a van, set it up and broke it down. We lugged all that shit up and down the staircase to our loft. And my B3 was a beast, the heaviest thing we had to move. One night, we carried it all the way up the stairs, and I'm not sure who let go first, but it slid back down the steep, rickety steps like a toboggan, gathering speed and smashing into the front door of the building. We were all so exhausted, we just stared at it stupidly without uttering a word, then turned and went to bed, abandoning it until late morning. It was beyond repair and it was time to switch to a more modern sounding keyboard to go with my Moog 15 synthesizer anyway. Fortunately, I'd had the good sense to take out an insurance policy on my gear, and that made it possible for me to buy a new organ, this time a new wave sounding Farfisa that I had recovered in cherry red vinyl.

Twyla Tharp, the legendary dancer and choreographer, had a studio directly below us, and I have to give her credit for putting up with all the noise. We played so loud when we rehearsed, but she never complained. We decided to name the band Siren, after the mythical sirens in Homer's *Odyssey* who used their seductively eerie voices to bewitch the captains of the ships, sending them crashing into the jagged rocks. All of it symbolized temptation, desire, and risk.

Living in the loft was far from glamorous. Because it was a commercial building, there was no heat during the bitter winter months between the hours of 5:00 p.m. and 8:00 a.m. Those were the exact hours during which we had to rehearse, so we wore our coats and gloves, which we cut the fingers off of so we could play. It was so cold we could see our foggy breath billowing through the frigid air. Conversely, during the muggy summer nights, we had no air conditioning, and most of the windows didn't open, so it felt like we were in a giant coffin. The intercom system was broken so we had to throw the keys out the window and pray it didn't kill whomever had stopped by to visit us five stories below. There was one toilet and a moldy shower stall, but even worse was the infestation of cockroaches. They would make their daily military roll call in the kitchen by the hundreds. The tiny bedroom that Anton and I shared opened right into the kitchen, so I was always afraid they would crawl over me when we were sleeping, and there were many times they did. We had mice too, but my cat, Lady, took care of them, although her way of showing me love was to lay a dead rodent at the foot of our bed. The first time she caught one, it lay there for days before the putrid smell alerted us that something dead was in our room. Those were pretty raunchy times, but I was the happiest I'd ever been.

CHAPTER THREE

THE DEMON, THE JOKER, AND THE ONE WITH THE STAR ON HIS EYE (KISS)

New York City, 1979

"Better hide your heart cos you're playing with fire…"
("Hide Your Heart" performed by KISS)

M ost everyone in the band was writing songs. I was dab-
bling with musical ideas but had never really attempted
to write a song by myself, certainly not a full song's worth
of lyrics. While I thought the material that Amanda and Keith were
writing had interesting parts musically, I didn't think they were very
strong lyrically or melodically, certainly not the kind of tunes that
were going to get us on the radio. On the odd occasion that Amanda
would come up with something really poetic I found it unrelatable
and hard to connect with emotionally. Anton took a stab at writing,
and Jimmy didn't seem to care if he wrote or not. So, I thought, *What
the hell, I should give it a try. After all, my songs couldn't be any worse*

than theirs. That's how I became a songwriter. I stumbled upon it and discovered that I was better at it than I thought I would be.

I loved the grunginess of our existence and the camaraderie we shared. We were sounding increasingly better with each gig, although I started to notice how bossy Amanda was. It seemed like she considered us her personal band. Keith had befriended Eddie Kramer, a well-known engineer and producer who'd worked with Jimi Hendrix, Led Zeppelin, KISS, and other legendary acts. Eddie also hailed from Cape Town, so the three South Africans in the band had the expatriate thing in common. Eddie was getting ready to produce Ace Frehley's solo album, and Keith sent Eddie a few songs, hoping the flamboyant lead guitarist of KISS might want to record one of them. Eddie liked one of them enough to play it to Ace, but Ace was more interested in the drummer than the song. He asked Eddie to find out whether Anton was available to play drums on his record, which, of course, he was, all while Siren continued writing and gigging around town.

Not only did Anton play on his record, but the two of them became fast friends and drinking buddies, and because I was Anton's girlfriend, I was often invited to indulge in whatever acts of debauchery and self-indulgence they got into. A typical evening would start with Ace showing up at the loft in a stretch limo and waiting downstairs. Once we got down, I would see the dark window lower and a hand emerge covered in diamond rings, the largest one forming the name "ACE." The hand would hold out a magnum of Dom Perignon, and then came his inevitable lunatic laughter. The Joker. All of this came from inside the limo as the driver walked around and opened the door for us.

Ace was the quintessential rock star. Successful, rich, and, by now, spoiled with a lot of "yes" people hanging around him, he got away with anything he wanted. As far as musicianship goes, he was the most talented member of KISS, and he was a lot of fun to hang out with. We would go out to dinner and have his driver take us all over the city in his limo with the moonroof opened so we could see the stars. Then we would hit the clubs. While we all snorted cocaine, I couldn't keep up with him, especially his alcohol consumption. He and Anton would reach a point of no return where I would have to call it a night and take Anton back to the loft in a cab while Ace's driver made sure to get him home in one piece.

Ace had a small apartment in Manhattan, but his main home was in Connecticut, and he invited Anton and me to stay there many times. In the lower level, he had built a state-of-the art recording studio with a guitar room. What appeared to be at least a hundred guitars, many of them vintage, hung from the ceiling, reminding me of Sam Ash. Ace had designed the basement to look like a real bar, complete with a KISS pinball machine in a corner of the room. It sat there, waiting to be fired up like something out of a Stephen King novel, and as we took turns playing it, it spewed out KISS tunes.

By now, Ace knew all about our band and generously offered to design our logo for us. He had designed the iconic KISS logo, making the "SS" look like lightning bolts. Unfortunately, KISS had received a lot of criticism for the artwork, saying that it bore a resemblance to the "SS" of the Nazi Schutzstaffel. Two of the main players in the band were Jewish and I never sensed any anti-Semitism from Ace, so to me, it seemed unfounded. The "S" in Siren looked similar, but I think that was just Ace's style. He said we were welcomed to use it for whatever we wanted, and even though it looked a little crude, we used it in the ads we ran to promote upcoming gigs because the mother-fucking lead guitarist from KISS had designed it.

At **TRAX FRI, JUNE 1**
Cor. 72nd and Columbus
Shows 11:30 and 1:30

The idea of free love and casual sex, which had started in the sixties, was at its peak in the eighties, so sleeping with someone you weren't in love with seemed pretty normal. When you're young you're supposed to do crazy shit. That's how you figure out what works for you and what doesn't. One evening, Anton, Ace, and I got so high, we stopped by Ace's midtown apartment to relax and come back down to earth. I'd never been to his apartment before, and it was surprisingly tidy, sparsely furnished like a hotel room, one that didn't get used very much. There were none of the usual personal touches like framed photographs, books, and artwork, or a lived-in patina, and I suspected the flat existed for such a night as this, a pit stop or place to crash in lieu of making the hour-long trek home to Connecticut. We ended up in bed together. I guess I was curious to see if sex with a rock star felt any different than with mere mortals, whether it was better or not. Truth be told, it wasn't better, and it wasn't worse. Of course, the fact that we were wasted didn't help, and it wasn't even a real threesome in the classic sense—the two of them never went near each other. I just took turns pouncing on them. I enjoyed it but I would have to say it was pretty uneventful. It didn't affect our friendship at all, and afterwards, we just carried on as if it had never happened.

The level of gigs started to improve. We played at CBGB, Max's Kansas City, Great Gildersleeves, and many other places in the tri-state area. Finally, we were able to hire a few roadies. And then one weeknight we got a lucky break when a band that was slated to play at TRAX canceled at the last minute, and the club manager agreed to take a chance on us. We asked all our friends to come, buy as many drinks as they could, and go wild when we played so they would hire us again. It worked, and the next time, he offered us a much better booking—a coveted, weekend night. All the local bands vied for the weekend bookings because those were the evenings that everyone in the city came out to hear live music. So once again, we invited all our friends to come down and go crazy—and buy copious amounts of alcohol, which they were all too willing to do. They loved our band anyway.

Within a month or two, we'd played there enough to prove that we were capable of drawing an ever-growing crowd of drink-buying patrons. The manager made us the house band, which meant we got to play there on a regular basis. With the favorable reviews we were getting, word started to get around that we were "the band to watch." Those were incredibly fun times, because now that we had established a residency at the famed club, we had the opportunity to play in front of some very special people. On any given night, the club manager or our friends would come back to the dressing room and tell us that Mick Jagger or David Bowie was in the house.

It was time to get a manager so we could start shopping for a record deal. Through Ace we met KISS's manager, the notorious Bill

Aucoin of Aucoin Management and Rock Steady Productions. As far as managers go, Bill was as good as it got. He was highly respected. On a marketing level, he'd masterminded much of KISS's success, after having first discovered them. His background had been in TV, theater, promotion, and marketing, and while he dressed in conservative business suits and looked nothing like a rock 'n' roll manager, I soon learned that he was as wild as they got.

One night, Bill came down to see us play at TRAX and after our set, he came back to our tiny dressing room to say hello. As we changed out of our wet stage clothes in front of him, he crossed his arms and said, "You guys were terrific!"

"Thanks Bill!" we all chimed in, half-naked and grinning at each other.

"I want to manage you," he said.

We looked at each other to confirm what we had just heard.

"Really?" Keith asked.

"Yes, really," Bill answered, smiling.

"Holy shit, that's great," we all yelped in some form or another.

Every band wanted Bill as their manager. As he was always busy with KISS, any other band he took on had to be one he really believed in, one that could achieve commercial success. At that time he was also managing Billy Squier and New England. His offer boosted our self-esteem. With Bill on board, we reached a new level of credibility, and it started to feel like our dreams just might come true. I often stopped by the uptown management office on Madison Avenue just to breathe in the sweet smell of pure unadulterated rock 'n' roll success that was evident everywhere you looked. I'd stare at the dozens of Platinum and Gold record plaques that lined the office walls like wallpaper, envisioning ones of my own on some future wall.

My favorite room was the boardroom, where an exquisite set of four-foot-high puppets, one for each member of KISS, hung from a wooden beam. These realistic looking puppets were exquisitely detailed and in the middle of them was a puppet of Bill, the likeness of which was uncanny. Their painted kabuki eyes stared back at me, waiting to be brought to life. It was hard to say whether Bill was the puppet master or KISS—maybe both, depending on the situation.

Then there was the insane amount of merchandise and collectable memorabilia, everything from T-shirts, action figures, lunchboxes, and comic books to KISS coffins and condoms. They were always giving us free stuff. My favorite item was a jacket made out of paper with the KISS logo and all four members, faces in bright orange and fuchsia. I have no idea what happened to it. To date, I read in *Forbes* magazine that KISS has licensed its name to over three thousand products to become a billion-dollar brand. Impressive.

On one of my visits there, I met Paul Stanley. He was the one with the star painted on his eye. I felt a little shy around him, maybe because he was the front man in KISS or that he was the best looking band member. Paul seemed to know all about Siren, which made me feel good and he seemed pretty normal, almost too normal. It was hard to imagine that this soft-spoken guy was the same person that got up on stage half naked in women's platform boots and makeup and yelled at the top of his lungs in an exaggerated southern drawl. They may have looked the part of partying heathens, but the truth was that both he and Gene never drank or got high—not once, according to them. Deep down, they were just a couple of nice Jewish boys with insatiable appetites for sex.

I met Gene Simmons when KISS was rehearsing for an upcoming tour at a rehearsal complex called S.I.R. on the west side of midtown Manhattan. We were there at the same time, preparing to record new songs for a demo. Now that Bill was managing us, we would run into them more often, and they were more than familiar with Anton's drumming on Ace's solo record. In fact, they'd been having problems with their own drummer, Peter Criss, who had descended into a downward spiral of drug and alcohol addiction. Once they'd heard Anton play, they were so impressed that they hired him to ghost play on their album, *Dynasty*. I was in the hallway when Gene came out of one of the rehearsal rooms and started walking in my direction. He was very tall, and his aura oozed narcissism and sexuality in a way that only rock stars get away with. He glanced at me as he walked past in slow motion, then did an about face and came back, taking both my hands in his and staring deeply into my eyes. Dracula.

"Hello, I'm Gene Simmons. How come we haven't met?"

"Um, I don't know, should we have?" I replied. My knees felt weak. He was charismatic, I'll say that much.

"Who are you?" he asked.

"I'm Holly, I'm in the band Siren that Bill started managing a few months ago. We're rehearsing in one of the rooms here."

"Ah, well we love Anton. It's very nice to meet you," he said as he smiled his most devilish smile. We chatted and flirted for a bit. He had this annoying way of staring up and down my body, deliberately being obvious about it; a typical male move that I couldn't stand. "Well," Gene said, "I'd better get back to rehearsal. Again, it was so nice to meet you!"

"Bye, nice meeting you too." I said as I watched him turn and head down the hall, approach a woman who worked there, and take both her hands in his as he said, "How come we haven't met?"

Up to this point, I'd never seen KISS perform. What little music I'd heard hadn't impressed me very much. However, everyone said that their live show was mind-blowing, and soon enough, they gave me a pair of tickets and passes to a show at Madison Square Garden. That's when I understood what all the fuss was about. Their show was a rock 'n' roll circus. Just the physical feat of running around in those massive platform boots was impressive enough, but when you added in the pyrotechnics and the feats of flying, all while playing and singing, you had to respect them.

Just as I had with Paul, I tried to connect the dots between Gene the flirt and mensch that I'd met, and the evil demon that puked blood all over himself and the stage. And that tongue was positively grotesque, yet fascinating. KISS' devotion to their fans was the key to their success. Their fans adored them so much, they would show up at the concerts dressed as their favorite member and called themselves the KISS Army.

We started running into them more frequently, whether it was up at Bill's office, the rehearsal complex, or the Record Plant, a recording studio on the west side. We had many lively conversations, especially with Gene, who was almost parental in his role towards us, something that he was known for with other bands. In fact, he had given Van Halen their start by producing their first demo after seeing them play at the Starwood on Sunset Strip in LA.

One day Gene called up Anton and said, "Hey, I'm going into a studio tonight to demo a new song I just wrote, and I wanted to know if you, Keith, and Holly are available to come in and play on the track." I was so excited that he had thought of us because there were any number of excellent musicians that he could've called. We were waiting downstairs when his stretch limo pulled up like a shark and whisked us uptown. The name of the song was "Dorothy Lamour," after a glam movie actress from the forties. Although I have no idea what the song was about, it was pretty catchy. We would've done the session for free, just for the thrill to play with one of KISS' own, but not only did he pay us for the session, he took us to the Stage Deli on 55th and Broadway afterwards and fed us.

The Stage Deli was an iconic eatery that was open twenty-four-seven and was always busy. It could be 3:00 a.m. and you might have to wait for a table. The clientele that frequented the place could be anyone from the theater crowd that spilled out after the shows, to the actors who starred in the shows, to tourists wandering around Times Square, to musicians who happened to be taking a break from recording at a nearby studio like the Record Plant or the Hit Factory.

Even without his makeup on, Gene drew attention when he walked into a room. The patrons couldn't help but stare at this behemoth with his black rock 'n' roll attire. He loved the stares. If they'd only known he was one of the members of KISS. I felt smug knowing his secret, that I was hanging out with rock 'n' roll's version of Bruce Wayne, privy to the fact that he was Batman. That night, one of the things that I found endearing was what he ordered. No bloody brisket or steak tartare for this demon: he ordered a slice of cheesecake with strawberries and whip cream, remarking, "I know this is fattening, but I'm going to enjoy every last bite of it." That was the sort of thing I would've said. Even superheroes have to watch their waistline if they want to fit into their costumes.

Nearly forty years later, the demo that we recorded that night ended up in a boxed set that Gene released in 2017 called *The Vault*. It was a huge collection of all the demos and scraps of ideas that he had recorded over the years. It came in a realistic looking vault, and he sent one to me. What a fantastic surprise. He had even included us on the liner notes.

On another occasion, Gene told me that he was a walking encyclopedia when it came to anything there is to know about horror movies. "Go ahead, ask me anything and I'll tell you all about it, who was in it, where and when it was made, who starred in it and directed it, go ahead. No one's ever been able to stump me." He folded his arms and smiled smugly at the ceiling. Without a second's hesitation, I shouted out *Suspiria*, a 1977 Italian horror movie directed by Dario Argento. Gene's face went blank. He was utterly dumbfounded. After that he gained a whole new level of respect for me.

Rock Steady Productions, Bill's production company, put up the money for us to record a five-song demo so he could start pitching us to record labels. We recorded the sessions at Electric Lady Studios in Greenwich Village, the same studio made famous by Jimi Hendrix, one of the owners, as well as other classic acts such as the Rolling Stones and David Bowie. Even today, it maintains its reputation as one of the most hallowed grounds for recorded music. There was carpeting everywhere, even on the walls, and you could feel the static electricity zap you as you walked around the place. One of the engineers handed me a spoon and told me to tap the walls as I walked through the hall, that it would keep me from getting shocked. I thought, *Yeah right, like I'm some idiot that's going to fall for that*, but as it turned out, he was right, it did get rid of the static.

It was so much fun recording as a band for the first time. My only experience until then had been a few demos in Ned's studio. The control rooms at Electric Lady were impressive with their huge consoles, and we recorded in Studio A, which was the big room. We completed the demos in a few days, and then prepared to showcase for record companies that Bill had targeted. Normally the trajectory of a band from inception to getting signed can be rife with years of frustration and repetition, but we were moving at warp speed.

Bill had his lawyer do a title search on the name Siren, and to our dismay, there was already a band using it. We had to come up with a new one. After much discussion and debate I suggested Spider. We were all huge Bowie fans, and it alluded to his Spiders from Mars. It was simple and easy to remember. We all agreed to the name and one more title search later we were clear and free to use it.

I'd wanted to change *my* surname for quite a while. Holly Erlanger just didn't cut it for me, it didn't sound rock 'n' roll, and people always mispronounced it. For months I put a lot of thought into it and came up emptyhanded until one night it came to me in a dream, cliché as that sounds. In the dream, my name was Holly Knight. Knight is actually a common surname in Britain, akin to Smith in the US. It was short, memorable, and went well with Holly. It was noble sounding too. A knight is a warrior, and that felt strangely relevant to me.

When I awoke, I was Holly Knight from that moment on and never again thought of myself as anyone else. I immediately had it legally changed. This was a quantum leap. It was a transformation of not just my name, but my entire being and persona. It wasn't so much that I created it, I just returned to something that had always been a part of me and gave it a name. I literally knighted myself. The sword I carried was a state of mind. I had merely recognized my true nature. I was a warrior.

Besides being a brilliant manager, Bill had quite the reputation. When it came to his personal life, he made no bones about being gay and flaunted it proudly, often cruising around the city in his private limo, on the prowl for pretty looking boys. We spent many a night up at his apartment in the famed Olympic Towers, a prestigious but ominous looking black monolith on Fifth Avenue and 54th street. The building had fifty-one floors, and only the top thirty contained residential condos. Below were high-end offices and retail spaces. Bill's place was *très chic*. He'd commissioned an up-and-coming interior designer to decorate it. On the living room coffee table was a copy of *Architectural Digest* with his apartment on the cover.

There was always a festive vibe when we visited Bill in his tower, disco music played loudly in the background while he poured drinks, but it was clear that he was far more interested in entertaining the guys during those visits. He made no bones about that either. He offered Valium to Amanda and me on more than one occasion in the hopes that we would pass out while he shared a steady supply of coke with the boys, hoping to get at least one of them into bed, especially Keith, the prettiest of the three. But Bill was so lovable and silly at times, we just told him to fuck off, never succumbing to his attempts. Everyone had the power to say no, so it really wasn't an issue.

Sometimes we wake up without a clue that something momentous is going to happen that day, something unexpected that ends up being a game changer in your life. I spent a good deal of time hanging out at the Record Plant. Many bands, such as KISS and Aerosmith, liked working there so much, it was like their second home. They would move in and lock down the studio for months or a year. It wasn't cheap, but they had lavish budgets.

It made sense for Bill to put us in there when we showcased for Casablanca Records, KISS's label. Unfortunately, the sound wasn't very good that day and they passed on us. We also did a few demos there, which gave me a legitimate excuse to hang out at the studio. As with almost every studio I've ever stepped foot in, there was a communal lounge the bands would walk through on their way in and out. Sometimes they'd even sit down. It was one of the best places to meet famous recording artists, but it had to be done tastefully. You couldn't drool or ask for a photo or autograph. You had to be cool and respectful and hope there was a way you could casually join in their conversations. Some of the studios had their own entrances and lounges so no one could get near the bands booked inside of them.

I became friends with a guy at the Plant named Jimmy Iovine. He told me once that he had started out sweeping floors in the place until he became a staff engineer and then started producing records for Springsteen, Tom Petty, Stevie Nicks, and U2. He introduced me to two engineers who he often worked with, Shelly Yakus and Thom Panunzio, who always seemed interested in what I was up to with my band. It meant a lot to me that such an elite group of men welcomed me and treated me with respect. Who knew Jimmy would become one of the most powerful and creative businessmen in the music business, cofounding Interscope Records?

One day, as I sat in the lounge, the door to Studio A opened and Gene Simmons sauntered out. I knew KISS was camped out there working on *Unmasked* as Anton had just played all the drums on it. No one was supposed to know that Peter Criss didn't play on those records, and they treated it like a military secret. Gene had once told me, "It's important that we don't confuse or disappoint our fans by showing any cracks in our armor or image. We want the KISS Army to view us as infallible and united." Gene looked over at me sitting on the couch, rifling through *Billboard*.

"Hi! I thought I saw you sitting out here before. What are you doing here?"

"I'm just waiting for a friend," I said.

"How would you like to come in and play on one of our tracks?" he asked. "We need some keyboards."

"Seriously?" I asked.

"I'm dead serious."

Still in disbelief, I said something dumb like, "You mean right now?" Gene walked over and held the door to the studio open. "Right now."

I leapt from the couch not even bothering to conceal my enthusiasm. Gene had just asked me to play on the new KISS record. I didn't have to be asked twice.

Vini Poncia, their producer, stood in front of the huge mixing console in the control room. Paul, who was sitting on a couch behind him, stood up and greeted me with a kiss on the cheek. I already knew Vini because he'd been dating Amy Sexauer, a friend of mine. We'd all hung out and gone to dinner a bunch of times and I liked him a lot, his demeanor was very New York-Italian. Vini smiled and said, "Hey, I hear you're going to play some keyboards on this track?" I smiled back at him and said, "Yep." I was waiting for him to tell me it was a prank.

"The name of the song is 'Shandi.' Have a listen." I sat in front of the console and listened quietly. It wasn't your typical KISS song. It was more of an adult contemporary ballad. I could understand why they wanted to put keyboards on it. "So, that's how it goes. Think you can figure something cool out for it?" Gene asked. That was when I realized that this was really happening. "Yes, absolutely," I said. "Just show me what keyboard you want me to play."

They didn't know this, but I'd never played on a record before, and I wasn't about to tell them. Vini pointed towards a keyboard that had been set up in the big studio room. I walked through two thick sets of doors, hearing the whooshing sound close behind me. I put the headphones on and gave them the thumbs up once I heard the track coming through. I started to go through sounds and asked them, "What kind of instruments or parts are you hearing?" "Mmm, maybe some kind of string pad for starters, but with more attack on it." I went through some patches until I found something that they all liked. After one listen, I already had the arrangement and changes worked out in my head.

I was confident that I would come up with something they'd like. I was more nervous about the situation itself. Everywhere I looked, there were men: the band, the producer and engineer, the assistant engineer and a few guys from management. The only other woman in the entire building that day was the receptionist. Vini turned to the engineer. "Let's roll the tape again." The song was so straightforward and basic that I started to relax as I played along. They really weren't looking for any virtuosity, just some coloring. I figured after this initial run through, I'd probably get it in one take. The song ended and Gene pressed the talkback button. "Can you give us a minute?"

That sounded foreboding. Vini walked over to Gene and Paul, their faces deep in conversation. I waited and watched, trying to read their lips, I saw their heads shaking through the plate glass window. It didn't look good. I hoped they hadn't changed their minds. Gene turned and motioned for me to come back in the control room.

"What are you doing the rest of the day?" he asked.

"Nothing I can't change," I answered.

"Good, because we really like what you played and we want to try something we've never done before, put keyboards all over the record."

This was turning out better than I could've imagined. "Fantastic! But I thought that was just a run through to learn the song."

Gene said, "Nah, it's perfect. We're finished with that one. So, can you stay and do some more songs?"

"Of course!" I replied.

How was it that a band who objectified women by keeping thousands of Polaroids with the names and dates of all the females they'd fucked hadn't thought twice about putting me on their record? A woman. Guess they were more open-minded than I had previously thought. They didn't give a shit who played on it as long as the musician kicked ass and gave them what they needed.

I stayed into the wee hours of the morning, recording keyboards on eight songs. It was a historical moment as KISS rarely put keyboards on their records, "Beth" being a notable exception. In the end, I think a lot of KISS fans loved it, and just as many diehard fans hated it. I know this much, from that moment on, people knew my name, even without any credit, and that's because the KISS Army is comprised of obsessive fans who want to know everything there is to know about KISS. That day I went from being an amateur musician to a professional one. It wasn't a hobby anymore because I was getting paid union scale to play on a record. It didn't hurt that the band sold millions of copies each time they put a record out either.

I couldn't wait to get home and tell Keith and Anton what had happened. I knew they would be impressed. I called my dad and told him, although he didn't know who KISS was. Still, he was very excited for me until he asked around about them. At first, he was worried that I had fallen in with a satanic cult, but once he found out Gene and Paul were Jewish, he was happy again.

Gene told me that I wouldn't get credit for playing on the record because the fans wouldn't understand seeing anybody else's name on a KISS record, other than the band members themselves. Even though it was a drag, I understood. I kind of expected it because they had gotten Anton to agree to it as well. When I received my checks, I made copies so I could prove that I'd recorded with them. I saved those motherfucking copies for forty years. After the record went Gold, the band sent me my first plaque with my name at the bottom. In their own way, they did acknowledge that I had played on the record. It's still there, hanging proudly on my studio wall.

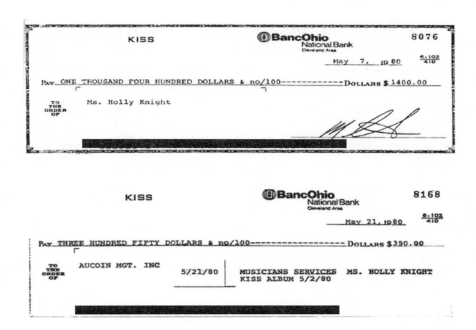

I ran into Bill Aucoin shortly after and he said, "I heard your keyboards all over the new KISS record. Congratulations, that's a big deal, Holly, and before you know it, Spider's going to have a record deal."

When it came to business, Bill suggested that the band form a legal partnership, something he said that KISS had set up between them, although I wasn't privy to their details, and maybe it was bullshit anyway because I can't imagine Gene and Paul sharing equally with anybody, not even the other two original members. For us, this meant that everybody would receive the same amount when it came to any monies received, including the money from songwriting, no matter who wrote what. The intent was to eliminate jealousy and competition, while fostering an "all for one and one for all" ethos. I wasn't happy about it, but the three South Africans were pressuring me to go along with it. It hurt me that even Anton had turned against me saying I should agree to it, even though I didn't think it was fair. Jimmy didn't write at all, and in my mind, I was taking my songwriting much more seriously than the rest of the band. The more Bill and everyone at Rock Steady took notice of my songs, the more confidence I gained as a writer. Reviewers of our live gigs often mentioned my tunes as the standouts. I naively thought that if I didn't agree, they would kick me out of the band, so I begrudgingly acquiesced.

It was clear that Amanda was not happy with the attention I was getting. Anton didn't like it either, and it began to drive a wedge between us, causing our relationship to crack. To be romantically involved with another band member, living, eating, breathing the same air twenty-four-seven was just too much. There was nowhere to run to, and within time we broke up, choosing to be bandmembers over lovers. Maybe if we hadn't been in the same band together and had been seeing each other under less stressful circumstances it would've lasted longer.

I found a small L-shaped studio apartment between 13th and 14th Streets on 4th Avenue, close enough to Tribeca that I could easily get to when we had to rehearse or have a band meeting. Across the street was Union Square Park, nicknamed Needle Park after all the heroin addicts who scored and slept on the benches. They even made a movie about it. Around the corner was the Academy of Music, a venue that featured big touring bands and whose name was later changed to the Palladium. A few blocks away, in the direction of the East Village, was the newly opened Ritz Theater, the same one that in a few years would see Tina Turner doing a famous live show that would seal her future as a solo artist, and indirectly tie my future to hers.

On one rendezvous to Aucoin Management, I met Billy Idol. He had a megawatt smile, and I figured if he wasn't a lead singer in a band already, he should be. He certainly looked the part with his white peroxide hair, flamboyant clothes, and diabolical smirk. Back in England, he'd already achieved some success as the front man for Generation X, who'd Bill recently begun managing, but now he'd come to New York to pursue a solo career.

Billy and I chatted for a bit, and I gave him my number, offering to take him around to some of the new clubs. Soon after that, he came over to my apartment to hang out, and together we hit the clubs, quickly becoming rock 'n' roll pals. Around the same time, Keith, my guitarist in Spider and I had seen a local band called the Fine Malibus perform and had commented on the savant guitarist, Steve Stevens. We told Aucoin about him one day and when Billy started looking for a guitarist, Bill thought of him. It was a perfect casting.

We were just kids, starting out with no money but with the same amount of drive and passion—and the same manager. Eventually we lost touch as our paths took us in different directions, but I watched from a parallel universe as Billy's career soared and he not only landed on the cover of *Rolling Stone*, but became a multi-Platinum artist.

Meanwhile, Gene and I considered each other friends by now, and once or twice he invited me up to his high-rise apartment near Columbus Circle. The first time I had to use his bathroom I burst out laughing when I turned on the light. Every inch of the walls was covered with Platinum KISS plaques. I can't imagine it was because he ran out of space in the rest of his apartment. I think it was just his sense of humor. It certainly made for some interesting reading material.

We both wanted what we wanted in the moment, and without much forethought, we ended up in his giant bed. It was fairly lacking for me and I'm sure for him as well. It's something I both laugh and cringe about now because I'd already slept with Ace. Rock 'n' roll. Lust. Opportunity. Stupid young puppies.

Once we finished recording the demos, Bill sent a few carefully selected A&R people copies. (Artist and repertoire were the people at the record labels who scouted for new bands and had the power to sign them.) Several producers had already shown interest in producing us. One was Eddie Kramer, whom we already knew liked the band, and another was Jack Douglas, who had produced a number of huge records for Aerosmith, John Lennon, and Cheap Trick. We loved Jack, but like Aerosmith, he had a bit of a drug problem at the time.

Another name cropped up by way of Gray Russell, an engineer whom I dated briefly. Gray was one of the staff engineers at the Record Plant and had worked on many post-punk era records like Lou Reed's *Street Hassle* and Patti Smith's *Easter*. He had recently been working with a producer by the name of Mike Chapman on Blondie's *Parallel Lines*.

"Holly, this guy is one of the top producers in the music business right now. He produced three number one singles in a row recently, Blondie's 'Heart Of Glass,' Nick Gilder's 'Hot Child in the City,' and, right after that, 'My Sharona' by the Knack."

"Wow, he sounds amazing!" I said.

Gray continued, "He's also a hit songwriter in his own right, something that most producers aren't."

"What's he written?" I asked, getting more interested by the minute.

"He wrote 'Ballroom Blitz' for the Sweet and Exile's "Kiss You All Over."

Those are great songs, I thought. Having a producer that could do both seemed way more appealing. It was double the ammunition.

Gray got busy with another record, and the burden to find Mike Chapman was on me. I often felt outnumbered when Keith, Anton, and Amanda joined forces. It felt like Amanda had the two of them wrapped around her finger. While the three of them were fixated on getting Eddie Kramer, I was much more interested in Mike. Bill was preoccupied with KISS and hadn't yet put much thought into who was going to produce us. He thought it was premature. He set up some showcases with some labels where we performed and the one most interested in signing us was Columbia Records, but they were dragging their feet and said they wanted to see us play live.

A few weeks passed, and Spider was invited to a private party at TRAX for the New Barbarians, Keith Richards's solo project. They had just played Madison Square Garden, and there were quite a few bands at the club. I was chatting with two members of the Knack when a cheerful blond man came up and joined us.

"Hello," he said in an Australian drawl to the guys.

Prescott, the Knack's bass player, said, "Hey Holly, this is Mike." They seemed to know each other pretty well and chatted idly for a few minutes.

Mike said, "Excuse me for a minute, I'm going to go grab another drink at the bar. Nice to meet you, Holly."

As he strode away, Prescott said, "Mike produced our record."

My heart skipped a beat. "Was that Mike Chapman?" I asked. I ran to find Anton who was floating around the club, knowing he had a copy of our new demo. "Hey," I said. "You're not going to believe this, but I just met Mike Chapman. He's here at the party!"

"Cool!" he said.

"Do you have a copy of the demo with you?"

"Yeah, but it's my only copy and I want to hold on to it."

"Are you crazy?" I sputtered. "Don't be an asshole. Give me the fucking tape."

"Okay, okay, here, relax. Jesus..."

I snatched it out of his hand, kissed him on the cheek and ran to the bar where Mike was nursing a martini and laughing with the bartender. I tapped him lightly on the shoulder. "Mike! I'm so sorry!" I said. "I didn't know you were *the* Mike Chapman. Prescott just introduced you as Mike. I'm so excited to meet you, you have no idea."

From there I explained who I was and told him all about Spider, how we were shopping for a deal, showcasing for labels, and how he was the perfect producer for us, how Bill Aucoin was our manager, and on and on. He quietly listened to my earnest little speech. When I got to the end, I was almost out of air and said, "Would you please listen to our tape?"

"Yes, of course I will," Mike said. He put the tape in his jacket pocket and patted it. I'll never forget that. Then he said, "Listen, at the moment I'm camped out at the Record Plant finishing up the new Blondie record, so it might take me a while to get back to you, but I'll definitely give it a listen. If you don't hear from me, feel free to call me and remind me that you gave me your demo. Keep calling, I'm kind of shitty about returning phone calls. But, eventually, I will listen to it, I promise."

For the next two weeks I relentlessly called him every day and it was always the same, someone would get on the line, apologize on his behalf and ask to take a message. One time, I could hear him saying in the background, "Oh, it's that Holly Knight chick again. I promised I'd call her back." He had given me permission to pester him, so I did. Relentlessly.

The Blondie record he was working on ended up being *Autoamerican* and contained two huge number one hits, "The Tide Is High" and "Rapture." After two weeks, my heart sank when he finally called me back and said he was finished with the record and was flying back to LA that evening.

"But I'll be a captive audience on the plane, and I definitely plan to listen to your tape. I'll call you in a few weeks." Eight hours later, the phone rang. It was Mike. "Holly, I listened to your tape three times on the plane and I absolutely love it. The songs are great, the band's terrific..." (*Holy shit!*) "...and I want to sign Spider to my new record label, Dreamland." (*Holy shit!!!!*)

Things happened quickly after I hung up the phone. Mike called Bill the next morning and the lawyers got to work hammering out a record deal. "Record deal," two words that once represented something unattainable, now fit into my vocabulary. Bill thought it was an excellent fit and was thrilled that we were signing to them. Word on the street was that the newly formed and independent Dreamland Records was quickly gaining a reputation for being hip and artsy, largely because of Mike's work with Blondie. He had a giant Andy

Warhol painting of Debbie Harry in his house that she had given to him as a thank-you gift. The guy was cool.

Dreamland, which was distributed by RSO Records, was based in Los Angeles, and Mike and his partner, Nicky Chinn, wanted to fly the whole band out there to record. I found the prospect incredibly exciting. While I'd been to California before in what I now considered a previous life, this would be my first time in LA. The label felt that by bringing us out west, we would have no distractions, that there would be one thing and only one thing to focus on when we got there—the record. Our friends threw us a party and then, at the eleventh hour, a few days before we left for California, I wrote "New Romance" with Anton, which would become our first single and one of our most popular songs.

My dad was so proud and happy for me. He had come to most of our gigs since the beginning, no matter how small or divey the club was. I often spotted him in the audience, as close to the stage as he could get, dancing and moving to the music like a little kid. And my mom? Nothing had changed with her—she was still the center of her own universe.. Why I even gave a shit was a mystery to me, but I did.

FUCK! We had just signed our record deal and we were heading to Los Angeles to cut our first album. California here we come!

CHAPTER FOUR

IN FUJICOLOR (SPIDER)

Los Angeles, 1980–1982

"We always wish for money, we always wish for fame..."
("Change" performed by John Waite)

Mike and Nicky pulled out all the stops for us. Their A&R guy came to greet us at the airport in a stretch limo stocked with champagne. It felt weird to be treated so lavishly. We hadn't done anything to deserve it yet, but we had no problem enjoying it. My first impressions were varied and panoramic in scope, things that screamed Hollywood and La La Land from every corner, and as we cruised down Sunset Strip, I marveled at the billboards that seemed to be everywhere. I was used to seeing them much higher in Times Square—New York is a vertical city where everything is crammed upwards into the sky. In contrast, LA is horizontal and spread out, so the billboards are much closer to the street. Most of them were massive advertisements for bands, such as AC/DC's *Back in Black*, the Stones' *Emotional Rescue*, and ads for upcoming movies like *The Empire Strikes Back* and *American Gigolo*. Everything was larger than life.

If New York was the film noir version of my life, then LA was a gigantic splash of Fujicolor. Known as the City of Angels, there was something utterly seductive about the place. New York was a melting pot of street culture, art, museums, diversity, and ethnic neighborhoods. It was a tough, gritty urban sprawl of attitude and survival where its residents could endure anything. In contrast, LA was a much younger city, spread out over 502 square miles. Instead of street culture, it had car culture. Without wheels you couldn't get anywhere. But so what? It had things that New York didn't. For instance, the weather was fantastic year-round, and not just socked in between a few measly weeks during the spring and fall like back east. It was versatile, you could surf in the Pacific Ocean during the early hours of the morning and ski Big Bear in the San Bernadino mountains by mid-afternoon. And being from Capetown, Anton would go surfing early in the morning before heading into the studio. You could hike, swim, and lay on the beach in the middle of winter. It was also a party town, way more than New York City. Heading further on Sunset, we passed a large, baby blue Tudor mansion. It looked like someone's home, yet we were in the business section of West Hollywood.

"That's it," our A&R guy said. "That's Dreamland Records. We're gonna circle back later once you're all settled in. First we're taking you to the apartment where you're staying."

West Hollywood was the epicenter of the music business; from Doheny Drive to Vine Street where Capitol Records was, it housed all the record companies. Closer to the edge of West Hollywood, before you reached Beverly Hills, was where most of the rock clubs resided. We stopped at a light, right in front of a car rental place whose marquee displayed the words, "Hertz Car Rentals welcomes the band SPIDER." I rubbed my eyes and squinted. It was still there. We all had a delayed response and then shrieked at the same time. (Dreamland had arranged for them to post it.) Directly across from

Hertz was Tower Records, whose exterior displayed a row of over-sized, newly released records that wrapped around the building. Later on, when our record came out, our album cover ended up on the building, right next to a couple of bands we worshipped.

Five minutes from Tower Records was Bill Aucoin's condo on Fountain Ave., a spacious place by New York standards. He often let his acts stay there when they were in town working. It was much more informal than his New York apartment, but it had four bedrooms and a full-time maid and cook. No doubt this was all going to show up on a recoupment statement down the line, but for now, we didn't care.

In a weird twist, my desire to work with Chapman had gotten us signed to his label, but because he had overcommitted himself for the next year, he couldn't produce our record. Instead, he paired us up with his long-time British engineer, Peter Coleman. To me, it felt more like he'd pawned us off on Peter, as if we weren't as important to him as the other acts he had signed. In reality, that wasn't the case at all. Before he'd even heard of us, he'd booked himself for the next year and beyond, but I wished he'd told us that in advance. I was gravely disappointed, but I reminded myself that I should be happy we were making a record at all.

We didn't waste any time. The day after we arrived, we went into a rehearsal studio for a few days with Peter. Mike made an appearance and asked us to play all the songs for him. He'd never seen us play live and seemed sufficiently blown away. "Well done!" he said and took off in his silver cloud Rolls-Royce.

Once the band settled in, we focused on nothing else but cutting the record, with the exception of the evenings when we were left to our own devices. No one asked questions as long as we showed up at the studio bright and early the next day, ready to record and capture on tape the hedonistic angst we'd gotten into the night before. It was 1980, the first year that would kick off the last decade of excess, reck-lessness, and decadence in the world. Little did anybody realize that a new phenomenon called MTV was about to explode and not only change the music business, but the entire planet in terms of how we viewed and received music.

———

The first night after we arrived, the whole band went over to Mike's house for a birthday party. The entire Dreamland roster was invited to his elegant mansion on Coldwater Canyon, and there I met another Holly, Holly Penfield, whom I quickly befriended, Shandi Sinnamon, Consenting Adults, and another band, Nervous Rex. I also met Holly's band members, one of whom was her bass player, Jim Hilbun, who became a sexy diversion for the rest of my time in LA while we made the record.

New York had CBGB, Max's Kansas City, and Irving Place, but Hollywood had the Rainbow, the Whiskey, and the Troubadour. LA might not have had the uber cool and artsy panache that New York had, but it had its own brand of rock 'n' roll. A lot of bands rose and emerged from the LA clubs, including the Doors, Alice Cooper, and a group of musicians calling themselves the Hollywood Vampires who had made the Rainbow their home away from home in the mid-1970s. Ronnie Dio's group with Ritchie Blackmore, Rainbow, was named after the club. On any given night during the seventies and eighties, there could be upwards of three hundred rockers hanging in the parking lot, and soon enough, I was one of them.

A few nights after the birthday party, Mike invited us to meet him at a trendy upscale restaurant on the strip called Le Dome. During the day, the place was a mecca for Hollywood power lunches among agents and their clientele, movie producers, and music industry execs—people like David Geffen, Berry Gordy, and Michael Ovitz. At the noon hour there was a long line of Rolls-Royces parked out front, but at night it turned into a three-ring celebrity circus, and that's where my induction into the inner sanctum of true Hollywood debauchery and the aforementioned hedonism commenced.

It was near impossible to get into Le Dome without knowing someone, but Mike's connection to the restaurant wasn't merely as a patron; he was one of several co-owners, and he would often go there after a hard day of work in the studio to tend bar. Serving and drinking martinis while flirting with all the beautiful women was one of his favorite ways to unwind.

It was a modern-day Sodom and Gomorrah, a surrealistic stage for people watching, people meeting, drugs, French cuisine, partying, and occasional sex in the downstairs bathrooms. In the front were tables that looked out through the dark, smoky windows onto the strip, a spot where people requested to sit if they didn't want to be disturbed. As I ventured further in, I saw a large round bar packed with young fashionistas and starlets. The bar led to the main dining room, which was filled with larger tables and brighter lighting to accommodate the people who wanted to be seen: the celebs, posers, wannabes, and everyone else who had managed to gain entry. A wonderfully noisy room filled with laughter, this was center stage, where all the action and excitement unfolded. That first night I thought someone was having a special birthday party but no, it was just a typical night at Le Dome.

We were led to one of the tables where Mike was holding court with a group of friends. He raised his glass when we arrived and announced to his guests, "Hey everyone, meet my latest signing, Spider." As everyone said hello, I shyly sat down and looked around. At a neighboring table, I saw Elton John and Bernie Taupin surrounded by an entourage of friends. (I found out later that Bernie was one of Mike's best friends.) Behind us, at some of the other tables, I spotted Burt Bacharach, Robin Williams, Rod Stewart, and Goldie Hawn. At another, Liza Minelli and her half-sister, Lorna Luft (another friend of Mike's), dined, and at another table, Sly Stallone sat with his family. I'd never seen so many familiar faces of people I didn't know in one room.

Sitting next to Mike was a sassy young woman he introduced as Tanya Tucker. He had produced her record and was now dating her. In her lap sat a little dog with a studded rhinestone collar. I'd barely sat down when a waiter appeared and poured me a glass of sparkling champagne. To my left, someone passed me a bowl filled with white powder. There had to be at least an ounce of pure, unadulterated cocaine in it. I couldn't even imagine what the street value of something like that would be. It was all out in the open, so I dipped my fingernail delicately into the bowl.

More often than not, that's how many a night played out. I was having a blast. Sometimes, it would be quiet there on a weeknight, and that's when I actually met the most interesting people. Mike introduced me to Bernie whom I would end up writing with years later, but at this point I had yet to discover that songwriting was going to be my main thing. At that moment, I only knew that I was in a rock band, and, like marriages when you're first starting out, I thought we would be together forever.

There were other places I went to that were just as fun for different reasons. There was the Whiskey, where I saw a lot of live music. There I met a completely different brand of people, everything from bottom feeders to visiting rock royalty all decked out in rock 'n' roll attire. The Rainbow was a trashy little club that was filled with rockers, male and female. The strip itself was as much an attraction as the clubs. The cars would honk their horns as they sped by, well above the legal speed limit, people yelling out the windows. Down the road was the infamous Hyatt hotel, otherwise known as the Riot Hotel, where several rock stars had thrown furniture off the balconies.

We cut all the basic tracks pretty quickly. I think it had a lot to do with the fact that we'd played most of the songs live for long enough that we were pretty tight as a band. Then again, we had Anton on drums. He'd actually turned down an official offer from KISS to be their new drummer in an admirable act of loyalty to Spider. He deserved a lot of credit for that.

Once Peter was satisfied that we had the basic tracks done, he gave us a schedule to record our individual parts. We fell into a rhythm: wake up, rock out, record, party, repeat. It took thirty days to record the record, which, by industry standards, is quite fast. It was an honest, live-sounding rock record with few bells and whistles. We packed a lot of living into those thirty days and by the time we finished, I was ready to go back to New York. You know the old adage, too much of a good thing?

We had a lot to do—shoot the record cover, film a couple of videos, plan the album release, rehearse, and go out on tour. We shot the album cover in Soho. After having done at least four photo sessions with the band, I realized how much I disliked them. They took forever. The hair and makeup could take hours and being in front of the camera made me feel self-conscious about my looks. I didn't intend to look so sullen and pouty on the cover, but we shot it outdoors in the middle of winter and I was only wearing a skimpy skirt and thigh-high boots, so I was freezing. We all looked pretty miserable when we had so much to smile about.

I'll never forget the first time I heard a song of mine come on the radio. If I were to keep a list of the top ten best moments of my life, that would be one of them. Somehow hearing the evidence of all our hard work hit me like a speeding train: thousands if not millions of listeners were tuned in to WNEW at that moment. As soon as I heard the first chord hit the airwaves, I recognized our first single, "New Romance." It sounded great with the radio compression. It just jumped out of the speakers. I ran over and turned my stereo up full blast and then started calling the band and anyone I could think of. "We're on the radio, turn on WNEW!!" I shrieked.

WNEW was a major station, what they called a P1. It was one of the hardest stations to get your song played on in the country, and, right out of the box, they added us, one of New York's own. Every time I heard it come on the radio, I felt such a rush. It was very empowering. The reviews were excellent. One review on the cover of *Billboard* magazine said, "It's a state of the art release from start to finish." In another music trade we were listed as one of the most promising bands of 1980. The critics loved us, and "New Romance" made it into *Billboard*'s top forty before we lost our bullet, that little black dot next to the song listing in the trades that indicated upwards motion. We did several small club tours that took us to a lot of states. The label asked us to do a bunch of radio interviews and "phoners" in whatever town we were playing to thank the station for adding the record or if they were close to adding it, to push them over the edge so they would.

We filmed three videos, one for "New Romance," another for our second single, "Everything Is Alright," and a third for "It Didn't Take Long." While the other two songs charted, they didn't make it as far as "New Romance." I felt it was a solid beginning and next time we would do better. After Spider finished touring in support of the record, we all headed back to New York to buckle down and write the next record. It'd only been a year and a half since we'd made our first album, but the label was anxious to get us back into the studio, and we really wanted to hit it out of the park this time.

We'd all become quite friendly with everyone at Aucoin Management, and we had a day to day person, Ric Aliberte, who had asked me to drop off a tape with the new songs I'd written. While I was there I ran into Paul Stanley, who was on his way to Europe to do some KISS dates. We chatted and flirted a bit, and I discovered that the more I got to know him, the more I liked him. He asked me for my phone number, and I realized that maybe it was mutual. A few weeks later, he called me from Germany to say he was thinking about me and wanted to say hello. I was touched and surprised. Then I didn't hear from him. It wasn't until several months later when I ran into him at the Ritz that we reconnected. I frequented the club a lot since it was only two blocks away from my apartment. That night, Paul came home with me, and after that we started dating casually. It was simple and sweet.

One evening, he picked me up in his Porsche and took me to a Diana Ross concert. She was riding the success of her latest single "I'm Coming Out," a song written and produced by Nile Rodgers and Bernard Edwards. Nile's signature guitar riff, one that threaded through many hits he'd written, started to play as Diana started singing backstage, and when she came out, the audience, including me, went wild. After the concert, Paul took me backstage to say hello. Gene Simmons, who was in a hot and heavy relationship with her at the time, was sitting in her dressing room, looking right at home. He greeted us, then introduced me to Diana. I reflected back on the days not that long ago when I would have to sneak backstage and gaze at the celebrities, an onlooker and outsider.

During that same period, I met another young man, Tony Guccione, at the Ritz. Tony was the son of Bob Guccione, the founder of *Penthouse* and *Omni* magazines. I thought he was rakishly handsome and charming, and we started dating, which was wild because, for the first time, I was seeing two very different men at the same time. Unlike his father, an Italian-bred New Yorker, Tony had been raised by his mother in England and had a British pedigree. He often brought me over to his father's house on East 67th street. We even slept over a few times in one of the most sumptuous bedrooms I've ever seen. The mansion was two townhouses merged together and was said to be the largest private residence in Manhattan at 22,000 square feet. Following in his father's footsteps, Tony was an emerging photographer, and he asked me. "How would you like to pose for a spread in *Penthouse*?"

I was flattered. I'd never thought of myself as hot enough to be asked, but I replied, "No, I don't think so, but I'd love it if we could do some artsy photos instead, with my clothes on." I was far more interested in being taken seriously as a musician. This was not the time to be objectified as a woman. I just wanted to be one of the guys. Tony agreed to do the photos on my terms and took me up to the *Penthouse* offices for a photo shoot. I still love and cherish the photos he took. They came out just the way I wanted, edgy and avant-garde.

It was time to make our second record. We had written a lot of songs, and once again, we sent them to the label so they could decide which ones were going to make it on the record. The process was still completely unbiased, Mike, Nicky, and the A&R people never knew who wrote what, they just picked the ones they thought had the most commercial potential. The band was pretty excited about the tunes we had, but the label felt we were missing the lead single, the one that would take us to the top of the charts and put us on the map. I personally agreed, but kept my thoughts to myself, hoping lightning would strike and I'd come up with a hit. As is often the case with recording sessions, the best songs come along at the last minute, like "New Romance" had. In the meantime, they wanted us to get started.

We were excited to fly back out to LA to record. This time the label had us set up camp at Ocean Way Studios in Hollywood, a much larger and prestigious studio where so many huge records had been cut. We stayed at the Oakwood Garden apartment complex on Barham Blvd. in North Hollywood, a rock 'n' roll haven where all the bands stayed when they recorded in LA.. The nicest part was that the label had rented each of us our own apartment. Of course, they'd be recouping that.

Some of the records that I had been listening to on repeat during that time were Queen's *The Game*, Bowie's *Scary Monsters*, AC/DC's *AC/DC*, and Talking Heads' *Remain in Light*, which contained one of my favorite songs, "Once in a Lifetime." Each one of these records had a profound influence on me. I was also a huge fan of the Pretenders and the Police.

Peter Coleman returned as our producer. As much as I adored him as a person, I found it increasingly frustrating that Mike would be unavailable again. We were the strongest act on the label, having had a top-forty single, and we were their best bet, so it didn't seem fair. But again, I wasn't privy to all of his other commitments. I only knew he was finishing up Blondie's *The Hunter*. Right now, it seemed that all we were getting from Mike was his executive skills as president of Dreamland. That sucked, and towards the end of making the album, I decided to do something about it. I thought, if I could get Mike to write one song with me, then maybe, just maybe, I could convince him to produce the track. I didn't discuss it with the band, because I was pretty sure they wouldn't like the idea of me going around them, but I figured if I could pull it off first then it might be easier to convince them that it was the right move.

I called Mike and, to my surprise, he went for the idea. "Meet me at the Dreamland offices tomorrow and we'll give it whirl," he said.

In a tiny office, there was a keyboard on a coffee table, and a small amp and guitar leaning against a wall. I felt a little shy around him, but I was finally getting some time with him.

"Okay, I have this title, Mike, 'Be Good to Me.'"

"Yeah, I like that, but what if it was a little more direct, like 'You Better Be Good to Me'?"

"Oh yeah, that's stronger," I agreed.

He plugged his guitar into the amp and turned on his Roland CR-78 drum machine, the same one he had used on Blondie's "Heart of Glass," and just like that we started to jam. It was fun and felt very natural. Mike started to mumble a great opening line, "A prisoner of your love, entangled in your web...." When we got to the chorus, he sang, "Oh you better be good to me." And I sang out "That's how it's got to be." He winked as if to say, "Nice one," then he sang, "'Cause I don't have the time, for your—something, something," and we both chimed in at the same time, "Yeah, you better be good to me." The lyrics were laden with attitude, and we finished it that day. I was so happy to finally be working with him. We had an instantaneous, mad chemistry together. That didn't surprise me one bit. It's funny, Mike didn't look rock 'n' roll at all, he dressed in polo shirts like some yuppie tennis pro, yet, in many ways, he was one of the most rock 'n' roll people I'd ever met.

Within a matter of hours we'd written an entire song, a really good one. I sat back, exhilarated. "What a cool song we just wrote, Mike. This is exactly what the band needs," I remarked. It had something Spider had been missing, rock 'n' roll attitude, and it was a great song for a woman to sing. It was way less complex musically than all the songs we had been doing. In fact, it only had two chords, but because the bass lines and melodies changed with each section it didn't sound like two chords. Mike was so pleased with the end result that he offered to produce it before I even had a chance to ask him. It was a much hipper song and vibe than anything Spider had done before and had we gone on to make another record, I suspect that that would've been our future direction. It reminded me of Lou Reed's "Walk on the Wild Side," one of the coolest songs ever written.

Mike gathered the band together and played them the song. (I was so relieved I didn't have to tell them what was about to go down on my own.) Even though they didn't voice it in front of Mike, I could tell they were pissed at me for the exact reasons I had anticipated. Amanda was too busy burning a hole into my skull with her eyes to appreciate the fact that Mike and I had just written a hit for the band, and he'd even agreed to produce it. I knew in my heart that even though they were disgruntled, I'd done the right thing. The guys told Mike they loved the tune. Once we got in the studio with him, one major difference I noticed right away between the two producers was that Mike was really good at drawing out tighter, more groove-oriented performances, and he got a great one out of Amanda. For the first time she was singing with attitude, focusing less on technique and more on real emotion. It was slated to become our first single.

One other significant thing happened while I was in LA. While Amanda put down some vocals on one of the last songs with Peter, the guys in the band and I went to the NAMM Show (National

Association of Music Merchants), an annual event in Anaheim. It's a trade-only business convention, catering to domestic and international dealers and distributors of gear and equipment. The product exhibits are an integral part of the show, allowing the dealers and distributors to see what's new, negotiate deals and plan their purchasing for the next year. Many musicians in recording bands end up getting endorsements by at least one of the companies, and as part of their agreement, serve as spokespersons for the product at NAMM. The guys in our band had endorsements from some of the major companies; Jimmy was a rep for Dimarzio pickups, and Anton was endorsed by Zildjian cymbals, so they had committed to make appearances at the booths.

Being a woman back then, no sponsors offered me any endorsements, but I went anyway because it was a musician's mecca and a great place to network. And on the last night, a lot of the bands would get together for one big jam. Ever since I'd gotten involved and interested in synthesizers when I was fifteen, I'd stayed as current as possible with every new keyboard and synth that came out. I was particularly interested in seeing the Fairlight CMI (Computer Musical Instrument), a digital sampling synthesizer, one of the first of its kind, along with the Synclavier. This one had an outrageous price tag of twenty-eight thousand dollars, and though I couldn't afford to buy one, I wanted to check it out anyway, hoping that one day my situation would change.

What I didn't know was that on that day I would meet my future husband. He was running the Fairlight booth and wow, was he gorgeous, this tall Viking with dark blond hair running all the way down his back. Every time he smiled, his eyes twinkled. I was too nervous to even flirt with him and just mumbled and smiled back as he introduced himself as Jeff Harris. I barely listened as he ran through his obligatory sales pitch, pointing out the computer's various features. He didn't seem at all interested in me the way I was in him.

"How long have you been working with Fairlight?" I asked, hoping to find out more about him.

"I'm actually a recording engineer on staff at the Village Recorder in Santa Monica. I'm just filling in today because we use their gear."

I told myself, "This is the guy I'm going to marry."

Keith and I had agreed to meet in a few minutes as we had a long drive back to the studio in Hollywood. Reluctantly, I forced myself to snap out of the trance I'd fallen into and tear myself away thinking, *Damn, I hope he calls me.* Then I realized we hadn't exchanged numbers, and I hadn't even thought to ask him for a business card. Neither had he. Obviously, he wasn't a very good salesperson. For the next week, all I could think about was the Viking. I told myself that I needed to stop obsessing over someone I didn't really know and was never going to see again.

Ned happened to be in LA on business, and we'd arranged to meet at Ocean Way before going out to dinner. When he arrived, after all the hugs and kisses, he said, "Hey Hol, I hope you don't mind, I invited a really good friend of mine to join us for dinner. He's gonna be here any minute."

"Any friend of yours is welcome. I'm going to go put on some makeup." I excused myself to freshen up, and when I came back, my jaw dropped. Ned's "friend" was sitting on the steps next to him laughing about something. It was Jeff, my Viking. Maybe I had made more of an impression on him than I had realized because he seemed really happy to see me. Completely confused, Ned stood up and looked at the two of us grinning idiotically at one another.

"Okay," Ned said. "What's up? Have you two already met?"

Jeff and I fell in love hard and fast. We spent every spare moment together when we weren't working. We even managed to run off to San Francisco for a few romantic weekends, staying at an eclectic Victorian bed and breakfast place called the Mansion, a magical place with just fifteen rooms, visiting chefs, magic shows, and late-night drinking. On one of the weekends, Holly Penfield and her boyfriend went with us. It became a favorite haunt of mine to escape to for years until, sadly, it closed its doors.

———————

As the recording of Spider's record wound down, I started to feel a deep sadness. I knew I didn't want to be without Jeff, but we were in a difficult situation: I lived in New York, he lived in LA, and sooner or later that was going to be a problem. In the end, we decided to remain positive, that we would figure something out.

Right before the release of our second record, Mike called me into his office and handed me a copy of the lyrics to "Better Be Good to Me." When I looked at the writing credits, it said, written by Mike Chapman, Holly Knight, and Nicky Chinn.

"Why is Nicky's name on the writing credits?" I asked.

"I know, I know," he said. "It's not fair, but he and I have this partnership where his name goes on everything I write."

"But he wasn't even in the country when we wrote it," I protested.

"You're right. Listen, just agree to it this one time and I promise it'll never happen again."

"Why is that?" I asked.

"Because I'm getting ready to dissolve our partnership."

I felt powerless to argue with him, worried that he might think I was an ingrate, and I didn't know him well enough to put up a fight. "Okay," I said in defeat. Nicky's name went on the credits and, since then, he's received one third of the income for a song he had nothing to do with. I still wonder how he sleeps at night.

Once we'd finished recording *Between the Lines*, we shot the album cover, and it was obvious that we had put a little more effort into our image this time. I, for one, had started working out and carefully put together a much cooler wardrobe. Even the guys devoted a little more time to their duds. In contrast to the dark look of the first record, the background to this one was all white. We flew back to New York to prepare for the release. There were big plans, and we were primed to kick ass. Our record came out just as we finished filming the video to "Better Be Good to Me," and the reviews coming in were incredibly favorable. But in a bizarre turn of events, the rug was pulled out from underneath us as a huge payola scam surfaced.

For years, rumors had percolated throughout the industry that record companies had been bribing radio programmers to add artists' new singles to their playlists with briefcases of cash, drugs, and other incentives, and the stations not only accepted the bribes but encouraged them. They pitted one record company's promotion guy against another to see who would go the farthest to get their artists added to the station's playlist. As signed artists, we never witnessed anything firsthand—like all bands, we just believed our records were worthy of radio play, and that doesn't mean they weren't.

The timing couldn't have been worse for us or anyone releasing a new record around then. Everyone in the industry scattered like rats, too scared to work on anything while they were under investigation. As a result, record sales during that period came to a dead halt, with the exception of mega bands whose fan bases were so strong, their new records sold whether or not they had hits on the radio. We were too new and our record ended up in the toilet. It was so heartbreaking after all the work we had put into it and felt like a colossal waste of a great record. I'm sure our fan base would've grown with "Better Be Good to Me." It took about a year for the industry to recover as a new precedence took hold on how singles got added to radio playlists, and it ended up being much fairer in the long run. At least I'd like to think so.

Dreamland sent us on the road anyway, first to Europe to do a few high-profile TV shows; one of which was a German show in Munich that Foreigner was also appearing on. After the show, we all went to a trendy nightclub together. I was pinching myself because they were one of my favorite bands. They had just released, "Urgent," which, in my opinion, is their best song. After Munich we flew to Amsterdam to do a few shows. I loved Europe, and because my father's side of the family was European, I felt very comfortable there. Rich in history with exquisite old architecture and art, it was so different from America. I made a mental "to do" note: must come back soon and often. After all the European shows, the label put us on a small US tour opening for Alice Cooper. We had our own tour bus this time, and that was quite an eye-opener. Bunking with the band was bad enough, but once you threw in the roadies, the smell of dirty socks and the snoring were intolerable.

I'd never seen Alice play live, and the first time I did, he performed his infamous guillotine act. It was so realistic, I thought he'd committed suicide. Alice, the Godfather of Shock Rock, was the predecessor to acts like KISS, and I loved his music, so touring with him was an honor. After we would finish our set, I would go back and sit on the side of the stage to watch him sing and kill himself every night. Backstage in his dressing room, Alice kept a large boa constrictor named Angel on a wooden frame. She was beautiful, but I didn't have any desire to venture into that space. One of our more exciting gigs on the tour was playing at the Joe Louis Arena in Detroit; their concert capacity was over 21,000 people. This was the first time we performed in an arena, and I was thrilled that my father and Rob flew out for it.

It was a difficult time because the record wasn't selling, Amanda and I weren't seeing eye to eye on anything, and, although she wouldn't say it, I knew she wanted me out of the group. I was sick of all the pettiness and drama within the band. Amanda and Keith were also having serious personal problems. The band felt like a pressure cooker waiting to blow. I thought that I should go talk to Amanda, buy her a drink, and make an honest effort to see if we could diffuse the growing tension between us, so I went to her hotel room and discovered that she had called a meeting with the band behind my back. They were all there looking sheepishly at me when I walked in.

"Since when is there a band meeting that I'm not a part of?" I asked them before turning to Amanda and looking her in the face.

"This is all your doing, isn't it?" Her guilty look said everything I needed to know. "Okay, fine, I'll stay until the end of the tour, and then I'm leaving. I'm done. You want me out so bad? You got your wish." Keith took me out to dinner and tried to talk me out of leaving, but I just didn't feel comfortable anymore.

Amanda and Keith divorced right after I left the band, then Amanda married Anton and had a child with him. Since I had been in a relationship with Anton prior to theirs, it made me wonder if their attraction for one another had existed even then. That might explain some of the tension between Amanda and me. Our lead singer was married to two of the band members at different times and had a child with each of them. Maybe that explains some of the underlying chaos within the band. Eventually, Anton and Amanda divorced, but, interestingly enough, Anton and Keith's friendship survived and continues to this day.

I hadn't planned on leaving, but I wanted to focus on songwriting anyway. It really was the truest source of pleasure for me and, apparently, I was getting better at it. There were aspects that I loved about being in a band, like playing live, making records, and the solidarity when things were good. I didn't even mind doing interviews. But the things I hated, all the stuff in between playing live—the endless traveling late at night after the shows, the photo sessions, the feeling of being ganged up on, the back-stabbing—I would not miss.

I had a lot to mull over. If I wasn't in a band, who would I write for, who would want to record my songs, and who would be my muse? I'd be out there, marooned in the middle of the ocean, on my own all over again. Bill Aucoin would be mad and Mike and Nicky might try to sue me. But I'd already drawn a line in the sand, and I couldn't go back even if I'd wanted to. Change is a scary thing, but if you look at it in a different way, as cleansing and cathartic, there's a certain thrill, a *je ne sais quoi*, to plunging yourself into the unknown.

There was also the undeniable fact that I was missing Jeff. Without any clue as to what I was going to do once I left the band,

I figured I had better let Chapman know. I honestly thought he'd be furious because they had invested so much time and money into the band, but when I called him, I was shocked at his response.

"Listen, Holly," he said. "I'm not upset at all. I mostly signed the band because of the great songs, your songs. I think the band is terrific and all, but if you're leaving, that's going to be a real problem for them. They may not realize it yet, but they will."

"Oh God, Mike," I cried. "I'm so relieved that you're not mad at me. I'm so lost. I'm not sure what to do next. I just know I want to focus on songwriting, maybe find another band that appreciates that." Now I was sobbing.

"Well, I'll tell you what I think you should do," he said. "You should pursue a songwriting career full time, at least for now, and see what happens. You're going to find out that while being a musician in a band has its rewards, being a respected, hit songwriter is much more unique, and therefore revered by the industry. Hit songwriters are considered royalty in the music business if you're exceptionally good at it, which you are."

"Thank you for saying that. That means a lot to me." I was still sniffling a little bit. "But where do I begin, what do I do?" I continued wistfully.

He said, "You begin by moving out to LA, and I'll sign you to a new publishing deal. I'll give you a small advance so that you have money to live on. We can write together all the time, and as your publisher, I'll hook you up with other songwriters. Plus, you'll have a direct line to whoever I'm producing, when and if they need a hit song from outside their own camp, which is often the case these days. With your talent, Holly, you really should be writing songs for other artists."

There was my answer. Mike had laid it all out for me. As an added bonus, this solved the dilemma of Jeff and me being bicoastal. I kept my word with the band, finished out the tour, then went back to NYC to pack my things and Lady, my cat. Within a week, I flew out to Los Angeles, and moved in with Jeff. Everything in my life had led right up to this moment.

Songwriter, I thought. *I'm going to be an independent, full-time songwriter.* I loved the sound of that.

CHAPTER FIVE

I WANT MY MTV

New York City, 1981

"Get off your ass and dance...."
("Here For The Party" performed by The Donnas)

M TV took the music industry by storm. If you were alive during the eighties, whether you were a child or an adult, you were part of the MTV culture. There was no escaping it. It was everywhere, and was both a mirror reflection of everything that was going on and an influencer of pop culture during that epic era. It never let you down whenever you needed a fix; any hour of the day or night, you could rely on it as sure as you could set your watch.

From the moment I woke up, MTV was always on, the new soundtrack to my life. As I went about my morning ritual, reading the newspaper, showering, drinking my morning coffee, MTV ran shotgun. As soon as I got back home, I flicked the channel back on, along with the lights. Sometimes I'd keep the sound off or keep it low, and if a song I liked came on, then I would turn up the TV so loud that the speakers would distort.

Music videos were constantly evolving with the times; MTV was a brilliant marketing tool and you couldn't exist as a band or solo artist unless you got your video on MTV. Part of MTV's legacy was that it transformed music into a multisensory medium, and while image had always been an important part of the equation, bringing high-end videos into people's homes twenty-four-seven placed every artist's image under scrutiny. The pressure to look good, or at least having an intriguing image of some kind, increased tenfold. Some of the record companies would spend millions of dollars to create videos that were literally mini-movies. Initially most of the videos they showed were mainstream rock.

The network hired a diverse group of personalities to be VJs (video jocks) and the original five became familiar faces in the homes of teenagers around the country—Alan Hunter, Mark Goodman, Nina Blackwell, Martha Quinn, and J.J. Jackson. I was twenty-five when the channel launched in 1981, and it was the best thing that could've happened to me.

CHAPTER SIX

LEARNING TO MAKE PAPER AIRPLANES (PAT BENATAR)

Beverly Hills, 1983

"Heartache to heartache we stand, no promises, no demands..."
("Love Is a Battlefield" performed by Pat Benatar)

ll I could hear was muffled talking on the other end of the phone. I had no idea who Mike Chapman was talking to, but he seemed to know this person pretty well and was enjoying the conversation. He called her "sweetheart." Okay, so he was talking to a woman. She must've said something funny because he started laughing. He paused to listen while the voice chattered away, then erupted into convulsions of laughter once again. His laughter was infectious, and it was hard not to laugh along with him, even though I had no idea what was so funny. Finally, he settled down as the caller continued. He moved the headset to his other ear and winked at me. The ticking clock on the mantelpiece was the only other sound in the room, and although I was trying not to listen to their conversation, it

70

was unavoidable, even as I looked the other way, staring at a framed Erté lithograph on his wall.

Mike, who was sitting at a massive office desk in front of a large set of open bay windows, spun his chair around to peer outside. As the conversation continued, I could see he was staring at one of his seventeen avocado trees. Earlier, he had told me that a squirrel had been working its way through his property, eating all the avocados. Then, without skipping a beat, he said, "Yes, you're absolutely right, you're gonna need a hit single for the live record," while aiming a BB gun at one of the trees and firing, punctuating the word, "record." I saw something drop out of the tree, but it was just an avocado. While I could appreciate the lunacy of the moment, I was relieved he'd missed.

"Well, your timing is perfect. I'm here with one of my writers, Holly Knight." My ears pricked up. "Uh-huh, yeah." Pause. "She was in Spider. I signed them to Dreamland." Listening. "Oh, you're right. I forgot John Waite was on Chrysalis too. Yeah, she wrote 'Change.' Listen, we actually got together today to write, so we'll focus on writing you a hit. Yeah, I'll call you as soon as we have something. Okay sweetheart." The suspense was killing me. He turned back around, and after a bit more banter, he finally said goodbye and hung up.

"Who was that?" I asked.

He grinned and said, "Pat Benatar."

From day one, I always let Mike take the lead. I thought of him as my mentor, and I was his protégé. While he was barely ten years older than me, he still seemed parental at times. I was more than happy to shine in his light. I was a baby next to him as far as experience goes, and I knew I could learn a lot. I wasn't that way with most people. I had a hard time with authority and didn't want to listen to anyone, but he had accomplished so much and achieved such a huge amount of success that I sponged up whatever I could. Any praise from him was precious to me. Everyone was dying to work with him, and I hadn't forgotten how many years it had taken for him to write with me. Yet, here I was, his new blood and cowriter.

Pat Benatar was a badass. She may have been petite, but she was full of piss and vinegar and had one hell of a voice. Trained as a coloratura, she had the power and range of an opera singer, and the attitude of a woman who wasn't taking shit from anybody. I felt an immediate connection to her. Her video, a cover of the Rascals' hit, "You Better Run," was one of the first played when MTV debuted. Dressed in a tight black and white striped t-shirt and black shiny pants that looked like they had been painted onto her legs, she literally growled into the camera. Her pants looked like they were made from rubber or spandex, and whatever they were, I wanted a pair. The short haircut completed her defiant tomboy image. By this point she had achieved megastar status with her first four records, and the reason Mike and Pat knew each other so well was because he'd produced and written three tracks on her first record. "No You Don't," originally recorded by the British glam rock group, the Sweet, was one of them. On top of that, he'd introduced her to the love of her life, her guitarist, Neil Geraldo, who ended up marrying her. After the first few records, Neil began producing her records as well.

"They're putting out a live record, and they need something new, a hit to help sell the record," Mike said.

"Well, this is an exciting turn of events," I said cheerfully.

People suffer for years paying their dues and waiting a lifetime to catch a break, and while I'd paid my fair share as well, the lightning speed at which things were beginning to happen to me had to be the work of some higher power. There were many things in my life I've tried to force or manifest into being, and no amount of willfulness could make it happen, but when it came to music, things always fell right into place, especially now that I'd moved to LA. That said, I never took it for granted and made full use of every opportunity that came my way.

If not for the giant Uri speakers, the kind found in most high-end recording studios, you would never have known that a world-class producer and songwriter used this living room to write hit songs, that's how simple and amateur-looking Mike's set up was. But we had everything we needed, a pair of loudspeakers, two amps, a beat up Strat, and his Roland CR-78. I had brought a keyboard with me. This was our second venture into writing together and if we pulled this off, it would certainly be an indication that the creative electricity between us was no accident. Writing for Pat Benatar marked my transition from being a writer in a band to a full-time, independent songwriter, writing for someone else.

I was there because Mike had recognized something different in me and I was glad I'd taken his advice to move to LA and go about my career in a new way. This first opportunity was critical. We had to write something close to a masterpiece. Not surprisingly, Mike liked to write with everything turned up really loud as if we were performing at a live gig. I loved the energy of loud music too. I was used to it after being in a rock band. His Uri speakers were so enormous, they looked like you could crawl in them and go to sleep, and I'll bet you anything that he or one of his buddies probably had after one too many drinks.

"Those are some big-ass speakers," I remarked the first time I saw them.

"Yeah well, I'm probably going deaf in one ear anyway. I once did a session with Blondie when the speakers fed back so bloody loud that everybody in the control room ducked under the mixing console."

From that day forward, whenever Mike and I wrote, we usually positioned ourselves on either side of the room with our backs to each other, yet we had this supernatural connection that allowed us to collaborate without even looking at each other. Every now and then, at some telepathically synchronistic moment, we'd turn and smile or wink at one another, especially when we knew we were onto something good.

"Do you want to hear an idea that's been brewing in my head for the last week or so?" I said. "Something I was saving for our writing session that might even be cool for Pat?"

"Of course," Mike said. "Let's hear it."

I played him the bass line and then the chord progression that went along with it.

"I like that a lot," he said.

Okay, that's a good beginning, I thought. Mike plugged his Strat into the small amp on the floor, and I waited until the feedback subsided. We played around with the idea and spent some time forming an arrangement.

Mike started to sing and phonetically mumbled some ideas over the chorus, then said, "We need to come up with a really weird title, one that's going to stand out and grab people's attention."

"Yeah, I agree," I chimed in.

Mike continued, "If we want to pull this off, we have to come up with something so outstanding that people will never forget it, something kind of twisted."

"Okay," I said, "Like what?"

"I have no fucking clue," he replied with comedic timing.

I could see him searching for words as he paced around the living room like a restless animal. Then he mumbled half to himself, "Something like, well not this, but something like this," and before he could take back the words, they flew out of his mouth, "Love...is a battlefield."

I could feel something electric pass through the room, a crack in the ether. "I love it," I whispered.

Mike stopped pacing and looked at me, "Really?"

"Well, I don't know what it means," I said, "but does it really matter?"

He picked his guitar back up and said, "No, not really, we'll figure it out as we go."

That's how songwriting is, you figure it out as you go. I've been asked many times where my inspiration comes from, what's the source? I'm not really sure where the ideas come from, because songwriters seemingly create something out of nothing. But there is one pretty good analogy I can think of that's akin to a Ouija Board. There's a planchette—a heart-shaped piece of wood that you lay your fingers on, letting your hands be led about by some inexplicable force of energy to form a word or message. My planchette is a guitar or keyboard. It's all abstract in the beginning and you follow it without knowing where it's going to take you. It's ephemeral, and sometimes elusive. Other times it's right there waiting for you. You keep chasing it until something starts to form. And once you arrive at a place where it feels or sounds like something worth working on, you keep going. If you hit a wall that's leading nowhere, you just stop and live to write another day.

We pretty much wrote the entire song that day, all the music and most of the lyrics—except for one line in the chorus. One fucking line. It wasn't that we didn't have ideas. We had a hundred, but we still weren't convinced that we'd found the right one, the one that sounded like it'd always belonged there. We weren't trying to reinvent the wheel as much as come up with something that was chorus-worthy and memorable, not so much a sentence as a statement. It should've been easy, but it wasn't.

This is how the afternoon went. "Okay, let's call this the verse, how about we start with—*You're begging me go, then making me stay, why do you hurt me so bad?*" "That's good!"—We kept going 'til we wrote the first verse. "Let's try going into the chorus with—*Believe me.*" "We should repeat that." "Okay, *believe me, believe me, I can't tell you why, but I'm trapped.*" "What do you mean you're trapped?" "No, I'm not trapped, that's the lyric." "Oh! I'm trapped by your...something, something." "Love?" "Yeah! That's good, *I'm trapped by your love.*" "I got it! Listen to this—*I'm chained to your side.*" "Nice, I like that—what do you think about going straight into the chorus and foregoing the pre-chorus?" "Yeah that's good." "*We are young, heartache to heartache we stand; love is a battlefield.*" "That's it right there, that's the hook!" "But what about the third line?" "I'm stuck on that one." "Yeah, me too." "Wait! Why don't we do the unthinkable: let's start the song with the chorus." We took our time, making sure each and every part of the song counted. If it didn't serve the song, then we got rid of it. There was nothing tame about the writing session so far—our ideas were boomeranging around the room.

We still had that third line to write in the chorus, and over the next week, I made the drive from my small apartment in Marina Del Rey to Mike's mansion in Beverly Hills to finish the tune. I liked being there. All I had to do was look around. He had a tennis court and a pool. Hell, besides the seventeen avocado trees, he had lemon and orange trees too and parked in his front driveway was his Silver Cloud Rolls-Royce. It wasn't all his wealth that I found so impressive (although how could you not be impressed?); what really struck me was the fact that here was living proof that it was possible to become highly successful doing what you loved to do. From then on, I aspired to that ethos with all of my heart.

The first day that I went back to finish writing "Love Is a Battlefield," about an hour into working on the lyric, Mike pulled a joint out of his shirt pocket and as he lit it and took a long drag on it, he asked me, "Do you know how to make a paper airplane?"

While it seemed a little random, I went along with it. "No, why?"

"Well, I'm going to show you." He passed the joint to me and took a sheet of paper with some discarded lyrics he'd scribbled on it earlier. Folding the paper several times, he held up a sleek airplane.

"That's incredible!" I said, taking a stab at it. It took several attempts, but I finally got the hang of it. Then he showed me how to make it soar perfectly.

At some point we found ourselves sitting on the concrete at either end of his pool, testing out the aerodynamics of our fighter planes. Somehow, I had gotten it in my head to unfold the wings of one of them, write a new lyric down and shoot it back across the blue expanse of the water towards him. Taking my cue, he would read it, crumple it up and toss it over his shoulder, then form a new plane, write something else down, and shoot it back. This went on for some time. Lunch. Smoke some more pot. Repeat. That was our process on the first day. We talked and laughed and acted silly. It was all part of the process. This was really the first time we were hanging out and getting to know one another. I liked him immensely.

The rest of the week we stopped horsing around and got down to business, especially when it came to the lyrics, because I already knew that once you sent a song out into the world, it would be out there forever. We were relentless until we were satisfied that we'd nailed that last elusive line.

"No promises, no demands." That was it. What was it about it that one that we liked? Why did we say yes to that one and forgo all the others? I can't say except that it sounded good, like it had always belonged in the third line of the chorus. I was a relatively young kid myself, and I found it relatable: when you're young, you don't have to commit to things the way you do when you're older. No promises, no demands. So, here was the chorus:

> "We are young, heartache to heartache we stand,
> no promises no demands—love is a battlefield.
> We are strong, no one can tell us we're wrong,
> searching our hearts for so long, both of us knowing
> love is a battlefield."

We made a bare-bones demo with Mike singing. While he wasn't the greatest singer, he captured the attitude and emotion of the song. Rock 'n' roll is 75 percent attitude—just take a look at Bob Dylan and Patti Smith. Do they have classically trained voices? No. But they more than make up for it with their emotional intensity and attitude.

We messengered it over to Pat and Neil and waited with bated breath for what seemed like days but in reality was a mere few hours.

Neil called us first. I could hear Pat in the background. I think she was trying to grab the phone from him, they were that excited. Finally, she got on the phone and told Mike how much they loved the song and to "make sure to tell Holly thank you." Jeff Aldrich, their A&R person, was over the moon. Everyone at Chrysalis Records was too. The label had a close working relationship with Mike because of Blondie and Nick Gilder, two other artists on their roster. Indeed, this wasn't my first foray into working with Chrysalis either. In 1982, another artist of theirs, John Waite, formally of the British rock group the Babys, had recorded a tune of mine called "Change," which Spider had originally recorded on our second record. It was the first cover of something I'd written. It's also one of my favorite songs that I wrote.

There was only one dark cloud that came to rain on the whole thing. Our demo had a midtempo eighth note feel. It wasn't fancy or anything, but it had an epic feel. It was weighty, like a chalice of red wine, or meat and potatoes. When Neil and Pat sent their recording back to us, we listened to it, looking at each other with the same reaction. *What the fuck? What did they do to our song?* We had sent them an anthem and they sent us back a dance track. They changed the tempo and meter, making it faster, and now it seemed to have a Bo Diddley feel to it. They put some weird synthesizer effects on the end of the chorus that reminded me of a Vegas slot machine.

Mike was one of the most successful and creative producers in the music business, and for us to have written such a potent and unique song, only to hear Neil's bizarre production, was a disappointment to say the least. It was strong enough on its own that all the bells and whistles Neil had added were distracting and only diluted its power. It must've been especially hard for Mike because he knew exactly how he would've produced it.

As a songwriter for other artists, you start to develop nerves of steel. First, there's the magic period when you conceive the song. It's safe and warm in the womb. Then you demo it and send it out into the world for people to hear. Once that happens, you brace yourself for the response—"I love it," "I'm not loving it," "It's a great song but we're looking for something different," "It's too pop," "It's not pop enough," "It's a hit," "It's not a hit." Once someone says they love and want to record it, it's feels like you're handing your baby over for adoption. You wave goodbye and hope like hell that they don't fuck up your little bundle of joy. Whoever is producing the song is more than likely going to make some changes. Sometimes, the only reason to change things is because they can.

We tried to choose our words carefully with Neil and Pat. We didn't want to create a shitstorm by telling them that we didn't like the recording. Thankfully, Pat's iconic vocals shined through. Mike had whistled a few notes at the beginning of the demo, I suspect he was just screwing around, and, ironically, it was one of the few things production-wise that Neil kept, though he added the whistling to the end of the record. The minute "Battlefield" hit MTV, it became an instant classic. They played it every hour on the hour, and over time we got used to the way it sounded. Dislike turned into love as it moved up the charts.

The video was groundbreaking. Bob Giraldi, a well-known director, fresh off making Michael Jackson's "Beat It" video, took "Battlefield" and, by adding dialogue to the beginning, set a new standard for music videos. As the music played in the intro, a father was shown yelling at his daughter, which had never been done before. "You leave this house and you can just forget about coming back." It was like watching a mini movie. Giraldi's interpretation of the song froze me in my tracks, and it took me a minute to realize why it was affecting me so physically.

It was a mirror reflection of my own life. My mother had yelled the same exact words to me on more than one occasion—before I finally left. Just like the video, my own journey had been about breaking tethers and forging a new life for myself. There is no way on earth that Giraldi could have known that he had captured my life on screen. It was an amazing coincidence that sent me hurtling back to my past.

Once again, I had that overwhelming feeling that everything I had done in my life had led up to this, even the most harrowing moments of my childhood had played a vital and prescient role in creating my story and the things I would write about in my songs.

Chapter Seven

A NIGHT IN HEAVEN ("OBSESSION")

Los Angeles, 1983

"I will have you, yes I will have you, I will
find a way and I will have you…"
("Obsession" performed by Animotion)

"I'm going to introduce you to Michael Des Barres," Mike said one day. "I think the two of you should try writing something together." True to his word, he was starting to set me up with other writers. Des Barres was the first.

Mike told me that Des Barres was from the UK, that he'd been in a British glam rock band named Silverhead, and that he was a former label-mate on Dreamland Records as a solo artist. Des Barres and I met just as Mike was about to go into the studio with Smokie, a British band with whom he'd had a lot of success during the British glam period of the seventies. He said that they could use a hit, so the three of us got together and wrote a lyrically edgy song called "Looking Daggers."

Not long after that, Des Barres came over to my place, excited about some lyrics he'd been working on for a song he wanted to call "Obsession." I suspected it was something personal, that it had something to do with his love affair with sex and drugs. I thought the lyrics were compelling, and I could certainly relate. I knew what it was like to obsess over something, or someone.

Immediately inspired, I sat down to write the music, starting with this infectious bass sequence I programmed on my synthesizer, and then added chords over it. We finished the vocal melody and tweaked the rest of the lyrics together in a day. After we recorded a simple demo, we played it to Chapman who said, "This is a bloody hit." Mike only dished out praise when he meant it, so we were elated. "Let's just record it as a master and I'll produce it," he said. (For anyone wondering what the difference is between a demo and a master, think of the demo as a "demonstration" or musical sketch of the song, and the master as the actual record.)

Chapman took a few days off from a project he was working on at Ocean Way Studios. First, we recorded the programmed drums and all the instrumentation. When it came time to record Des Barres, once the tape started rolling, he came to life and started ranting in what sounded like Japanese but was just some gibberish he'd made up on the spot. You can hear it on the record. Some of the best stuff happened like that—spontaneously. I laid down all my vocals and it ended up as a duet.

The people assigned the job of pitching songs to the labels and film companies were called song pluggers, and Chapman had his send "Obsession" to a film company that was distributed by Twentieth Century Fox. The music supervisor wanted to license it for a movie they were filming called *A Night in Heaven*, starring Christopher Atkins, whose claim to fame was *The Blue Lagoon* with Brooke Shields. He played a college student who becomes a male stripper to pay his bills and discovers he's quite good at it. They worked "Obsession" into a club scene where he danced and thrusted his crotch into a pretty but frumpily dressed schoolteacher's face, played by Leslie Anne Warren. It was a steamy scene, and while the movie was cheesy, it made its mark, serving as predecessor to Chippendales and the *Magic Mike* movies. Cheesy or not, I was just thrilled to hear my music being played on the big screen for the first time.

A year after the movie came out, a new LA based band named Animotion heard the song and decided to cut it. They had both a male and a female singer and reminded me of Human League, which had the same vocal setup, so it seemed like a natural progression from "Knight and Des Barres" to them. While our version was more druggie sounding and cool, theirs was more pop and fit the MTV eighties format. I think that's why it did so well.

"Obsession" went to number six in the Billboard Hot 100 and became an international smash, going to number one in several different countries. In the video, there were hot young men dressed as Romans parading around the poolside in skimpy little togas and helmets, serving hors d'oeuvres. To this day I've never been able to figure out what that had to do with the song, but that was the wonderful zaniness of the times. It didn't matter if a cow walked through the set. The more random the better because no one really cared. It was all entertainment, and everyone had a sense of humor. Even though it was such a silly video, it became a staple on MTV, whose weekly fashion show, *House of Style*, used it as its theme song. "Obsession" has a life of its own and is probably one of my most licensed songs.

Michael Des Barres introduced me to Kathy Valentine, bass player for the Go-Gos. The Go-Gos had recently split up, and whatever turmoil Kathy must've been going through, I give her a lot of credit for being the funny, and fun loving character she was. We had the same wicked sense of humor, as well as music in common, and we immediately took a shine to one another. Kathy was always making me laugh and vice versa. It was nice to have a girlfriend who understood the pitfalls and trappings of the music business. It was also refreshing to find someone to hang out with and do things that had nothing to do with rock 'n' roll. For instance, one morning on New Year's Eve day, we'd decided to drive up to Big Bear, a small ski resort about an hour and a half from LA for a few days. Kathy's mother, whom I liked, came too, but she wasn't a skier. I don't think Kathy was either, but no matter. We were so excited to be going skiing that we wore our ski clothes on the drive up so we wouldn't waste a single moment when we arrived. We'd be able to walk right up to the chair lift with our already-purchased lift tickets and hit the slopes. We were in such high spirits during the whole road trip, we didn't pay attention to much else. By the time we arrived at the slopes it was quite warm and we were sweating with all the gear on. Still, we kept babbling on about how great it was going to be up on the mountain in all that fresh pristine snow. We were able to park close to the slopes, which I thought was a little odd. Usually it was impossible to get this close to the lifts. Kathy and I got out of the car, still yapping away, "This is going to be so—"

We both stopped in mid-sentence as we looked around and up the mountain. There wasn't a drop of snow to be seen *anywhere*, not on the ground, not up the mountain, not falling from the sky. Kathy asked the obvious, "Where's the snow?" "Fuck !!! " I yelled. "We should've checked the Weather Channel." (There were no apps or smart phones back then.) For a few minutes we stood there not sure what to do or say. Then we burst out laughing. We laughed so hard I think I peed in my ski pants. We fell on the ground laughing and couldn't stop. Kathy's mother just looked at us like we were idiots. The three of us ended up having a marvelous time anyway, sunbathing and greeting in the new year together.

On September 14, 1984, I went to the first MTV Video Music Awards show at Radio City Music Hall. Billy Idol was my buddy date. I had run into him months prior at an event and he pointed at me grinning that big toothy smile of his, while I pointed and grinned back at him. The last time we'd seen each other was back in New York when we were hungry musicians struggling to get a foothold in the music business. Just a few years later and we'd both "made it."

"You did it, Billy!" I exclaimed. "You're a fucking rock star! Success suits you."

"Yeah and look at you, you're writing hits for everyone!" We were so proud of each other. We had both been planning to go on our own to the video awards show, so instead, we decided to go together. He was nominated for five awards for "Dancing with Myself" and "Eyes Without a Face," while Pat Benatar was up for Best Female Video with "Love Is a Battlefield." Chrysalis hired a limo for Billy, so we were going to arrive in style. Everyone in my hotel lobby stared at him when he walked in to pick me up. It was obvious he was used to it. I, on the other hand was never comfortable with strangers staring at me, so songwriting was the perfect gig for me.

When we arrived, we went in through a back entrance, and an usher showed us to our seats. They were in the front row where we had a bull's eye view of Madonna's crotch as she writhed around on stage singing "Like a Virgin," a brilliant song my friend Billy Steinberg had written with Tom Kelly. I'd dressed to the nines and had on a long white fitted coat that opened at the front from my waist to reveal thigh-high black leather high-heeled boots. All my jewelry was the color of amber jewels and I had a makeup artist help me with my hair and makeup. It was my debut, my coming-out party in many ways. All my life I'd been the outsider, never fitting in with any group, never having lasting friendships, always running away, and now I was sitting in the VIP section, the front row to the first MTV awards show. I finally felt like I was part of something, a family of super talented misfits and renegades.

Some of the presenters that night were Mick Jagger, Rod Stewart, Ronnie Wood, and Hall & Oates. Roger Daltrey smashed a guitar during his presentation for Best Live Performance; Best Group Video went to ZZ Top for "Legs"; David Bowie won Best Male Video for

"China Girl," which Iggy Pop accepted on his behalf; Billy presented the Viewer's Choice Award for "Thriller," which won three awards in total, but Michael Jackson wasn't there, so Diana Ross accepted on his behalf; Video of the Year went to the Cars for "You Might Think," beating the Police's "Every Breath You Take"; and Best New Artist went to Eurythmics for "Sweet Dreams." Amongst some of the performers were Rod Stewart and Tina Turner. Pat Benatar lost out to Cyndi Lauper's "Girls Just Wanna Have Fun," but what a startling year of music and videos it was. To say it was an iconic year is an understatement.

CHAPTER EIGHT

BANG, BANG, I AM THE WARRIOR (PATTY SMYTH)

Los Angeles, Malibu, 1984

"I don't wanna change your animal style, you
won't be caged in the call of the wild..."
("The Warrior" performed by Patty Smyth)

ittle did I know when I first wrote "The Warrior" back in 1984 that it wouldn't just be a big hit, but also serve as a kind of theme song for the rest of my life. It didn't feel autobiographical when I wrote it, but as I've learned, sometimes we don't write songs—the songs write us.

Mike had just met with Patty Smyth, a feisty singer from New York (not to be confused with the poet/singer Patti Smith) whose band Scandal was getting ready to do their first album. I loved her voice. She didn't sound like anybody else, yet she had what I like to call a radio-friendly voice. Previously, Scandal had released the catchy "Goodbye to You," which was on an EP they had put out that reached number five on Billboard's Album Rock Charts. It was a good start and Mike was excited about producing them. He thought Patty, if not the band, was a star. The label clearly felt the same because when the record came out, they billed it as "Scandal, featuring Patty Smyth."

Mike said they had written some good songs for the record, but they were sorely in need of a hit that would put them on the map. As my publisher, he had been wanting to introduce me to Nick Gilder, a Canadian singer for whom he had produced "Hot Child in the City." It became a huge number one hit. Just as he had with Michael Des Barres, he wanted to set me up with Nick to write. "I need a hit for this record," he said.

I was excited at the opportunity to work with Nick; he was a great vocalist whose voice was in an unusually high range. In fact, the first time I heard "Hot Child In The City" on the radio, I thought it was a woman singing. Nick lived in LA, so I invited him over to my place. I liked his vibe. While he seemed pretty chill, I sensed that beneath his quiet demeanor was an artistic and twisted soul. I told Nick that we needed to write the kind of male-driven lyrics that men were known for, but that a woman with balls could sing instead. I felt that would be much more enticing. These were the kind of things I was starting to strive for.

I played Nick the chord progression I'd started, which I thought would make a great sounding chorus. Our process was similar to how I wrote with Mike—we phonetically sang random nonsense until the words and melody came, bouncing ideas back and forth over the music. I knew I wanted to write something with "Warrior" in the title.

"What do you think of this? 'Shooting at the walls of heartache...'" Nick asked.

"That's great, now try 'I am the warrior.'" I said.

"Yeah, that's good," he shot back, "Hey let's repeat that."

And then I came up with "heart to heart you win if you survive," and so on. It went back and forth like this until we had most of the song. We got together one more time to finish the lyric and that's when Nick came up with my favorite part, the "bang bang" after the first line in the chorus. It was so hooky and iconic. We demoed it with Nick's vocals—he sounded great.

> "Shooting at the walls of heartache, bang bang,
> I am the warrior, well I am the warrior.
> Heart to heart, you win if you survive,
> The warrior, the warrior."

Here was a song that resonated close to my heart. I was thrilled and couldn't wait to send it to Mike. I knew we had written something special. Whenever I wrote a really powerful tune, I would be on cloud nine for days, I'd literally look up at the sky and say, "Thank you," my heart bursting with gratitude. Kind of like being in love. Of course, I don't feel that way about everything I've written. There have been more than a few bad ones that no one will ever hear, but I try not to write bad songs anymore. On the other hand, there have been many times during my career, so many, in fact, that I've lost count, where I wrote what I believed was a hit and no one wanted to record it. Some of my best work is still sitting on ice, waiting to be discovered. I never give up on sending songs out if I believe in them, no matter how old they are. I think of them as vintage Knight songs, waiting to find a home.

I messengered "The Warrior" to Mike, and his response was disappointingly lukewarm. "It's not bad," he said.

I was crushed. Nick, who loved it as much as I did, said, "That's fine with me because I want to record it." The problem was that he wasn't signed to a label anymore, which I found strange since he had recently scored a number one hit. Either his label hadn't renewed his contract or he'd left. I'm not sure. A week went by when Mike called me up, "Hey, can you please resend me that tune? The warrior one?"

No doubt his mind had been elsewhere the day he first listened to it, but my guess is that he'd been walking around singing the chorus and couldn't get it out of his head. I dropped the cassette in his mailbox. A few hours later, he called me.

"This song is a fucking hit, and I'm going to record it with Patty."

Hallelujah. Delayed reaction or not, I was happy he had seen the light. Nick, on the other hand, wasn't thrilled because now he wanted to keep "The Warrior" for himself. He thought it would help him to get a new record deal, and it probably would have. I could understand what he was feeling, but Mike decided to play hardball.

"Look," he said, "I'm a publisher on this song. You wrote it for an artist I'm producing because I asked you to, and if you don't let me have it, I won't grant the license to you or anyone else to record it."

"The Warrior" was released as the first single and became a huge, iconic hit. I always get a kick when someone learns that I wrote it and starts singing the chorus to me. The song went to number one in Canada and number seven in the United States, as well as number one on the US Rock Chart. Over the years it's been recorded and licensed over and over again for many things.

Patty's label had hired David Hahn to direct the video. The plot line made absolutely no sense, and the makeup artist should've been shot, although it was probably the director who told him (or her) to make Patty look like a multi-colored bolt of lightning had struck her in the face. The band looked like extras from the Broadway production of *Cats*. It was a big rock song, yet there wasn't a single shot of the band playing. And the hair stylist made Patty look like the Bride of Frankenstein with her upswept 'do. Did they really think she looked anything like a ninja warrior? Surely, that's what they'd been going for. There's one scene where a large man dressed as a cat is keeping tally on an abacus of sorts, keeping score of what I know not. Still, it was typical of the eighties' silliness, and the programmers at MTV loved it. It remained in heavy rotation for months. I often wondered what Patty thought of the video, and it was only thirty years later when we got together for lunch in New York that I learned she hated it as much as I did. We shared a good laugh over it.

Luckily for me, it turned out that the producers at MTV found it newsworthy that a young woman was the songwriter behind quite a few of the rock videos being played repeatedly on the channel. Because of that, they often mentioned me on the newsbreaks they did every half hour on the hour. You'd hear Alan Hunter or Mark Goodman say something like, "And that was 'Change' by John Waite, a song written by Holly Knight," or, "And that was Animotion's 'Obsession,' followed by Patty Smyth's 'The Warrior,' back-to-back songs by songwriter Holly Knight." There was also Martha Quinn and Nina Blackwood, the other two original VJs. "That was another Holly Knight tune, she was spotted at the Prince concert in LA with Robin Zander...." Unlike other songwriters, I never hired a PR agent. I think part of the fascination with me was that I was a woman who had not only infiltrated the male-centric landscape of rock 'n' roll but was writing empowering songs with attitude for female artists. We set it up beautifully for singers like Alanis Morissette to come along and sing about standing up to their asshole boyfriends and telling them to fuck off.

While I enjoyed the free publicity, some of the bands I'd worked with weren't happy about it, especially when they mentioned only me. I didn't want the bands to think it was coming from me, and I thought I'd better send a message through my attorney, Gary Gilbert.

"Dear MTV. While I am extremely grateful and delighted with all the press you have been affording me with, could you please turn it down a notch? It's pissing off the bands I work with. You guys rock. Thank you, Holly Knight."

Nevertheless, because of all the newsworthy blurbs they shared, viewers and fans who otherwise would've had no knowledge of me became familiar with my name. One day, Ned called me up and said, "Buy the new issue of *Rolling Stone*." When I asked him why, he said, "Just go get it."

I ran to the newsstand on the corner and rifled through it until I saw what he was talking about. *Holy shit!* I'd been named one of five in the Best Songwriters category in their eleventh annual Readers' Poll. There was my name, along with Bruce Springsteen, Billy Joel, Paul

Simon, and Phil Collins. I'm not sure I merited that kind of recognition—these guys were legends—but I loved that the fans thought I was worthy. I also found it encouraging that of the five, I was the only woman and the only independent songwriter writing for other artists. The rest wrote for themselves. It was thanks to MTV.

THE WINNERS

Readers' Results

Bruce, Madonna, Genesis and Peter Gabriel score in the eleventh annual poll

Artist of the Year
Bruce Springsteen
Peter Gabriel
Phil Collins
Madonna
Steve Winwood

Best Album
Bruce Springsteen and the E Street Band Live/1975-1985, Bruce Springsteen and the E Street Band
5150, Van Halen
So, Peter Gabriel
Life's Rich Pageant, R.E.M.
Invisible Touch, Genesis

Best Single
"Sledgehammer," Peter Gabriel
"Higher Love," Steve Winwood
"Addicted to Love," Robert Palmer
"Amanda," Boston
"You Give Love a Bad Name," Bon Jovi

Best Band
Genesis
Van Halen
R.E.M.
The E Street Band
U2

Best Male Singer
Peter Gabriel
Bruce Springsteen
Phil Collins
Steve Winwood
Robert Palmer

Best Female Singer
Madonna
Tina Turner
Janet Jackson
Stevie Nicks
Annie Lennox (Eurythmics)

Worst Album
Eat 'Em and Smile, David Lee Roth
Heartbeat, Don Johnson
True Blue, Madonna
Raising Hell, Run-D.M.C.
Dancing on the Ceiling, Lionel Richie

Worst Single
"Heartbeat," Don Johnson
"Dancing on the Ceiling," Lionel Richie
"Walk This Way," Run-D.M.C.
"True Blue," Madonna
"True Colors," Cyndi Lauper

Worst Band
Run-D.M.C.
Cinderella
Bon Jovi
Mötley Crüe
Genesis

Worst Male Singer
Don Johnson
David Lee Roth
Lionel Richie
Bruce Springsteen
Prince

Worst Female Singer
Cyndi Lauper
Madonna
Janet Jackson
Stacey Q
Tina Turner

Best New British Band
Pet Shop Boys
Simply Red
The Outfield
Level 42
Communards

Best New American Band
Bruce Hornsby and the Range
Cinderella
David and David
Bangles
The Rainmakers

Best New Male Singer
Don Johnson
Bruce Hornsby
Mick Hucknall (Simply Red)
Andy Taylor
Peter Cetera

Best New Female Singer
Anita Baker
Janet Jackson
Stacey Q
Belinda Carlisle
Whitney Houston

THE BEST AND THE WORST
Bruuuce! Bo-zo!

Best Producer
Nile Rodgers
Phil Collins
Dave Stewart
Don Gehman
Hugh Padgham

Best Songwriter

Phil Collins

Billy Joel

Paul Simon

Bruce Springsteen

Holly Knight

Best R&B Artist
Aretha Franklin
Anita Baker
Run-D.M.C.
Janet Jackson
James Brown

Best Country Artist
Alabama
Willie Nelson
Dwight Yoakam
The Judds
Kenny Rogers

DON JOHNSON
Voted both the Best New Male Singer and the Worst Male Singer of 1986, the Stubbly One demonstrated that, like his native mediums, he has the power to cloud minds.

E.J. CAMP/ONYX

CHAPTER NINE

"WE FELL OUT" (DIVINYLS)

Los Angeles, 1985

"It's a fine line between pleasure and pain
you've done it once you could do it again..."
("Pleasure and Pain," performed by Divinyls)

E ven though I was busy conquering the world as a songwriter,
I had to admit that I was waxing nostalgic about being in a
band. In a band, I could take more risks artistically compared
to when I wrote for other artists. I missed being part of something
and I really missed performing live. Even though I was spending all
my time writing songs, I still practiced piano almost every day for the
sheer joy of it.

Of course, I hadn't forgotten about the things I didn't miss, the
reasons I'd fled from my last band. Still, I felt a stab of envy every
time I saw a new video or new band on MTV.

One day at Mike's house, I brought it up. "Sometimes I miss
being in a band. It would be nice to make music a little more artsy

and outside the box, if for nothing else, to express my personal style of music without worrying if it's a hit."

"Yeah, I get it." He replied. "But why do you think you can't be in a band anymore?"

"What do you mean?" I asked, intrigued.

"You could make a record."

"Ugh! I don't want to go through shopping for a deal again. It's so time-consuming and stressful doing all those showcases, and it's such a long shot," I said, thinking out loud. I was spoiled now.

"C'mon, Holly, you know I have a great relationship with Chrysalis."

"Yeah, I know they love you, but what's that got to do with me?" I asked.

"They love you too. You've given them some big hits, and if I were to speak to them about it, I bet they'd be interested in signing you."

"Seriously?"

"If you want, I'll talk to them and see how interested they are. It doesn't hurt to ask. I could tell them that I'm going to produce the record."

"You'd actually be interested in producing the record?"

"Why not? It's not a bad idea and it could be fun."

I left Mike's in a happy daze, totally unprepared for this turn of events. I'd expected him to shoot me down and tell me to be happy that things were going so well, and that I would fuck up everything up by trying to change things. Now that the possibility existed, I started to picture the kind of band I wanted to put together as I drove home, rain splattering on my windshield.

I would write great songs. I'd work hard to make sure of that. Because I had become known for writing for women, I wanted to change things up and find a male lead singer, someone with a low voice yet incredible range and a tone all his own. And someone with a great look. I loved to write bass lines, so I decided that I would play the bass—but do it all on a lo-fi keyboard. That would give the band some low end sonically. I also knew how to play bass guitar, which I had been teaching myself over the last few years. I could use a portable keyboard! Why be stuck behind a stack of instruments off to the side? This was *my* band and I intended to be just as visible as the guitarist and singer. I wondered if I could get something wireless where I would have the freedom to run across the stage without tripping over the cords. And the guitarist had to be exceptional.

Mike called me up the next day and told me to come over right away. I walked into his living room, unsure what the urgency was about.

"They said yes."

"Who said yes to what?" I answered dumbly.

"I spoke to Jeff Aldrich at Chrysalis, and he thinks it's a great idea. I even spoke to Chris and Terry." Chris Wright was the "Chrys" and Terry Ellis was the "alis" in Chrysalis Records, the two founders.

I was stunned. "But they don't even know what it is yet," I stammered, still in disbelief.

"It doesn't matter, they love you and they know there will be hits on it."

"Wait," I said. "Don't I have to actually put the band together first?"

"Nope."

"Holy shit! This is incredible, this is so utterly fucking fantastic!" I sputtered. "Wait! You're not just pulling my leg, are you?" I squinted at him suspiciously, scanning his face for cracks in the armor even though I knew that Mike was not in the habit of making shit up.

"No, I am not." he said seriously. "It's real. Call them yourself if you don't believe me."

I had been living with Jeff for three years when he proposed to me. We got married in the Marina at a lovely hotel and invited our friends and families. Even my mother flew out. We went to Europe for our honeymoon, and as soon as we got back, I decided I would make it my mission to start putting the band together, especially finding a vocalist. How hard could it be?

The first night I went clubbing in the San Fernando Valley, and in the middle of nowhere, I discovered Gene Bloch, an incredible guitarist. *Surely, it couldn't be this easy*, I thought. Gene was someone who would become not only one of my favorite musicians to play with, but a dear friend for the rest of my life. He was able to slowly transition out of his other band and join my band, and while that happened, he and I started writing for the record. He decided to change his surname to Black, something he had been intending to do anyway, and which, as an added bonus, went well with my surname... Black Knight.

To my utter dismay, finding the perfect singer turned out to be much harder and was a long and arduous process that took almost two years. During that time, I continued writing for other artists.

While Jeff and I lived together happily for three years, one short year after we tied the knot, things began to unravel pretty quickly as my career continued to blossom. We loved each other very much, but our schedules were so different, we barely saw each other. I was focused on my songwriting, as well as trying to find a lead singer for my band, which involved traveling. I didn't have the wherewithal to make both things work. I realized I would be happier keeping my autonomy and having the freedom to take advantage of the numerous opportunities coming my way. There was no doubt in my mind that I wanted to have children one day, but not then, not in my twenties. When the marriage ended, there was no drama, just sadness as I watched Jeff move out and I continued to live alone in the duplex.

I was already a fan of the Divinyls, an Australian band that Mike was about to produce, when he asked me if I would write a song for, them. It was for their second record, *What a Life!*, and they'd already spent two years working on it by the time they contacted Mike. He produced just two songs, but they were the best ones on the album, one of which was a song we ended up writing together, called "Pleasure and Pain." It was a dark title and song I'd started writing when Jeff and I broke up, the concept being, *the harder you love, the more you hurt; the closer you get, the further you drift apart.* Mike set up a meeting between Chrissy Amphlett, the lead singer, and I to see if she'd want to finish writing it with me. I can't remember why, but we met in a hotel room. What I do remember is that she walked in carrying a violin case. It was her purse. *How eccentric*, I thought. *She's very cool.* Chrissy had a distinctive voice, which people either loved or hated. I was a fan, I loved the band and thought they were going to be really big one day.

We laid some lines of cocaine out on the table and started to have a pleasant enough conversation. I asked her if she and Mark, the lead guitarist, were a couple, because it seemed like they were a perfect fit and they were seen together a lot in photographs. It seemed like an innocent enough question. I'd been in a band and had a relationship with the drummer, so it was no big deal. Instead of answering, she stood up and said, "I think I'm going to go for a walk." Then she left and never returned. It was bizarre. The next day, I called up Jeff at Chrysalis and asked him if he had heard from her. He said she was upset that I'd asked her such a personal question. Apparently, she didn't want anyone to know about them and now she didn't want to write with me.

I ended up finishing the song with Mike and they recorded it anyway. He produced it and it came out exactly as I had imagined it in my head. That was the beauty of handing a song over to Mike. I knew I could count on him to do the song justice. It's one of my favorite songs that I cowrote. Chrissy never apologized, but I did, although I'm not sure for what. The song did not do well on the American charts, but their video got heavy rotation on MTV anyway. That was the power of the cable network. Even if you didn't have a hit on the Billboard charts, which reflected radio airplay and sales, you could

still get tons of airplay on MTV and end up having a hit anyway…
and the Divinyls did just that.

Rolling Stone described the music as "loud and hard-edged, as
purely physical as any metal band, but tempered with swaggering
rowdiness." Another reviewer said, "Literally any Divinyls song ever
recorded could have been called 'Pleasure & Pain.' Chrissy Amphlett's
titanic voice was all about pushing prettiness until it became punishing. 'Pleasure & Pain' is a leather boot, pinned directly into your chest."

What a Life! is the only record I've had a song on that didn't list
the songwriters. I wrote "Pleasure and Pain," but my name didn't
appear anywhere, and I thought, *What the hell?* By now, I knew most
artists want everyone to think they wrote all of their songs, but this
wasn't even legal, on top of which it was hard not to feel slighted.
The credit was important to me because it was my "business card"
and it got me more work. It was also nice to be acknowledged for my
efforts. By then, I should've been used to feeling slighted.

The single did much better in Australia, getting to number
eleven. I love her vocals and Mike's production. Several months after
the song came out, Chrissy and Mark appeared in the Random Notes
section of *Rolling Stone*. Wearing garters, she was crouched on top of
Mark, their limbs intertwined, looking very much the couple. Maybe
they were just perpetuating the myth, being provocateurs, but it was
what she said that really made me laugh. Discussing their new single,
"Pleasure and Pain," she said, "I was supposed to write that song with
Holly Knight, but we fell out, so she wrote it with Mike Chapman
instead." Falling out would've been more gratifying than her walking out on me with no explanation. But surprisingly, we moved on
and became good friends. In 2013, Chrissy died at her home in
Manhattan after a long battle with breast cancer. I was devasted. She
was only fifty-three.

First photo of Spider. (from left) Anton, me, Keith, Amanda and Jimmy.
(Photographer: Michael Obliwitz)

Spider video shoot for
"Better Be Good To Me."

Hanging out at Aucoin Management.

Photo shoot in the *Penthouse* offices, 1982.
(Photographer:Tony Guccione)

With Mike Chapman.

With the infamous Fairlight.

One on One Recording Studios in
North Hollywood.

With Kathy Valentine backstage at the
Eurythmics show in Rome.

Video shoot for Device's "Who Says."

The "thirty toes." (from left) Me, Ann and Nancy Wilson of Heart.

With Patty Smyth.

After Tina teased my hair backstage in Germany, 1985.

Device photo shoot.
I love hanging out on rooftops.

Filming "Hanging On a Heart Attack"
in London.

One of my many '80s looks.
Pebbles hairdo, big loop earrings.

In my living room after a makeup artist
got his hands on me.

With Don Johnson in his trailer on the set of *Miami Vice*.

At one of Rod Stewart's soccer games.

With Jon Bon Jovi at his house just hours before I got thrown in the pool.

With Steven Tyler at Little Mountain Sound Studios in Vancouver.

With Nancy in my apartment,
the Kitty Cave, on Wilshire.

With Tina at the Hit Factory in
New York City.

Cruising in my Maserati.

With Kathy and a local hottie in Venice.

With Elektra, "Warrior Princess."

About to be inducted into the
Songwriters Hall Of Fame in 2013.

My recording studio, The Jewel Box.

CHAPTER TEN

HOW I MET THE ACID
QUEEN (TINA TURNER)

Los Angeles, 1985

"Walk tall, cool, collected—savage."
("One of the Living" performed by Tina Turner)

Tina was forty-four when she embarked on her solo career. In 1983, legend has it that in an A&R meeting to listen to potential songs for her debut solo record, *Private Dancer*, Tina jumped out of her seat and pranced around the room as "Better Be Good to Me" blasted from the office speakers. "This is the perfect song for me!" she exclaimed. She thought it had an empowering message and lots of rock 'n' roll attitude.

Private Dancer was released in 1984 and "Better Be Good To Me" became her second single. I was excited, but I had no idea how big she was about to become or what impact she would have on my life. The record triumphantly went on to sell twenty million copies and firmly established her as "The Queen of Rock 'n' Roll." It won the coveted Grammy for Record of the Year while "Better Be Good to

Me" earned Best Rock Vocal Performance, which was a win for me too. I couldn't have been prouder. It really established me as a successful writer in more ways than I could've ever dreamed of.

With the massive success of *Private Dancer*, she had become the biggest star on the planet, and even though I had met and become friends with Roger Davies, her Australian manager, the opportunity to meet Tina hadn't happened, which wasn't unusual. More often than not, the songwriter didn't meet the artist recording their song. If you collaborated with them, that was a different situation, but even then, you could only get so close.

One late spring afternoon, Roger called me.

"Listen darling, Tina's just wrapped up filming the second sequel to *Mad Max* and George Miller, the director, wants her to record a new tune for the opening scene. How would you like to take a stab at writing something for her?"

"I'd love to!" I answered enthusiastically.

I was so stoked that Roger had called me when he could've called anybody. I'd never assumed that just because we'd had some success together, Tina would record another song of mine. This time, I would not only tailor something just for her, I was going to write the song by myself.

Roger arranged to have the script and some movie footage sent over to me right away. It was important to capture the dystopian nature of the movie in the lyrics. I had read *Cosmos* by the late great astronomer and author, Carl Sagan, in which he had said that if there was a nuclear war, the living would envy the dead, so I paid homage to that:

"No, you can't stop the pain of your children crying out in your head....They always said that the living would envy the dead."

Within a week I'd written and demoed "One of the Living," a postapocalyptic metal cruncher. I wrote the song on bass guitar because I wanted it to have that low drone on the bottom end while chunky eighth notes on guitar gave it an ominous edge. I messengered it to Roger, who overnighted it to Tina in Europe. She was on tour but that didn't stop her from getting back to him right away.

He called me up as soon as he'd heard from her. "I have great news, Holly. Tina wants to record the song. She absolutely loves it."

Holy shit, holy shit. "Really? That's fantastic!" I exclaimed.

The first two *Mad Max* movies had already become classics. Warner Bros. wanted the song delivered by a certain date; they'd already scheduled their big blockbuster releases for the summer, and this was a priority. The movie was called *Mad Max Beyond Thunderdome*, and Tina played the corrupt ruler of Bartertown, Aunty Entity, a real badass and my kind of gal. Just as I was hoping, Roger wanted me to be involved in the recording session.

"I'd love to work on it. What do you think about getting Mike Chapman to produce it?" I asked.

Roger said, "Yeah, he'd be good."

Then I pressed on, "Why don't you let me cut the track with my guitarist Gene before Tina comes back to LA? Then all she has to do is walk in and sing it."

"I was thinking the same thing and the sooner the better."

"Great! Although I do have one concern. I want to make sure we record it in the right key. I don't have to tell you what a disaster it'll be if she comes in to sing it and it's not in the right key."

Roger murmured, "Yeah, that's a good point. Why don't you just make a cassette with a verse and chorus in four or five different keys. I can give it to her in person. I'm flying to London in the morning to meet up with her and the tour."

I took a breath, not wanting to seem difficult, and said, "Unfortunately, that won't be very effective."

"Why not?" he asked.

"What if her Walkman is running at a different speed than mine because the batteries are half dead? That's going to affect the key."

"We'll just plug it into a power outlet," Roger replied.

I said, "Yeah, well the electrical current between the two continents is different. That could affect the key too." This was long before the convenience of digital recordings, the internet, Dropbox, and chatrooms.

He was quiet for a few seconds, deep in thought, and then he said, "Do you have a passport?"

"Yeah, why?"

"Pack your bags and your passport, you're coming to London with me in the morning."

The next morning, we met at the airport, and Roger helped me check in. We were flying first class, which was a first for me. I napped, watched a few movies, ate a few meals, chatted with Roger, and before I knew it, the captain announced we were landing at Heathrow Airport. Tina and her road manager (another Aussie) surprised us by picking us up in a stretch limo. My heart was pumping as I climbed into the car, dressed in my usual black from head to toe, black leather pants, black fox fur coat, black stiletto heels. Tina quickly put me at ease laughing at Roger's dry jokes and banter. She was in a chatty mood and had a great sounding laugh, low and hearty.

Then she asked me the oddest question. I would've expected anything but this.

"Holly, do you have nice tits?" she said.

What? Was this a prank? Some sort of test to see how uptight or cool I could be? I had to think fast. *Fuck it*, I thought. I lifted up my shirt to show them my bodacious tat-tas and we all had a good laugh.

Roger had booked a room for me in the same hotel that he and Tina were staying in near Bond St. The name conjured up one of my better memories growing up, going to see all the early Bond movies with my dad and brother the minute they came out. Surely, that has to be the reason I have a weakness for men with British or Scottish accents.

Rock stars usually stayed in five-star hotels while everyone else, the backup band and the roadies, slummed it out in a Holiday Inn or something similar. I didn't take it for granted that Roger had put me up there with them. After we checked in, plans were made to meet the following morning. The porter had already taken my bag up to my room and handed me an old-fashioned skeleton key. I headed to the bar for a drink, looking forward to unwinding after the long flight. Twenty-four hours before, my most ambitious plans had been to do my laundry, eat some unidentifiable leftover food in my fridge, and watch reruns of *Saturday Night Live*. Now, here I was in London for the second time; the first had been on my honeymoon with Jeff. Here I was in one of my favorite cities with Tina Turner who was about to record another tune of mine. Did it get any better than this?

Two hours later, and slightly inebriated, I lay blissfully sprawled out on the queen bed in my room, surrounded by a cloud of crisp Frette linen sheets. I stared up at the ornate ceiling fan slowly rotating above me and thought, *How did I get here, how did I arrive at this very moment?* I wished I could go back and tell the frightened little girl I used to be to be patient, that it wouldn't always be that way, that lots of wonderful things were going to happen to her in about twenty years. But would I have even believed it?

Even though I'd written for many successful recording artists by this time, to me this was a whole new level of success, bigger than anything I'd experienced before. Tina wasn't just your run-of-the-mill rock star, she was a supernova.

There was a quiet tap on the door. I raised my head and called out, "Hello?" I heard a soft posh voice coming from behind the door.

"Sorry to disturb you, it's Reginald. I'm your butler for the evening."

A butler? Really? I grabbed one of my stiletto heels just in case the person behind the door wasn't a butler and cracked open the door to see a little man in a hotel uniform with impeccable posture. I discreetly tossed the shoe behind me.

"If there's anything you need, a pot of chocolate, or a cup of tea, just ring the front desk. I'm at your service."

"Um, thank you, Reginald. I'll keep that in mind."

He handed me a beautiful plate of cheese and wine. "Compliments of the house. Enjoy." He tipped his head, turned, and vanished. The only thing missing was a purple puff of smoke.

The following morning, I met Tina and Roger in the lobby. We headed over to the rehearsal studio, a small room with a piano, that had been arranged for us. I thought I already had a pretty good idea what the key was going to be, but, surprisingly, we settled on half a key higher after she sang the chorus. It was exciting, standing there in the room with her, hearing the live version of what I had imagined in my head as I wrote for her. It really suited her. I knew the other key would've worked, but one step higher and she would hit those harmonics and rasp in her voice that she was famous for. It dawned on me that I'd just traveled five thousand, four hundred and thirty seven miles—ten thousand, eight hundred and seventy four miles if you count the return trip—all for a five-minute meeting. And I would've gladly done it again.

Mission accomplished. We had our key and were good to go. I'd learned from my days in a band that it's vital the singer like and sound good in the key they're going to sing in. Invariably, every time the band has to change the key, the guitarist or someone whines that their instrument doesn't sound as good in the new key. But here's the thing—nobody walks out of the arena singing the guitar or drum parts.

I had a week before I had to cut the master back in LA. *Well, damn,* I thought, *here I am in London, what to do? Maybe I should visit Stonehenge or see the dungeons underneath the Tower of London.* Who was I kidding? What I really was dying to do was to go to Tina's next concert, but I didn't want to be pushy by inviting myself. Her next gig was in Switzerland. Tina looked over at me, smiling, all-knowing. "How would you like to come on the road with us for a few days before you head back to LA? You have a few free days, don't you?" I didn't need to be asked twice.

You hear about life-changing experiences, and when one happens to you, you never look at life in the same way. It's the kind of thing that happens, maybe once or twice in a lifetime, if ever. For me it wasn't the elegant hotels in Munich and Paris, or the Michelin restaurants, the running around on the tarmac from planes to buses. That was glamorous as hell, but it was life-changing because not only did I have the opportunity to see Tina perform live for the first time, it was also the first time I saw tens of thousands of people singing along with her, singing the words to my song. They were more like one big entity than thousands of individuals and Tina held them in the palm of her hand. Our first stop was in Basel, Switzerland, where she played to a sold-out audience at St. Jakobshalle. I had the best seat in the house, sitting on top of a beat-up road case on the side of the mammoth stage.

She performed "Better Be Good to Me" much faster live than on the record, probably because she fed off of the energy of the audience. Once she hit the stage she never stopped moving. (I read that her legs were insured for three million dollars.) Her fans not only knew the lyrics, they sang along with so much passion. It hadn't even occurred to me when I wrote the song with Mike that one day, in another part of the world where they spoke a different language and led completely different lives, that they were going to relate to the words we had written. Music is the great connector, and at the end of the day, no matter our differences, we all bleed red.

> "Oh yes I'm touched by this show of emotion
> Should I be fractured by your lack
> of devotion? Should I ?
> Oh! you better be good to me,
> That's how it's got to be now
> 'Cause I don't have no use for what you
> Loosely call the truth.
> You better be good to me."

I was a member of Tina's tribe now. To see and feel this collective love was something I hadn't expected as a songwriter. I thought you had to be in a band to feel that. Without intending to, I'd figured out a way to quench my deep need to be loved in a brand new way. Of course, the audience believed Tina had written the song, and that's because she made it her own, putting everything she had into it. Was it enough that I knew? Maybe, maybe not—that was a struggle I was going to endure for the rest of my career. To this day, when I hear a song of mine playing in a grocery store or a restaurant, much as I'd like to, I can't exactly turn to a complete stranger and announce, "Hey that's my song!" Instead, I've gotten used to it—I've learned to smile inwardly, enjoying the moment and carry on doing whatever I happen to be doing at that moment.

I was always welcomed in Tina's dressing room, even when she was getting ready, until those few minutes before she hit the stage, when she needed to be alone to chant. She had several large Louis Vuitton wardrobe trunks packed with designer outfits and high heels. God knows what those suitcases cost, maybe fifteen or twenty grand apiece. One of them was filled with stuffed animals, probably gifts from her fans and family.

We had gotten to the venue pretty early, so we sat around, noshing on the lavish food the promoter had set up for her and the band. I told her, "I love the way your wigs are styled, they make you look like a wild cat."

Since she had some time to kill before the show, she said, "Hey Holly, come over here, you should let me tease your hair, I'll make it look like mine. Wouldn't that be fun?"

I submitted, thinking, this is going to look strange on me, but how could I refuse an offer like that from her? It did look pretty silly, but I didn't mind at all. I loved the attention. Someone took a polaroid, and I laugh every time I see it because it was one of those girlie moments, one that females often bond over, doing each other's makeup and hair.

Everyone stayed in the same hotel when we got to Munich and some of us met in the hotel bar at night. Timmy Cappello, Tina's sax player, who flaunted his testosterone-driven abs on stage every night by playing shirtless with his skin oiled to a glistening sheen, walked into the bar wearing a girl's baby doll dress and his hair in pigtails, carrying a stuffed teddy bear. No one seemed to notice, or if they did, they couldn't have cared less, which I thought was pretty cool. The band members were all nice guys who had been with Tina for a while, and they treated me with respect and kindness. They knew I had written one of the songs that they performed every night.

After she performed another riveting show at the Rudi-Sedlmayer-Halle in Munich, she did one more show in Württemberg and then we flew to Paris where Tina brought me with her to visit her good friend, Azzedine Alaïa. He was one of the top couture designers in the world and had been designing all the clothes for her tours. He understood a woman's body. His clothing embraced and emphasized women's natural curves. I drooled in the background watching the two of them going through one outfit after another. Tina picked up a beautiful black leather pencil skirt, looked over at me, and tossed it in my direction. "Here," she said. "This would look great on you. Keep it."

Before we left, she threw a few more items my way. "No, no, I can't possibly...Oh, wow, thank you so much!" No one was going to believe this when I got back to the States.

After that, I was thinking it was time to head back to LA and get cracking on cutting the song. Party time was over for now. It had been an unforgettable experience, but now I was anxious to get back in the studio.

As soon as I got home, I called Mike, who said he'd booked us at Cherokee Studios. Mike and I did most of our recording there. We each owned Fairlight computers by then; there were certain samples and sounds you couldn't get anywhere else at the time. I used a certain mallet sound for the intro to "One of the Living," and down the road I used it a lot with my band Device, as well as other acts I wrote for. In many ways, the Fairlight defined the sound of the eighties, and were I to play a bunch of records, I could say to you, "There's that sound."

With the exception of Gene Black's wicked guitar parts, everything on the track was programmed. We did this to make the track sound industrial and apocalyptic. I programmed the drums, the bass, several layers of haunting keyboards, and sound effects. And we were ready to go. On the day that Tina was set up to record the vocal, I waited about half an hour before going down to the studio so she would have time to warm up on her own with Mike. I expected everything to go smoothly, I knew I had gotten the key right, and the track sounded incredible. But when I got there, I could feel something was wrong. The friction between her and Mike was palpable. I said hello to her and gave her a big hug, then told her I would be right back and went in the control room. "Is the mike turned off?" I scribbled on a sheet of paper. He nodded. Looking through the glass at her I asked him, "What the hell is going on? Why is she packing up her things?"

"She said she's finished. She sang it a few times and she's happy with the vocal, wasn't interested in my opinion. I haven't even finished getting her bloody mike sound yet." Mike was used to being in control. Now I understood why he looked so annoyed. Tina was having none of it. She was the one calling the shots that day. Who could blame her? She was a superstar who knew her voice better than anyone.

"Let me talk to her and see what's going on." I said. I walked back into the studio. "Is everything okay? It looks like you're leaving. What happened with you and Mike?" She didn't explain anything and to this day I don't know what was said between the two of them.

"I'm going down the street to another recording studio to do the background vocals and I want you to come with me," she said. "They're already waiting for us."

That put me in a really awkward situation. Mike was my frequent writing partner as well as my publisher, not to mention my friend. If I left with her, he would be livid and call me a traitor. On the other hand, if I didn't go with Tina, I might never work with her again.

"OK," I said. Let me just tell him I'm going with you." I figured that Mike would get over it, and I didn't know her well enough to know if she would.

Tina opened the door and led me out of there without so much as a word to Mike while I gestured to him that I would call him later. He did not look happy. Someone grabbed the two-inch master tape and we headed to the other studio. Since I was the songwriter, I can only guess that she wanted me there to make sure she got the vocal backgrounds right because they were the only thing left to record and they were very specific. Plus, I think she wanted me there for moral support. It certainly made a statement to Mike that she was running the show, and fair enough: she'd been told what to do and how to sing by men her entire life.

Roger had somehow managed to reach Humberto Gatica, the well-known engineer who'd worked with Michael Jackson. He must've lived close by because he arrived at the studio at the same time as us. Tina had taken over the production. But that was her prerogative, after all—she was motherfucking Tina Turner.

I remained in the control room while Tina went into the studio and let the assistant engineer adjust the mike in front of her. Then she pressed the talk-back button and said, "Holly, I love the background vocals on the demo. Is that you singing?" I nodded a timid yes. "Well, get in here 'cause I want you to sing them with me. Humberto, let's get another set of headphones in here please."

What? My mind was racing and tumbling, tripping over itself as I walked in and stood next to her. I couldn't believe she wanted me to sing. I wasn't a vocalist, and she was one of the greatest singers in the world, but she was dead serious. Sure, I had sung background vocals on other records, but she was in her own league.

"Roll the tape. Come closer," she directed as she pulled me next to her and positioned me where she wanted me to be as the track started to play. I was standing so close to her, I could smell her expensive perfume, could see the lines on her face and the sweat glistening on her brow. It was lovely.

The background vocals came out great. We sang all the choruses together and all the "yeah, yeah yahoos." Not only that, but we had fun doing it. That day with her stands as the most memorable session I've ever done, and the quickest. It's definitely a top ten moment in my life.

> "Walk tall cool collected—savage
> Walk tall bruised sensual—ravaged.
> It's every man for himself, every woman, every child,
> A new breed, ferocious and wild."

Mike didn't talk to me for a while. He was pretty pissed. It wouldn't be the first or last time he didn't want to talk to me, but we were close enough that I knew we'd work things out. We always did.

I discovered that there were two mixes of the master recording that sounded very different from each other. No one ever told me, so I'm not sure how or why it happened, but I knew what went into the making of that record. One was done by Humberto and was used for her video and in the movie. There was far too much reverb on the vocal and the whole track sounded like it was under water. Frankly, I thought it was a terrible mix. On the record and CD, they used a mix Mike had done and damn if his didn't sound better. You could hear the vocals clearer because they weren't drowning in a sea of reverb, and the band sounded crisp and tight. The track packed way more of a punch.

"One of the Living" is the first thing you hear when the opening scene to *Mad Max Beyond Thunderdome* begins. It goes beautifully with the shot of an empty desert that slowly becomes populated with a large group of derelict people coming over the dunes, walking, staggering, and riding all kinds of DIY concoctions of dystopian vehicles. The beginning lyrics to the song worked perfectly: "In the desert sun, every step that you take could be your final one."

I had no way of knowing when I wrote it that it would play over a desert scene.

Once again, Tina received a Grammy nomination for Best Rock Vocal on "One of the Living," the same year that Pat Benatar also got a Grammy nomination (and won) for another song of mine in the same category, "Invincible." In the coming years, Tina would end up cutting nine of my songs, one of which would become her signature song, a song she has been quoted as saying she wants to be remembered for, more than any other.

CHAPTER ELEVEN

NIGHT OF THE THIRTY TOES (HEART)

Los Angeles, 1985

"Never let them shoot us down, never, never, never…never run away."
("Never" performed by Heart)

" I called you because I think you're a fantastic songwriter and I really want to get you together with the girls. I think you'll love each other, and I can only imagine what would come out of a writing session between the three of you," said the upbeat British woman on the phone.

"That would be amazing." I exclaimed. Over the years I had often fantasized about writing with "the girls," even now when they weren't doing so well.

"They have a new record deal with Capitol and it's vital that they have hit songs on this next record," she continued. "We've put them together with a few other writers, and they've written some really good songs, but I just have a feeling that writing with another woman, especially someone of your caliber, would produce something special."

"One of the reasons I've made it this far is because they inspired me so much when I was first starting out." I exclaimed.

"Aw, that's really lovely!" she said. "Right now they're rehearsing at SIR in Hollywood. They've already recorded some of the tracks and are about to go back in soon. Let me set something up for you to meet them in the next day or so, and I'll call you back."

The woman's name was Trudy Green, and she handled the managerial duties with HK Management for Heart. The "HK" could've stood for Holly Knight, but it actually stood for Howard Kaufman. He co-managed many, many bands with Irving Azoff over the years, most notably the Eagles, Stevie Nicks, Def Leppard, and Aerosmith, so they were in good hands.

Heart had reached the pinnacle of success in the mid-seventies and had stayed there for many years, but they were now in a similar position to many other bands. They'd reached a plateau and weren't selling records or selling out shows like they used to. The "why" was usually the same reason as it was with most bands—burnout, either from grueling tour schedules or the hedonistic lifestyle, boredom, love/hate relationships within the band, or a combination of all of them. Whatever the reason, it produced the same result. They'd stopped writing great songs.

I loved Heart from the moment I'd first heard "Magic Man" and "Crazy on You." They were the first hard rock band that I knew of to be fronted by a woman. But it was their third record, *Little Queen* with "Barracuda," that really made me a fan. To this day, I consider "Barracuda" with its iconic guitar riff and Ann Wilson's voice soaring above the track like a renegade jet, one of the best rock songs in existence. I learned a lot about songwriting just from that song. There's a dramatic pause at the end of each chorus when there's nothing but Ann's declaration, "Ooh…barracuda." Acapella moments like this work because they are so razor-focused on the vocal and the hook.

I know it seems odd that a band like Heart would need or even agree to write with anyone outside the band, but times were changing;

a lot of bands that normally would've said "no way" to the notion of venturing outside their own band were becoming more receptive to the idea. They had to be if they wanted the label to support their records. Lots of bands were starting to collaborate with other song-writers. They had nothing to lose, really. Most of their fans would still believe they wrote their own material. This jumpstarted a new era for me of being brought in to write with artists, as opposed to writing for them. Things were about to get much more fun.

The next afternoon, I found myself walking into a huge rehearsal room at SIR. The biggest rooms were called sound stages, and a lot of bands rented them to rehearse for upcoming tours. I got there a little early, so I stood in the back where it was dark and I could watch undetected, listening to the band run through a song, just taking it all in. "This is your life now," I told myself. "You were invited." The song they were playing must've been new because I didn't recog-nize it, but three of the faces were familiar to me, Ann, Nancy, and Howard Leese, their guitarist. Trudy must have spotted me in the back of the room because she walked over to me and shouted over the music, "Hi, Holly? I'm Trudy. It's so lovely to meet you." We smiled and shook hands.

"Hold on, hold on," Ann said in the distance to the band. They stopped playing, and I could hear Ann telling Denny Carmassi, their drummer, "You're dragging a bit, you need to pick up the pace. Let's try it again, okay?" He nodded, counted off the song, and they started playing again, this time faster, and it sounded better. After they fin-ished the song, they huddled for a minute, then put their instruments down and scattered off the stage in different directions. "Come on," Trudy said. "Let me introduce you."

Ann and Nancy were sitting on the edge of the low stage laugh-ing about something when Trudy brought me over. "Hello, ladies! Look who I've brought with me. Holly Knight, meet Ann and Nancy of Heart, girls, meet Holly Knight, songwriter extraordinaire."

They grinned at me and said, "Hi! Cool braids. Can I touch them?"

I'd just come back from another trip to London in my ongoing search for a lead singer. I liked to stay at the Portobello Hotel in Notting Hill, a notorious rock 'n' roll haven filled with musicians passing through town or just living there indefinitely. It was London's version of New York's famed and funky Chelsea Hotel, only much smaller and less seedy and violent. On the other side of Hyde Park, on Kings Road, where the last remaining punks still hung out, clinging to an era that no longer existed, were some of the trendiest hair salons.

I walked through the front door of the first one I saw that looked decent, and spoke to the man dying a woman's hair purple, "Hey, can you give me some long, braided extensions, maybe two or three in black, and one in blue?" Another guy, sporting a huge mohawk and dressed in a tartan kilt and army boots, walked up to me from behind and said in an East London cockney accent, "Of course, darling. How long do you want them?"

"Down to my ass." I told him.

"Yeah, they're not real, they're extensions," I said to Ann and Nancy.

"Damn," Ann said, examining them in her hands. "They look real!"

"It is real hair, it's just not mine."

"I like the blue braid," Nancy joined in. "It's rad."

It was clear from the moment we met, there was a strong feeling of simpatico between the three of us, something very much missing in my life. Other than Kathy and Gene, I didn't have many friends. I had a lot of acquaintances and people I spent time with because we worked together, but not what I would consider real friends.

"I've been a Heart fan since the very beginning and I'm really honored to meet you," I gushed.

"Wow, thank you and thanks for coming down," Nancy responded. "We love your songs."

We talked for a bit. and then I excused myself to go to the bathroom, and like girls do, the sisters said they had to go too and followed me in. Before I knew it, Ann had whipped out a vial of coke, and shyly asked, "Do you partake?" My eyes lit up. "I do, but I had no idea that you did." I had always thought of them as pretty straight. I think they were happy to know I was into partying as well. It would be something else we would have in common. I pulled out a small vial of my own and offered them some.

There has always been available contraband for renegades. In the twenties and early thirties, during the prohibition, it was bootleg alcohol, in the fifties it was heroin, in the sixties and seventies it was pot and acid, and in the eighties it was coke. Almost everyone I knew or worked with in the music business was ingesting it; it was practically a staple. Musicians did it, record execs, journalists, managers, lawyers; you name it. It was the fuel of the era. Most did it for recreational purposes, but I'll tell you why I started doing cocaine. There were actually a few reasons, but the main one was pretty simple; I felt a lot of pressure to be thin. Men seemed to respect you more if you were, and when I tried to eat as little as possible, it was still hard. So, for dessert, I would always take a tiny spoonful to keep me from eating more. It was the one thing that helped me to stay thin. It also was a way to stay up all night and work, which was my favorite time to write. The Vampire Hours, as I came to call them, were magic hours for me. And as in the case of the bathroom, it was a way to socially engage with other people. I never did massive amounts, it was more like a sniff here and there. I did it for many years this way.

We talked a little more, even touching upon the existing patriarchy that was rampant in the music business and the world in general, and how things needed to change. Ann said, "We better get back to rehearsing…can you stay for a while? We can go to dinner afterwards if you're free."

I was surprised at how natural and sweet they were, given their rock-goddess status, and I soon discovered that their sense of humor was just as deep and wicked. They were no fools, these women. Sharp, sexy, and street smart, they felt kindred to me. Or at least what I aspired to be.

We went back to the rehearsal room and they introduced me to the rest of the band. Trudy was thrilled the three of us had already hit it off so well.

"So, did you discuss a plan as far as writing together?' she asked.

"When's our next free day?" Ann asked Trudy.

"Day after tomorrow, does that work for you Holly?"

"Yep, perfect."

After they finished rehearsing, the whole band decided to join us for dinner. At one point, Tommy Lee, Mötley Crüe's drummer, who'd been dining at another table, came over to say hello. He was fawning over Ann and Nancy, and I loved it because it was a complete role reversal of what I was used to seeing. I could tell they were used to it. Howard stared at me with puppy eyes throughout the meal. I liked the attention and smiled back at him. When dinner ended, the girls and I firmed up plans for a writing session.

"I hope you don't mind driving all the way to the Marina. It's not very fancy or anything," I said apologetically.

"Oh please, we don't care as long as there's a place to write."

Everyone was a little tipsy, but in good spirits as we hugged goodnight.

A band's first record is often their best because they have all the time in the world to write it and rehearse it live. It's often the most honest and least contrived. As time goes on, especially if they become highly successful, the demands change, they're always on the road with less time to write, and when they do it's usually in nondescript hotel rooms with windows that don't open. After years of giving the best of themselves, they can run out of fresh ideas. That's where someone like me comes in.

I had a few ideas prepared to get things rolling. I was acutely aware that I had to come up with something that didn't compromise their unique style and image. It had to sound like something they would've come up with themselves on a good day. At the same time, I wanted to step outside the box and give them something new, a fresh vibe. It could be as simple as an odd time signature.

Later on, as I started writing more with the bands and solo artists, even if I pretty much wrote the whole song, I left enough of the lyrics or music unwritten so they could finish it with me. I could've finished it myself, but that wasn't the point, the point was to get songs on as many records as possible with the best artists, Either way, the worst thing that could happen in a writing session was for everybody to just sit there with blank looks on their face, hoping like hell that lightning would strike. I knew that you only got one shot on the first day. If it went well, you would more than likely be asked to get together again. If it didn't go well, you were history. When I wrote with someone on a regular basis, like Mike Chapman, then of course, we had the luxury to just jam and really have fun. That was always my favorite way of writing.

Gene came over the next day to pick up a guitar he had left at my house and while he was there, he played me an idea that might work for our new band. I loved it, but rather than saving it for us, I asked him if I could play it to the Wilson sisters. I wanted to bring him in on a few cowrites so I could keep him busy while we were searching for our singer. Gene was too good to lose. His idea was funkier than anything Heart had done before, and he was excited at the prospect of writing with them, especially if this was the comeback album everyone was hoping for. His riffs became the verses while I wrote a chorus melody and chord progression that had an anthemic vibe. With one idea already prepared, if Ann and Nancy liked it, we could finish the song pretty quickly. My only question was—would they think the verses were too much of a departure? Gene and I also came up with another song idea just in case they didn't go for the first one, which I planned to play them as well. It was less funky than the other one, a straight-ahead rocker.

The next day when Ann and Nancy came over, I said, "I have an idea I started with my guitarist yesterday that I thought you might like—can I play it to you?" They didn't seem to mind that there would be another writer on the tune.

"Sure, let's hear it!" they said enthusiastically.

I played them the recording we'd made. "This is great! Let's work on it."

"I have some thoughts on what the song could be about," I said. "We were talking about this in the bathroom the other day—how it's time to take a stand and stop being defined by other people…" Ann chimed in. "Or being told what we can and can't do."

For the chorus I came up with, "We can't go on just running away." We threw in some sexual innuendo too: "Walk those legs right over here, give me what I'm dying for." Whether it was about business or love—"One chance, one love, your chance to let me know"—it made the same point: "Never run away." There's a little hook in the chorus that I threw in, the "Whoa-oh ooh-oh."

"We could call it 'Never Run' or something like that," I said.

"What about 'Never'?" Ann suggested.

With that, we had most of our first song. Before we finished for the day, I said, "I have another idea that Gene and I started," then played them the recording I had made, grinning as it blasted through the speakers.

"That's really cool too!" Nancy said. "Why don't we get together again tomorrow. We can finish the lyrics for 'Never' and work on this as well."

They returned the next day, and we finished writing both songs, then recorded the demos in my makeshift studio, which I had set up in a second bedroom. The name of the second song was "All Eyes."

When it came around to recording "Never," Ann and Nancy invited me to the Record Plant in Hollywood. I was so excited to see them record the song we had just written. That didn't happen often. I loved being in the studio. It was my favorite part of the process, even more than playing live, because there was this underlying vibration of creativity and history being made, especially when it was someone legendary like them. When I got there, Nancy introduced me to their producer, Ron Nevison, who had produced a lot of rock bands—Led Zeppelin, Ozzy Osborne, Thin Lizzy, KISS, and many others. Ann and Nancy were obsessed with Led Zeppelin so it was easy to see why they had hired him.

"I've been hearing a lot about you," Ron said as he stood to shake my hand.

Lunch was brought in and we chatted as we ate. They made me feel so welcomed. Then the rest of the band walked back in from having lunch somewhere else, and Ron said, "Hey, you want to go in there with the band and play the keyboards on 'Never'? Just double the guitars like you did on the demo."

I looked around the room to see what the rest of the band thought, and they were all grinning, giving me the thumbs up. These guys were used to working with two very strong, talented women so of course it made sense that they were into it. I stood up and boldly announced, "Let's do this!" and shot into the studio before Ron could change his mind. A stack of keyboards was already set up and ready to play. "Is it in the original key?" I asked, just in case Ron had changed it. Mark Andes started playing the bass line and it was the same. Ron rolled the tape, Denny counted off, "One, two, three…" (the four always silent to leave a clean space), and off we went.

As I looked around the room, everyone was smiling. What was there not to smile about? It sounded great, and we were all were getting paid to have fun and make music. For me, it didn't get much better than that. I really did miss the camaraderie of being in a band, but soon enough, I would be playing with my own. There's a connection and passion for music that exists between musicians when they're sharing this space together. It's like nothing else. All distractions, cares, and woes take a back seat. In fact, songwriting and playing music are the only times I'm truly in the moment—100 percent. I know this because I lose track of time. Twelve hours can go by and feel like minutes.

Ann was in an isolated vocal booth so I couldn't see her, but I could hear her through the headphones. I was doubling the guitar and bass parts note for note, so I had to maintain eye contact with Mark and Howard. Whenever I wrote a song, I could hear the end result in my head, and to hear it come alive the way I envisioned it was so gratifying. I had programmed the drums on the demo, but nothing sounded better than real drums. For a brief second, a shot of adrenaline pumped through my body as it dawned on me, *Holy shit, I'm recording with Heart.* We played through it three times before Ron said, "OK, guys, I have what I need."

Afterwards, Denny and Mark came up to me and said, "Great song, man." Howard stopped me on my way out.

"You should come up to Sausalito," he said flirtatiously.

Ann and Nancy had already invited me to come up for the weekend. I kissed him goodbye.

"We'll see." I smiled.

The band moved back up to the Record Plant in Sausalito where they had first started the record. Everyone had a room in one of the oldest and most charming hotels in town, a rambling multileveled place called Casa Madrona, and I got a room for myself too. During my visits, the Wilson sisters and I bonded even more. We had so much fun, always playing pranks on each other. What started as one weekend became another, and then another. Howard and I started seeing each other and for a while it was fun. He attended the Grammys with me in Los Angeles and things were great until I found out he was living with someone in Seattle. Not only was I pissed at him for his duplicity, it was awkward because I had a professional relationship with the band, and a budding friendship with the girls. They had wanted to tell me all along but they were in the middle: Was their loyalty supposed to be to their guitarist or to their new friend and cowriter? After that, Howard was reduced to dog status with me. Lesson learned: (at least in this case) don't shit where you eat.

The Record Plant in Sausalito was completely different from the Record Plant in LA and New York. It was more rustic, and the studio was in the woods, surrounded by tall, majestic redwood trees. Even the interior was built with indigenous wood from the area. The studio felt like it was magically hidden from the outside world by design, so that whoever was recording there had no distractions. They were there to do one thing—make great music and get it down on tape.

The first track they worked on was a beautiful song called "These Dreams," cowritten by Martin Page and Bernie Taupin. I had fond memories of working with Bernie. We'd written a song with Mike Chapman called. "I Engineer." Animotion, who'd had a hit with "Obsession," recorded it. Ron had decided to have Nancy sing the lead instead of Ann, and as it happened, on the day she went in to sing it, she had a sore throat. She'd played it to me and asked me what I thought, adding, "Don't listen to my vocal. It's just a guide track, and I'm going to redo it."

After I listened, I told her, "You should keep that vocal! It's gorgeous and so honest. I love the raspiness in your voice, even though that's not how you usually sound. If I were the producer, I'd tell you not to do it again." Fortunately, Ron came to the same conclusion, and they ended up keeping the rough vocal.

On the songs we wrote, as well as other cowrites the girls did with other writers, Ann and Nancy combined the writing credits of their two names into one, coming up with the name "Connie." I remember reading it and saying to them, "Who's Connie?" "It's us," Ann replied. To this day, I'm not sure what that was about. There was something else I noted about the two of them which I found incredibly endearing. They were as close as two sisters could be. They finished each other's sentences and practically had a language of their own. I'm sure that's what kept the band together for so many years. Ann and Nancy had a third sister, Lynn, but she wasn't in the music business, and I never met her.

They decided to call the record *Heart*, as if presenting the group for the first time, which I thought was a great idea. No one could have predicted that the record would do as well as it did, not only in America, but internationally as well, especially in countries like Germany where rock was huge. "Never" was the second single, and got to number four on the Billboard charts, becoming the second highest charting song off the record. "These Dreams" went to number one. It was a first for them, and in a way, I imagine that it must have felt odd that their first number one was a song with Nancy's vocals. That had to be hard for Ann, the lead singer. "All Eyes" also made it on the record. I was so proud when I got the advance copies. They were back on the map, more successful than ever, and I was happy that I had been a part of their success. The record sold more than five million copies and garnered four hit singles.

Gene and I were invited to come and watch them film the video for "Never." I befriended the director, Marty Callner, who was one of the top directors for rock bands like Aerosmith, KISS, and ZZ Top.

It was always fascinating to see what the sets and bands looked like in person and watch the between-takes chaos of techs blowing smoke everywhere while the makeup artist and stylists sprinted in to primp up the band members and make sure their makeup wasn't melting under the harsh lights. It was the era of big hair, and even Heart fell prey to the look. Take after take—it had to be exhausting for them.

"Never" went into heavy rotation on MTV when it was released. In fact, Heart became one of the darlings of MTV, along with Pat Benatar and Tina Turner—a great plus for me. MTV was incredibly supportive of female rockers and artists.

It was a small pool, this alternate reality we dwelled in, where we not only navigated but flourished in a sea of men. We were hardworking and successful, and we didn't have to sleep with anybody to get where we were. If I went to bed with someone it was because I wanted to. We were the bosses of our own respective careers and destinies.

As time went by, I became much closer to Nancy. Ann was the star and, like most lead singers, had a wall which you could walk through only if she held the door open. Sometimes the drawbridge would be up and entry was barred. Nancy had a place outside of Seattle in a small town called Woodinville while Ann had a place in Seattle. Whenever they came to LA, we would try to get together, although with the success of the record, they had less time. One day, after the record had been out for a few months, they came to LA to do some radio interviews, and, as they were heading over to do one at a major station, they invited me to participate. It was so generous of them to include me. Who does that? Most artists want to keep the limelight to themselves, and certainly don't want to highlight the fact that they've worked with outside writers. Not Ann and Nancy. We had a blast during the interview; I even had the DJ laughing his ass off.

In an utter testament to my friendship with Nancy, Heart had come to play the Forum. After the gig, Nancy came over to my apartment. While she was there, I realized I had misplaced part of my publishing advance, a check for twelve thousand dollars, so I was stressing out.

I was easily distracted and constantly misplacing things. I would come home and put my keys in the refrigerator, spacey things like that. I probably had attention deficit disorder, although I've never been diagnosed as such, but I'm definitely *something*.

Nancy helped me search for it, and then insisted, "We need to go through your garbage. All of it."

"Shit, you really want to do this?"

"We have to, it's the only place we haven't looked," she said.

We emptied a large, smelly, black trash bag and laid it all out on the ground of my back patio. Sure enough, we found it, soggy but intact. I remember saying to her, "Here you are, a rock star, going through my garbage with me, the same night you played a sold-out Forum. Thank you, I'm really touched." We had a good laugh over that one.

My most memorable night with the three of us happened about a year later when Heart had another show in LA. They invited me to their hotel the night before the concert. We wanted to see each other, but they needed to rest up, and I was pretty tired myself. So, we lay down in the king-size bed together, got under the covers, talked, sang songs, and caught up. It reminded me of the sleepovers that girls love to do when they're young, a rite of passage that always strengthens friendships. My mom didn't allow me to have sleepovers growing up, so this more than made up for it. I can't remember much of what we talked about with the exception of this very special moment that will live in my heart forever.

We had pulled the covers up so high that all our feet were exposed. There lay thirty toes lined up, one next to the other like little sausages, all painted with red nail polish and Nancy started laughing.

"Look! Thirty toes!" she cried out.

We laughed so hard we were nearly crying.

"We have to christen this moment, 'The Night of The Thirty Toes,'" Ann exclaimed in a fit of laughter. It was charmingly silly and, at the same time, very sweet. Over the next few years or so, we had several more "Nights of The Thirty Toes," not necessarily hanging out in bed together, but having some pretty fun moments, especially when they recorded their next record in New York. Even after things got busier and we saw less of each other, all we had to say was "Night of The Thirty Toes" and it would bring us all back. It was our code, one that defined our friendship and support of one another—the rock girls at the top of the heap. We were all doing great. Life was good and getting even better.

I continued writing for or with Heart. In 1987, they released *Bad Animals*, featuring the single "There's the Girl," which Nancy and I wrote and she sang lead on. It reached number twelve on the

Billboard Hot 100. After the success of "These Dreams," the label wanted to make sure that Nancy had a chance to sing lead a little more often. In 1990, I cowrote two songs with renowned songwriter Albert Hammond, the Beatles-ish "I Love You," and, one of my favorites, "Tall, Dark, Handsome Stranger." Ann's vocal on that track is kickass.

CHAPTER TWELVE

"WELL DONE, YOUNG LADY!" (ROD STEWART)

Los Angeles, 1985

"I want to feel the breathless end that you come to every night."
("Love Touch" performed by Rod Stewart)

Rod Stewart was many things: superstar, character, mischief-maker, soccer player, blond-lover, instigator, storyteller, and, for me, something of a traitor.

Most of my stories start with a phone call and this one came from Stiefel Management.

"Please hold for Arnold," the woman on the other end said before putting me on hold.

"Hi Holly. It's Arnold Stiefel, nice to talk to you." I had no clue who he was or why he was calling. Then he said, "I manage Rod Stewart."

This is the point where I realized I had reached a new level. My name was getting around in the industry, I was part of the conversation when it came to matching writers with recording artists, and fortuitously, I'd been part of a conversation with Rod Stewart. That blew my mind. Rod was rock 'n' roll royalty, right there in the upper stratosphere with Tina.

"Rod's working on a new record and wants to meet with you about possibly writing together."

"I'd love to."

"Can you come up to our office sometime this week?"

"Of course!"

Writing for famous artists was more difficult than you might imagine. It was always a fraught guessing game trying to figure out what they might need at any point in their career. There was usually a list of things to consider: What was their vocal range and the keys they liked to sing in? What was being written about them in the trades and tabloids? For instance, were they getting married, or going through a divorce, did they just meet someone new? It helped to stay one step ahead of them because then I could pitch them an idea that was more likely to resonate with them. And finally, how far outside of the artist's box should I try to venture? After all, they were calling me for fresh ideas.

Cowriting with a famous artist had its risks too. On the one hand, if we wrote a song together, the chances of it ending up on their record increased because they were one of the writers. For them, that was a huge incentive. They'd have a writer's credit and make money from their share of the music and the publishing. However, if they didn't end up recording it, then I'd be stuck with a song that had their name on it, and that could be the kiss of death. No other recording artist wanted to touch it after that, the logic being, "If so-and-so didn't cut it, it probably wasn't strong enough, so why should I record it?" I already had quite a few songs like that in what I referred to as my boneyard, songs that would probably never see the light of day.

In preparation for our meeting, I cancelled my plans for the next few days and hunkered down in my studio. Recently I had bought something called a plasma globe, a large, round glass ball that generated electrical currents inside. It looked like something out of Frankenstein's laboratory, but it had its purpose. Cheaper versions became popular a few years later, but mine was huge and was an art piece that cost two thousand dollars. Whenever I would go into my studio to create, I would turn it on because I always imagined songwriting as akin to catching lightning in a bottle.

Lyrically, I wanted to write something romantic for Rod because that was his wheelhouse. If I was going to step outside his zone, it would be better to do it musically. At the time, I was romantically involved with a man named Jonathan who lived in London, and that night, I don't know where it came from, right before I'd hung up the phone, I said to him, "Baby, I wish I was there and I could give you a kiss right now, but since I can't I'm sending you a love touch."

Wow, I thought, *what a great title for a song! I'll just start with that.* I had a sound I'd discovered months ago on my Fairlight, something I'd been waiting to use on the right song. It was a sample of steel drums, and I thought if I used it on this, it would give the track a summery, nostalgic feeling.

A few days later, I was ushered into the boardroom at Stiefel Management in Beverly Hills by Randy Phillips, one of Arnold's associates. I had my cassette with "new idea" in tow. To my surprise, Rod was already sitting at the head of a long table waiting for me. Usually, I was the one waiting for them. It's always such a strange feeling to meet or see someone in the flesh whose image and persona you've seen and heard so many times. You feel like you know them already, that they're familiar, and you have to remind yourself that you don't know them at all.

Rod was decked out in a light pastel-colored suit and looked every bit the rock star. He stood up grinning and shook my hand. "Hello, darling, lovely to meet you," he said, his hand lingering in mine. He was a total flirt, very attractive and charismatic, if not necessarily my type, but that was a relief. I didn't want any distractions.

"It's wonderful to meet you," I said, grinning back. I had taken great pains to pick out something fashionable. I had on the black leather Azzedine Alaïa skirt that Tina had given me in Paris. With my red lipstick and dark hair, I was going for a Bettie Page look. "Would you like to hear an idea I started for you?" I asked. "Something we can finish together if you like?"

"Of course, I want to hear it. What's the title?"

"'Love Touch.'"

Rod smiled and said, "I like that."

After asking Arnold to pop the cassette into their stereo, I stood close to Rod and sang the verse and chorus in his ear. This was a strategic move as I didn't want the song to sound too finished, lest he think, *What's left to write on this?*

As the music played on, Rod started to sing along with me. He had the chorus down pat after one pass. That's always the most thrilling moment for me, imagining how a song is going to sound with somebody in mind, and then actually hearing them do it and knowing you nailed it. As a songwriter, I lived for those moments.

"Well done, young lady!" Rod exclaimed when the music stopped.

I couldn't help but giggle. He sounded like a school headmaster, not the singer of "Hot Legs," "Maggie May," and "You Wear It Well."

"Do you want to finish it with me?" I asked him.

"Yeah, of course I would. Where's your studio?"

"I live in the Marina, it's not very fancy."

"No worries, luv," he said. "I'll get my limo driver to take me there."

"Hey, I have this great guitarist and he always comes up with really hooky parts. We wrote together for Heart about a month ago. How do you feel about him joining the session? I think you'll love him. We can even try writing something else while we're all together."

"Yeah, if you say he's good, then great!"

Rod seemed good-natured and open-minded. I liked him. The following week, a stretch limo pulled up to my run-down apartment complex, something you didn't see every day in my neck of the woods.

Locals walking their dogs, or parking their cars, all slowed down to peer at the great white whale with the black obsidian windows, not even bothering to be discreet about it. They wanted to know who the hell was inside. They were like monkeys. I almost expected them to start climbing all over of the car and beating it. As I walked out to greet Rod, I could see some of my neighbors' jaws dropping, staring at me, even though in all the years I had lived there, they had never bothered to say hello to me. When Rod got out and hugged me hello, I think one of the neighbors nearly passed out. It might as well have been the second coming of Christ. She ripped the front of her shirt down the middle and shoved a marker into his hand, asking him to sign her 44DD breasts. Only two years before, during the 1984 Summer Olympics in LA, the marathon had run right through the same parking lot we were standing in. Not one of these fools had given as much of a shit about that as this. Embarrassed, I hurried Rod to my apartment.

Once inside, I introduced Rod to Gene, who had come over an hour earlier and was already set up. I led them upstairs to my studio. I didn't often include a guitarist on the credits if they came up with riffs for a song. That was their job, but Gene wrote hooks that helped shape the songs significantly, giving them signatures, and that's why I had included him on this one. If you've ever listed to "Love Touch," you'll immediately hear what I'm talking about. My objective was to get Rod to write some lyrics in the verses. We played and jammed over the verses, hoping to strike gold, but instead of contributing ideas, Rod kept cracking jokes and announcing it was time to take another break, the kind that involves your nose. It was hard to say no to him, so we just kept getting higher and higher and further and further away from the song. We were having a ball laughing and screwing around, but we weren't accomplishing anything and that was worrying me. Eventually, we stopped and went out to dinner. It was dark by the time we finished eating, so we made plans to get together the next day to finish "Love Touch."

The second day went the same as the first. Rod was too busy being mischievous to be interested in writing, which under any other circumstance would've been endearing, but for me the pressure was on to deliver. I recorded the writing sessions, as I always did on my Sony Walkman so I could have a record of all the little gems and ideas we put down. We got bored going over and over the same verses, so we took a break from it and started to mess around with another idea. Rod kept singing "red hot in black." It was the kind of song that he had done before, and I liked it, but we never finished it. (Some thirty-five years later, I discovered that Rod cowrote and recorded "Red Hot in Black" on the same record as "Love Touch" with two of his band mates: Kevin Savigar, his keyboardist, and Jim Cregan, his guitarist. I still have the cassette from those two days of writing, or attempting to write together. Personally, I like our version much better. It had a catchier hook.)

As the end of the night was approaching, I could see everyone was running out of steam and still, Rod hadn't contributed anything. It was not only annoying because I really wanted to turn in a hit song to his label, but also frustrating because I knew it would be easier finishing it without him. It was also disappointing because I knew that Rod had written some really great songs in the past.

At this point, I cared more about the song than his feelings. My sentiment was always, "whatever serves the purpose of the song, not the people writing it." Looking back now, I'm amazed at the balls I had to say to him, "Rod, listen, this has been a blast hanging out with you, but we haven't come up with anything in two days. I would like to finish this on my own, with your blessing, and hand you a finished song. I have an idea where this needs to go. Would you be okay with that?" I don't know what I had been so worried about, because Rod didn't seem at all bothered about it. He was in good spirits and didn't put up much of fuss.

"Yeah sure, you two seem to have this under control."

That was a relief because I knew that if he didn't cut it, without him listed as a writer it would be much easier to get someone else to cut it. I knew the song was a hit, and I was pretty sure he was going to cut it anyway because it really suited him.

Over the next day or so, I tried to finish the lyrics, but I had messed around with the song so much now that I had hit a wall. I was burnt out. I needed a fresh pair of ears that I trusted, so I called Mike and told him what had happened, and asked if he would like to hear the song and finish it with me.

He loved what he heard and helped me to finish it in one afternoon. We produced a simple demo that I sent to Rod. In return, Rod sent me a large, beautiful vase of flowers with a card that read: "Thank you for a wonderful song, can't wait to sing it." I took a Polaroid of the flowers, so that once they died, I'd still have something to remind me of the moment.

I pitched the idea of Chapman producing the song to Rod's management and was delighted when they went for it. As we got nearer the date to start cutting the track, Rod invited me to dinner with him and his usual group of pals and leggy blond models.

Soccer is a huge passion of his, not only as a spectator but as a player, and he invited me to a couple of the games that he regularly played in North Hollywood with his mates on the weekends. He was almost at a level where, from what I could tell, he could've played professionally. Many of his friends that he'd grown up with had moved over to the States and were on his team, and I suspect there were a few professional players that showed up as well. Rod would come over and say hello to me, dressed in his soccer jersey and cleats, and then go back to the game. Afterwards, we would all go to a local pub. It was so nice, how he included me in a part of his life that had nothing to do with music.

Mike and I did the preproduction together. This involved preparing the tracks, first by programming all the drums, which was popular during the eighties. Real drummers were not happy that they were being replaced by drum machines, and I don't blame them, but like many things during the MTV era, it became part of the sound. Our plan was to replace them with real drums, but we liked the way they sounded so much that we decided to keep them. Since that time, I've gone back to using real drummers on everything, although programming drums can be convenient when I'm writing a song, or if I want to produce something more industrial sounding.

Gene came in and recorded all the guitars, and while he was cutting them, I thought I was going crazy...I could hear "Love Is a Battlefield" playing somewhere in the room.

"Do you hear that?" I asked Gene.

"Hear what?" he asked. "Wait, is that 'Love Is a Battlefield'?'" We looked around the room trying to figure out where it was coming from. It was bizarre. Then Gene started laughing. "It's playing through my guitar pickups. Sometimes they pick up local stations."

How badass is that? I thought.

The track was coming out great. Chapman hired Mike Porcaro, one of the three famed Porcaro brothers in Toto, to come in and record the bass. He was one of the top session players in the world, and yet he had no ego playing what I asked him to play, note for note. I was so used to session players getting irritated with me for telling them what to play, I don't know if it was because they were so accomplished, or if I was a woman. Probably both, so this was a nice change. We didn't even bother with any charts, I just sang him the parts. Before he left, he said to me, "Holly, your bass lines are killer. Thank you for inviting me down to play on it. It was an honor." That acknowledgement from him was priceless to me because I knew my bass lines *were* integral to the songs I wrote. Indeed, I often started a song with a title and a bass line. But most of the time, when another producer stepped in to produce one of my songs, it would drive me crazy when they'd change the bass, which they did every fucking time! Chapman never did, though. In fact, one of his highest praises to me was that I came up with the best bass lines and that he always relied on me to do so.

One day, I vowed, I was going to be sitting in front of the console, producing records myself. Being the producer meant you were in charge; I had been in the studio for years now with some of the top producers and learned so much. I was a human sponge who watched and picked up everything. I even paid attention to the producers who had no business being producers, learning what not to do. Hell, I had no issues with leadership but it seemed like the music business, which was still pretty much run by men, did. It was going to be a very long time before that changed, if ever.

Rod never came to the sessions, but we figured he'd be happy with the way it was coming out. He seemed to go along with everything, and I wondered if that was just his nature, or he couldn't be bothered, which was common among a lot of superstars. They wanted to walk in, sing the song a few times, then leave and let everyone in the trenches figure out the rest.

Before Mike Porcaro left, he asked for my phone number, which I happily wrote down. Not only did I want to work with him again, but we also had a mutual attraction that was fairly obvious, and sure enough, we started dating for a bit. He was a sweetheart. The first time I ever drove up the California coast to Big Sur was with him. While our romance didn't last long, we remained good friends with a lot of respect for one another. Tragically, in 2015 he died from ALS (amyotrophic lateral sclerosis) at the age of sixty.

Once we finished cutting all the musical parts, Rod asked Mike to send the masters over to him so he could record the vocals on his own. Imagine a movie star telling the director that he's going to shoot his scenes alone without any of the film crew or the director and send the footage to the director when he's done. We didn't know what his reasoning was. It was hard to imagine Rod being shy. This was the same man who strutted in front of tens of thousands of screaming fans and shook his ass in a pair of leopard pants so low that you could see his butt crack every time he spun around.

Whatever the reason, Rod recorded the vocals and sent them back to us. As we listened back, Mike and I looked at each other with the same what-the-fuck expression. A lot of his phrasing and melody was wrong, as if he had completely rewritten certain sections. We wondered whether it was a case of him not taking the time to learn the parts, or that he had his own ideas. It was one thing for a singer to embellish the notes and put their own style or signature on the song, that was a good thing, but that's not what this was. We had taken great pains to write a vocal with great lyrics and melody specifically for him. It was all there on the demo we'd given him.

"Let me call and talk to him," Mike said.

I went in the lounge and dumped a handful of quarters into the Space Invaders machine next to the coffee maker. Everybody was obsessed with that game. Even the Pretenders had recorded a song on their first record called "Space Invaders." It was an instrumental, but it had the sound effects from the game. I had just made it to the fourth level when Mike walked in.

"Okay, I talked to him and he's agreed to come down here today, but he said he doesn't want anybody in the control room when he's singing except for me."

"And me, right?" I asked.

"No, he doesn't want you here either."

"Did he say why?" I asked, surprised and a little hurt. That would've made sense, had he been recording the song with another producer and band, but I'd been putting together the entire track with Mike from the get-go. It wasn't like Rod and I were strangers.

"No, and I didn't ask him," Mike said. "Listen, I just want to get the bloody vocal done. I wouldn't take it personally."

Dejected, I went home and sulked.

Later that day, Mike called to say, "Rod did the verses, and they're sounding terrific now, but he's asked if you can come in and sing the backgrounds on all the choruses before he sings them."

I'd never heard of a singer wanting the background vocals to be cut before the lead vocal. That meant that the backgrounds would dictate the phrasing of the lead vocals, instead of the other way around. That just seemed backasswards to me. On top of that, instead of hiring, say, three professional background singers, he had specifically asked for me—just me. I spent the rest of the day doing stacks of vocals, and even improvising at the end. The next day, Rod came back and finished his vocals. Now, everything sounded great. By the time the song was mixed, it sounded like we had been in the same room singing a duet together.

While we waited for his record to come out, I continued to hang out with Rod and his inner circle. He threw a big party at his house, which was huge. The living room felt like a hotel lobby. I tried to imagine what it would be like to live in such a big house when it wasn't filled with a hundred people in that cavernous room, and it was just Rod sitting alone having his afternoon tea and biscuits in his skivvies.

One evening when we were driving around in his limo, he said, "Hey, Holly, do you think I'm sexy?" It was so direct, and because he had had such a big hit with the same title, it caught me completely off guard. I burst out laughing and nearly sprayed my drink all over the car.

I said, "Well Rod, you know, you're not really my type, and I know I'm not yours either. For starters, I'm not blond and I don't have long enough legs."

Soon after that, Rod invited me to join him, along with his usual entourage, at an awards show. When we arrived, we were ushered through the VIP back entrance and into a large room set up for all the stars and industry people. As we entered, everyone turned and looked at Rod, greeting him or calling out to him. Besides me, he had several blond models in tow, so I imagined that I stood out with my dark hair and long black dress. The women on each of his arm were Marilyn Monroes. I was Morticia Addams.

Paul Stanley and I spotted each other at the same time. We hadn't seen each other in years, not since I had left Spider, and since then I'd had a lot of success. When he saw me walk in with Rod he did a double take, probably wondering what I was doing with him, and came up to say hello. It was wonderful to see him. He asked for my phone number, and shortly after that, we started dating again.

"Love Touch" was released in May, right before the summer, as the first (and only) single on his record, *Every Beat of My Heart*. I hadn't realized it, but the album had been produced by Bob Ezrin, with the one exception being "Love Touch." It dawned on me that I must've been brought in to write towards the end of the project when they probably realized they were missing a single. They'd called in the big dogs. Hah, I was a big dog now.

Right before "Love Touch" was released, my publishers pitched the song to Universal Pictures for a movie called *Legal Eagles*, which was directed by Ivan Reitman, the same director behind *Ghostbusters*. It starred Robert Redford, Debra Winger, and Daryl Hannah. The film came out in June and really helped to promote the single. There were scenes from the movie interspersed with shots of Rod dressed in a denim prison outfit, pleading his innocence to a jury of scantily dressed women. Like that would ever happen in real life. The video ended with him lying on a cot in a jail cell. Even though it was kind of shallow, it was a popular video on MTV and stayed in heavy rotation for months.

About a month after "Love Touch" soared up the charts, Randy Phillips called me up.

"We've just booked a short tour of Asia with Rod for three weeks and his keyboard player can't do it. Rod suggested you. How would you like to fill in?"

I had every reason to say yes: I missed playing live, it was only for three or four weeks, and it was Rod Stewart. Hell, I could afford to take off a month to do this. There was nothing to think about. "I would love to!" I told him excitedly.

Every morning when I wake, before my feet even hit the ground, I say a thank you to the Universe. It was times like these that it didn't feel like a job at all, even though a tremendous amount of work was involved. I couldn't believe how much my life had changed in the last twenty-four hours. I was going to Japan and China for the first time, not as a tourist, but as a touring member of Rod Stewart's band. Visas and passports had to be arranged and I barely had time to put together a stage wardrobe. I was looking forward to meeting the guys in his band and feeling that same camaraderie I had felt as a guest on the Tina Turner tour, only this would be even better as I would be playing in the band instead of watching from the sidelines. The management messengered all of Rod's records to me. I only had a week to learn his whole repertoire by the time rehearsals started. Luckily, I knew a lot of the songs and had a good ear, so I learned them all as best I could in time. It was going to be so much fun, I thought. I couldn't have been more wrong.

The first day of rehearsal, I walked into the room wearing a pair of ripped jeans, a *Clockwork Orange* T-shirt, and a pair of Converse sneakers. I knew it would be a bad idea to dress in anything feminine or hot-looking if I wanted to be one of the boys. I had been told ahead of time that the band was going to be scaled down to an efficient, tight-knit group for this tour, just drums, bass, guitar, and keyboards. That meant no backup singers, horn players, or percussionists. If a band of macho guys like KISS could welcome me on board, I was confident that Rod's band would too. He hadn't arrived yet when I walked in smiling and said a friendly "Hello," foolishly thinking I'd be like a sunny breath of fresh air. The guys looked at me blankly like, "Who the fuck are you? We didn't order food."

I walked up to the guitarist and offered my hand, which he limply shook in slow motion, staring at me as if he'd never seen a woman before. "I'm Holly Knight, I'm filling in for Kevin."

The guitarist didn't bother to tell me his name (I knew he was Jim Cregan). His only response was, "Really. No one said anything to us about you."

This was awkward. "No shit? I'm sorry about that." I smiled insincerely as I scanned the room, hoping to see a road manager or someone from management to help me out, but there was no one other than the band and a bunch of guitar and drum techs. Maybe if I told him I wrote the new single for them it would give me some cred and he'd relax. "I wrote 'Love Touch' and Rod asked me to do the tour, so I said yes. I'm only filling in until Kevin comes back." Why the fuck was I having to explain myself to this ginger-headed putz?

Jim said nothing and continued to tune his guitar. One of the roadies walked up to me, introduced himself, and kindly showed me to the keyboards that were set off to one side. The rest of the guys just kind of gawked at me.

About half an hour later, Rod finally walked in. He greeted all his band mates warmly. It was obvious that they hadn't seen each other in a while, and then he saw me and came over and gave me a light hug. Something felt different, like he had to act more formal with me in front of the guys. I thought, *Why are they so pissed?* I tried to see it from their perspective, and sure, some of it I could understand. After all, Rod's first single had been written by an outside writer, and I suspected that they wanted to get their own songs on his record. To add insult to injury, they hadn't even been hired to play on the recording, and they had probably played on the rest of the new album. The outsider was a woman, and to make matters worse, their beloved leader had taken it one traitorous step further and invited the wench on tour.

Still, this wasn't high school, and they needed to realize that I wasn't the enemy. In fact, I'd written Rod a song that was climbing up the charts, just as they stood there glaring at me. Did they not realize that even for them, this was a good thing? Having a hit song meant they would sell more records and tickets when they went on tour. It reminded me of the pettiness in Spider.

We started to run through the songs, and the guys seemed to relax a little when they saw I had not only learned all the tunes but played them well. Still, they never said a kind word to me. When we would take a break, I would go hide in the bathroom and sometimes cry softly, then fix the mascara that had run down my cheeks. In later years, I heard that they thought I kept going in to powder the inside of my nose and not the outside. If that was the case, they were probably pissed that I wasn't sharing with them. But it was one of the few times I wasn't doing blow. I already felt paranoid enough without making the situation worse. I was hurt that Rod wasn't his usual ebullient and funny self with me. I'm sure the guys had given him more than an earful of grief for inviting me into their inner sanctum. In all the years that I'd played in bands and been a songwriter, this was the most uncomfortable and hurtful experience I had ever had. Never before had I felt the harshness or the stench of the man cave this bad.

This continued the whole week of rehearsals, and I started to dread going to a foreign country with this lot, even with Rod. As bad as it felt here, in my own country where my home and my friends were, over there I would be alone and isolated with these guys. That scared the shit out of me, but it was too late to back out, and the last thing I wanted to be was a quitter.

We moved into Rod's garage for one last rehearsal. I remember he had parked his bright, candy apple red Lamborghini in the garage. At some point, his son, who was maybe five at the time, came out. Somehow, he had gotten hold of the garage opener and pressed the button to make the overhead garage door close. I could see him laughing with delight. No one seemed to notice what was about to happen but me, and I shouted out at the top of my lungs, "STOP!" Everyone turned and scowled at me until they realized that I had actually saved the roof of the sportscar from being sliced in two.

Soon after that, I got a call from Arnold, telling me that the tour had been cancelled. I never asked why because frankly, I was relieved. I had other projects I wanted to get going on, especially my own band. More importantly, I felt that I needed to take care of myself by being around people who appreciated me. "Love Touch" reached number six in the Billboard Hot 100, higher than any other single Rod had had in the previous six years. *Legal Eagles* came out and earned $63 million at the box office, which wasn't too shabby back then. After, the cancelled Asian tour, I didn't hear from Rod for thirty-seven years. No more invitations to his soccer games, or dinner outings. I chalked it up to him being busy, but I missed the early part of what I thought was our friendship, because I had liked him so much.

In 1990, Rod released *Storyteller: The Complete Anthology: 1964–1990*, comprised of four CDs that contained sixty-five tracks, including "Love Touch." He also released a second compilation, *Encore: The Very Best of Rod Stewart Volume 2.* "Love Touch" was also on that compilation, only this one had liner notes for each track. I was so excited when I got a copy of it, I scrolled down the track list till I found my song. I couldn't wait to see what Rod had to say about it, because it had done so well, and he had told me how much he loved it. Hell, he'd even sent me flowers.

I was stunned by his words: "One of the silliest songs I've ever recorded." I couldn't believe what I was reading. I read it three times to make sure my eyes weren't playing tricks on me. How in God's name were the lyrics silly? I mean, c'mon, this, coming from the singer who wrote "Do Ya Think I'm Sexy"? I couldn't help but recall how Rod's demeanor had completely changed once he'd walked into rehearsal and had to face his good old boys club. Someone, and I don't know who, had whispered some negative crap in his ear, and he had believed it. I can't imagine any other explanation. Had I been able to talk to him and ask him what he meant I would have. But I never got that chance. I searched my soul, trying to be objective. Was he right? Were the lyrics silly?

This is the answer I came up with, and it's just my personal opinion. Of course, I may not be entirely objective, but I think it bares saying: "Love Touch" is one of the best songs I've ever written, that Mike and I have written together. The lyrics are beautiful and deeply romantic:

> "Why can't I climb your walls and find
> somewhere to hide?
> Can't I knock down your door and drag myself inside,
> I'll light your candles baby and maybe
> I'll light your life,
> I want to feel the breathless end that
> you come to every night..."

I'm sorry, but that's fucking poetry.

Rod and I never really discussed the lyrics, and maybe we should have because I meant it in the most cerebral way. For example, you could send your beloved a "love touch" from across a room, an ocean, even over the telephone. Your love would be so deep that you could just look at that person and give them a love touch without so much as a word and they would feel it. To me that was very sexy. Sure, the verse setup was about a man and a woman who had had a fight, and he was trying to get back in her good graces, but at the core of the song, what they had together was spiritual—"I want to be good for you, I didn't mean to be bad."

Then one day I had an epiphany. I am, after all, a woman, and it's fairly obvious that men and women are wired and conditioned differently. Maybe that's why, after all these years, my songs have had a greater impact with women, not just the recording artists who sang my songs, but the listeners and fans as well. As women, we are much more complex and stronger than we are given credit for. I started out at a time when women wanted to hear from women, and I had plenty to say. I still do.

143

Maybe Rod thought, "But darlin' I'm still the best that you ever had," referred to the best lay, when what I meant was "the best love." At the end of the day, it doesn't really matter. Sure, my feelings were hurt, but who knows if he actually said it that way, or if he even said it at all. And if he did, I forgave him. I let it go.

Years later, Rod achieved huge success redefining himself by recording songs from the Great American Songbook, the kind of songs that Frank Sinatra and Tony Bennett were famous for. I love that genre of music.

In 2017, I was in New York having lunch with my friend Lissa at The Boathouse in Central Park when Rod walked in with his family and sat down at a table behind us. She whispered, "Hey, isn't that Rod Stewart?" I turned around and sure enough it was. "Go and say hi to him," she prodded.

"No, I don't want to bother him, he's with his family."

"Nonsense," she said. "Get up and go say hi."

"But there are bodyguards everywhere," I shot back.

"So what. Go!" she insisted.

I stood up and walked the three feet to his table. The bodyguards started to move in, but before they could pounce, I tapped Rod lightly on the shoulder. "Rod? Hi, it's me, Holly." To my surprise, he stood up and gave me a kiss, European style, one on each cheek. The bodyguards slithered away once they saw that their charge was happy to see me. I was so relieved he was nice to me because I'd carried around this comment of his for decades and even though I had forgiven him, I didn't know how he would act towards me.

It was as if it'd never happened. He turned to his wife Penny and his young sons and introduced me, "Holly and I wrote a beautiful hit song together called 'Love Touch,'" Huh? Then he corrected himself and said, "Well, she wrote it and I sang it. Fantastic song." We chatted for a few minutes, and he wrote down his phone number on the back of a card.

And they say women are crazy. It made me happy to see him again, especially since I was back in his good graces. Maybe I never was out of them in the first place.

There's something valuable I've learned as I've moved through life: there are people you work with who you get very close to because you spend a lot of time together, years, and you get under each other's skin. You start to think of each other as real friends, and in some ways, you are, but it's really just for the time you spend together or a chapter in your life. They're not soul-deep friends, the ones you can count on or trust with your life. Instead, they're what I think of as "part-time" friends. It's always nice to run into them and give each other a hug, but then you go your separate ways until next time. If there is a next time. Thinking this way has helped me to not personalize things so deeply.

I saw Sir Rod Stewart again in 2018, in London's West End when the Tina Turner musical debuted at the Aldwych Theater. Three of my songs were in it, "Better Be Good to Me," "Be Tender with Me Baby," and, of course, "The Best." Mike Chapman was there too, sitting next to me. Rod and his wife, Penny, were sitting directly behind me, and just as we were saying a friendly hello, the lights in the theater dimmed. The audience, which was abuzz with excitement, heard Rod go, "SSSSSSSSShhhhhhhhhhhhh," really loud, and the whole room went dead quiet, thinking the show was about to begin. Then Rod yelled out, "Just kidding!" and everyone cracked up. That's the mischievous prankster I fondly remember, and he was in a naughty mood the entire evening. He kept tapping me on the back and whispering to me, asking me who wrote every song, and whenever one of my songs was being performed, he hit me on the back saying, "That's one of yours!" He was proud of me and that made me smile deep inside. When the show climaxed with "The Best," the audience rose to their feet and sang along. I could hear Rod singing along behind me, and it gave me the chills.

It suited him. It was another one of those top ten moments in my life, sweet and genuine.

Everything had come full circle, all was well with the world. We are all merely human with flaws and baggage. I've learned to laugh at myself, and to laugh at the absurdity and beauty of life a lot more.

CHAPTER THIRTEEN

WE WILL BE INVINCIBLE
(PAT BENATAR)

Los Angeles, 1986

"And with the power of conviction there is no sacrifice..."
("Invincible" performed by Pat Benatar)

I went to New York every few months, circulating around all the clubs, looking for that elusive rock star to complete my band. I liked the idea of an Anglo-American band, so I made several trips to London. I bought records of British underground bands I liked and approached some of the singers. I even met a few buskers on the street who had a lot of charisma and took them into a local studio that Chrysalis had set up for me. They all looked the part but couldn't sing anything other than their own music. One of the singers was a squatter in a boarded up house in Camden. That brought back a few memories.

Now that I was signed to Chrysalis, I spent a good amount of time at their London offices whenever I was there, just as I had with Aucoin Management in earlier days. It was nice to have a place to go to with some friendly faces, and one bright and sunny day, I met Huey Lewis, who was a Chrysalis recording artist. Huey Lewis and the News were huge, their videos played constantly on MTV. His music appealed to the working class, someone you'd have a beer with while you watched the World Series on the TV above the bar. Originally, Mike Chapman had written "Heart and Soul" for the band Exile, but it was when Huey's band recorded it that it became a huge hit. The choppy guitar on that song is quintessentially Chapman. I loved it the first time I heard it. Huey took me out to lunch, and we had a wonderful time. He was kind of goofy and sexy all at once, and he didn't come across like a rock star, more just a regular guy with a stunning cleft in his chin.

Mike had worked with a singer based out of London named Simon Climie who he had suggested I meet. Simon had been part of a British duo called Climie-Fisher, the latter part of which had been in a band called Naked Eyes. They'd had several huge hits like "Promises, Promises" (which I loved) and a remake of the Burt Bacharach classic, "Always Something There to Remind Me." Mike must've known that if we met, we would end up in bed together. I was crazy about him. He was so funny in the most self-deprecating way and so British. During my search, I continued to write for other artists, and because Simon and I got on so well and he had a mini studio in his flat with a Fairlight, I asked him if he'd like to try writing a song with me for a movie TriStar Pictures was making called *The Legend of Billie Jean.* I had a copy of the script that they had sent me, and given the story, I thought Pat Benatar would be the perfect singer to pitch the song to because, once again, it needed a strong, ballsy approach from a woman.

The story was an empowering one about a young woman who became a fugitive and icon for her generation, especially women who were tired of being pushed around and sexually abused, and like Joan of Arc, she'd chopped off all her hair, which made her all the more striking. The movie had a #MeToo theme to it, long before the real

#MeToo movement existed. I already had a title, "Invincible." Simon and I spent twelve hours straight writing the song from start to finish, then we recorded a demo with his vocals. When I returned home to LA I got Chapman to put another vocal down. He brought the fire, always.

> "What are we waiting for?
> We've got the right to be angry
> What are we running for when there's nowhere we
> can run to anymore?
> We can't afford to be innocent stand up and
> face the enemy,
> It's a do or die situation, we will be invincible."

The great thing about Pat Benatar was that I could write anything and know she would be able to sing it with that supernatural range of hers. The melody on the chorus is not an easy one to sing because the notes move around a lot, by design. TriStar was thrilled that I was going to pitch it to her, and just as I hoped, once she heard the song, she wanted to record it. To this day, it remains one of my absolute favorite tunes that I've written. I would have to say it is quintessentially me. Dark and edgy, it was anthemic with an epic melody and powerful message, especially for women.

Giving the song to Pat came with one caveat, a ballsy move on my part because she could've not only said no, but never worked with me again. Since "Battlefield," Neil Giraldo had produced everything she did and I wanted Mike Chapman to produce the track. I didn't trust Neil to record "Invincible" the way I heard it in my head, the way the demo sounded. Mike had produced tracks on her first record and would do a great job staying true to the song. I braced myself for the rebuttal. Surprisingly, Pat agreed without argument, and Mike did an excellent job. I especially liked the way the drums sounded. I'm sure Myron Grombacher, their drummer would agree. "Invincible" charted as soon as it was released and soared to the number ten spot on the

Billboard Hot 100 chart. The movie director loved the song so much, he had the chorus melody orchestrated and used it all over the movie. In addition, the song was on the movie soundtrack and was released as the first single on Pat's record, *Seven the Hard Way*, which she was in the process of finishing.

The video stayed on the heavy rotation playlist for months. I never would have known that Pat was four months pregnant when she filmed the video if I hadn't read it somewhere years later. They shot her in a beautiful, long brocade coat and featured a lot of close-ups of her face. I don't think she ever looked more beautiful or radiant.

Paul Stanley called me up early one morning and said, "I'm going to Eddie Van Halen's house tomorrow for a barbecue. Would you like to come with me?"

Did he even need to ask? I mean, who wouldn't want to meet one of the world's greatest guitarists? "Hell yeah, I'd love to!" I replied.

Eddie and his wife Valerie Bertinelli lived on a bluff in Malibu that led down to the beach. Their house was a modest but cozy place with a stunning view of the Pacific Ocean. Often, on the weekends, they invited friends over for food, drinks, and beach volleyball.

Paul picked me up and we headed up the Pacific Coast Highway. I was excited to meet Eddie. I'd heard he was a sweet, down-to-earth guy, and as soon as we arrived, he came out to greet us.

"This is Holly," Paul said. Usually, I liked being introduced the way he'd just introduced me, but when it came to meeting someone special in the music business, especially someone like Eddie, you'd think Paul would've introduced me as "Holly Knight," along with something interesting like, "She's a successful songwriter," or something to that effect—for the obvious reason that Eddie would take me more seriously when the conversation inevitably got around to music. Yes, it sucks that I had to think this way, but I was pretty damn savvy by then, and I understood how things worked. Celebrities trusted and respected you more when you were successful. You weren't a "wan-nabe" anymore, you were "one of them."

Eddie shook my hand, and said, "Hey there."

"Hi Eddie, I'm so pleased to meet you. I'm a big fan." It probably wasn't the first time he'd heard that.

"Thanks," he said, "Nice to meet you too."

He invited us into the house where he introduced me to his wife, Valerie, the award-winning actress who'd starred on a show called *One Day at a Time.* She was super friendly and warm towards me, especially considering her celebrity status, she could have been stuck up, but she wasn't. Paul and Eddie hung out together most of the day, so I did too. While I repeatedly tried to join in on their conversation, which was entirely about music, they both ignored me. I noticed it most when they started talking about songwriting, they were both explaining how they approached it and again, I tried to join in, but this time Eddie looked at me as if to say, "No one asked you." Eventually, I just gave up and left, certain that they didn't even notice.

I walked into the living room where Valerie and her girlfriends were drinking and having a much livelier time. Valerie said to her friends, "Guys, this is Holly. She came with Paul Stanley." Their female energy was much more fun. I noticed that the TV was tuned to MTV, and "The Warrior" came on. Valerie yelled out, "Oh, I love this song!" She and her friends started singing along, "Shooting at the walls of heartache, bang bang, I am the warrior." What a contrast from this room to the one next door.

I glanced over at Valerie and shyly said, "I wrote that song."

As it continued in the background, Valerie looked at me and said, "Get out of here. You really wrote 'The Warrior'? You're a songwriter?"

"Yes," I smiled.

She turned to her friends. "Hey, Holly wrote 'The Warrior'!" All of a sudden, the girls surrounded me, curious and wanting to know what else I had written.

About an hour later, Paul found me and said we had to go and to meet him in the garage, so I hugged Valerie and my new friends, gathered my things, and headed outside. Paul seemed to be deep in conversation with Eddie, and then Eddie turned and came over to me.

"Oh my god, I'm so sorry. I wish Paul had told me when he introduced you, that you were the songwriter Holly Knight. I feel like such a jerk."

I smiled at him sweetly and said, "It's okay, you didn't know, but thank you for saying that. I meant it when I said I'm a fan." I'd spent the good part of the day being snuffed by him, but the fact that he had just admitted to being a jerk was quite decent of him. He had at least acknowledged his misogynistic crap, which men rarely do. I left in much better spirits.

I even experienced a similar encounter with my idol, David Bowie, a few years later, although the circumstances were entirely different. One night, my friend Paul Chavarria, who was the head of production on Bowie's 1987 Glass Spider Tour, invited me to a concert at Anaheim Stadium. It was the first time I saw Bowie perform, and it was phenomenal. Not only were the band and Bowie fantastic to listen to, but the visuals were magnificent. On stage, Bowie was joined by guitarist Peter Frampton and a troupe of dancers (choreographed by longtime Bowie collaborator Toni Basil, who had had a hit of her own with Chapman's song, "Mickey").

After the concert, Paul Chavarria brought me to the after-party, a spacious room filled with music industry people and celebs. When the right moment presented itself, Paul grabbed me and brought me to David.

"Hey David, this is Holly, a good friend of mine," he said.

Bowie shook my hand and, smiling, said, "Lovely to meet you, Holly."

"I love you David," I blurted out like a complete dork. I was nervous, something I rarely am when meeting celebrities, but this was one of my idols; as a writer, he was one of my biggest influences, I'd even named my first band after him. I would gladly take crumbs, anything from this man, and I had finally met him and shook his hand. Maybe the energy coming from it would transfer over to me. Of course, I knew that for him, meeting me was uneventful, that he had to say "Nice to meet you" a hundred times to a hundred strangers that night. Still, I was grateful to have met him, to be able to stand twelve inches away from his iconic face in the flesh and stare, even for the briefest of moments, into his alien eyes.

As Bowie made his way through the room making his obligatory greetings, I studied his every move. Like all bands that performed, this was work, there was nothing "party" about this after-party for him, it was meet-and-greet time, and in a big city like LA, the work-load was heavier than usual. Then I noticed Paul saying something to him. Back and forth in each other's ears they talked over the hub-bub, and then the unimaginable happened. Bowie turned around as if he was looking for someone in the crowded room. When his eyes locked on me, he walked right over. "Holly Knight!" My knees went weak. "Paul just told me you were *the* Holly Knight. I didn't know and I'm sorry, I am so impressed with your work. It's lovely to meet you. Really," he gushed.

I was flabbergasted, "Well, I wouldn't expect you to know, *oh my god*, thank you so much for saying that, you have no idea what that means to me," I gushed back.

He gave me a warm hug. Another top ten moment in my life. Paul was proudly grinning the whole time and later said, "You see? I told him all about you, and he knew your songs."

Every day, I witness women having to constantly fight for their place in the world, and I'm no different, always fighting for my place in the sun, fighting the good fight with love in my heart, maybe not all the time, but as much as I can muster. Bang bang, I am the warrior.

CHAPTER FOURTEEN

22B3 (DEVICE)

Los Angeles, 1985

"Sometimes you go so far you're so hot you can't stop"
("Hanging On a Heart Attack" performed by Device)

While this was all going on, I kept searching for a lead singer. I was annoyed and frustrated that it was taking so long. Everything else had been so easy. The talent pool just wasn't what I thought it would be, neither in America nor across the pond. I'd been ricocheting between three major cities and everywhere in between for a year and a half and was feeling antsy. *Maybe I'm being too picky*, I thought. I started to lose perspective and objectivity. Mike had other commitments and wanted to get some of the record done while we could. *Build it and they will come*, I thought, just like in *Field of Dreams*.

So, we did something crazy. We started recording the record without a singer, cutting the tracks in keys that Mike could sing them in. This was so he could put vocal roughs on the masters as references for whoever would eventually step into his shoes. just as we had always done when demoing songs for other artists. It was risky because it locked us into finding someone who could sing in Mike's range. Fortunately, his range was pretty common. If we found a singer who had a higher or lower range, we'd be screwed and would have to recut everything. These days, with digital recording, it's pretty easy to change keys and tempos, but back then it was impossible without rerecording. I didn't want our singer to literally sound like Mike. His reference vocals were only intended to show how the melodies went.

Singers were constantly sending me tapes and bios with photos. More often than not, I would find someone who sounded great singing their own material, but once I took them into the studio to sing my material, never sounded as good. Some looked like rock stars but couldn't sing, and others sang well, but had no attitude or vibe. Out of curiosity, we flew Simon Climie to LA to see how he would work out, and even though he had a his own sound, it wasn't a good fit for the band.

Then a singer named Paul Engemann sent us a photo and tape. He had sung a song on the *Scarface* soundtrack as well as a few other things with Giorgio Moroder. He had a strong voice that sounded oddly similar to Mike's, and he was good looking, so we had him come in. He had a good ear and picked the songs and vocals up quickly.

Here's the first mistake we made. Because Paul's range and tone sounded so similar to Mike's, and because we were so used to hearing Mike's voice on the demos, when Paul opened his mouth to sing, he was able to emulate Mike so well that it kind of worked. We were so worn out trying to find a lead singer that when Mike and I went into another room and looked at each other, we both said the same thing—"He's pretty good, right? He'll do." That pretty much said it all, "He'll do."

"What about his stage presence?" I asked Mike.

"You can get someone to work on that with him," he said.

I came up with the name Device. I had made a list of edgy words that contained the letters "d" and "v", words like: divine, device, deviant, destiny, darkness, depth, and violet, vines, victory, versatile, vice, vital, villainous, valiant. The definition of a device is "a thing used for a particular purpose." In a way, the band was my device where I could write all the songs and music that I wanted as an artist. So, Device it was. Just like that, we were able to finish the record.

Mike Chapman came up with a futuristic but obscure name for the record: *22B3*. When we asked him what it meant, he only gave us a cryptic answer. "When the record is a hit, I'll tell you what it means." We looked at him like, *Yeah right, you're full of shit*, but we went along with it.

In terms of musical sophistication, we were badass. "Hanging On a Heart Attack" was an epic opener with cascading, intertwining sequencer lines and massive drums. I'd found an oboe sound and written a melody for the intro that sounded like a snake charmer. The bass line was sequenced as well, and Gene's guitar playing showcased his versatility, whether it was the funky strumming in the verses or his stunning solos. Lyrically, the song was about going right up to the edge of something that gives you an adrenaline rush and having the control to pull back before its too late, anything from having an orgasm to driving a car over the edge of a cliff.

> "Can you make it last, make it rock to the bone?
> And if you do it faster will the hunger drive you home?
> Right down to the basics of it, right down
> to the wire…"

In many ways, I think, *22B3* is a masterpiece, and I'm proud of it. However, I'd have to say that the vocals were the weakest part of the record for me. I'm pretty sure Gene and Mike would agree. And, interestingly, a lot of fans disagree.

Chrysalis spared no expense for the "Hanging On a Heart Attack" video, hiring Brian Grant, whose company with David Mallet, MGMM, was the most successful UK production company of the eighties. They were a venerable who's-who of the most iconic videos of the decade, including the Buggles' "Video Killed the Radio Star," Peter Gabriel's "Sledgehammer," Queen's "Radio Ga Ga," David Bowie's "Fashion," Billy Idol's "White Wedding," and Duran Duran's "Hungry Like the Wolf" and "Rio."

We flew to London to film in an abandoned warehouse. We also shot the album cover there. The end result was a fast-paced and haunting video. One of the elaborate sets looked like a ward in an insane asylum with patients strapped to each bed. Another set had our instruments in what looked like a frozen ice cave, with mist and smoke. That effect happened to be real. It was the dead of winter and that mist was the air coming out of our mouths as we froze our asses off.

Personality-wise, Paul couldn't have been more different from Gene and I. He had grown up leading a somewhat sheltered life in a Mormon household, so his perspective was going to be different. When it came to photo and video shoots, talking to the press, and performing live, it became exhausting trying to explain to him what our vision of the band was. The last thing I wanted to do was tell my singer how to be a rock star. I realized it wasn't his fault. He did everything we asked of him, he just didn't get it. For instance, the lyrics to our songs were extremely dark and romantic and I wondered if he had even taken the time to understand what the lyrics he was singing were about. We asked him if he could try to come across a little more intense and serious. Gene and I tried to befriend him, but it was hard.

Once we returned to LA, I met with Freddy DeMann, Madonna's manager, and played him a few of the songs from the album that everybody around me was flipping out over. When the music ended, I sat back in my chair and waited for him to tell me how much he loved the record.

"I don't get it." he said.

I looked at him, confused. "You don't get what?"

"Is this a real band, or is this you and some hired musicians... what is this?"

"It's a band, my band...what are you trying to say?" I started to feel angry and defensive.

Freddy said, "Look, I'm sorry, I'm just being honest. I think you're an amazing songwriter, and I was genuinely interested in seeing what your new band would be like, but I'm not buying this whole Device thing. It sounds fake, like something put together. And the singer sounds robotic. He sounds like you propped him up and told him what to sing."

Bingo.

I was so upset I stood up and said, "What the fuck do you know about real singers? Look who you manage," before storming out, going to my car and sobbing uncontrollably.

While everyone around me was kissing my ass and praising the record, Freddy had seen the truth. I had settled for a singer I didn't like. It was as if Freddy had sucker-punched me in the first round and I was defenseless because I knew he was right and I just didn't want to admit it, especially after having worked so damn hard on the record. Had I found a true star and the kind of singer I really wanted, the entire trajectory of the band would've been different.

I felt like an asshole for telling Freddy off. I actually loved Madonna, so it was a stupid remark said in a moment of defensive arrogance. I had been riding on such a string of success, that I was long overdue for some kind of failure. Still, too much money and time had been spent putting this project together, and I had poured so much of my heart into it, so I held my head high and kept going. I wasn't about to give up years of work just because some manager had told me he wasn't buying it.

We released the record to incredible reviews and "Hanging On a Heart Attack" entered the Billboard Hot 100 pretty quickly. We hired Patrick Ranier, a pleasant but somewhat benign manager, and started rehearsing for a small club tour while we did local gigs at outdoor events and headlined a club called the Palace in Hollywood.

Finally, there was something I could feel good about—playing live again. I loved running around the stage with my portable bass keyboard and right up to where Gene was standing. I had a few portable keyboards powder coated one color (including the keys), one in grey and one in bright blue, which look really futuristic. I did end up with a wireless setup, which had only recently come on the market and allowed me the freedom to go anywhere on stage without tripping over wires in my stiletto heels. I was in the best shape I'd ever been, and I had these black, sleeveless leather jumpsuits custom-made that zipped up the front. I felt confident and sexy, even tomboyish in them.

Once again, MTV was my ally. We released the video and it immediately got added to heavy rotation, which was rare for a new group. That helped Device to get noticed a lot quicker than it otherwise would have. Leading up to this, every time I would do interviews, there seemed to be a lot of curiosity as to what kind of band I was going to come out with. I promised it would be "different." Any time people would see a band with a woman in it who wasn't the lead singer, the woman always stood out because it was unusual. That was a good thing, and I hoped that more women and even young girls would take notice and realize that they, too, could end up being in bands not just as singers, but musicians.

"Hanging On a Heart Attack" got as high as thirty-five on the Top 100 before it lost its bullet. Device made it into the top forty, just as Spider had done. We appeared on *The Dick Clark Show*, a milestone for any band. Chrysalis released a second single, "Who Says," and because I had learned a lot from the first video about what not to do, I came across much better. I got rid of the hair extensions and focused more on how I wanted to be perceived. Paul, instead of improving, took our advice from the previous video shoot to heart and overcompensated this time. His expressions went from smiling too much to looking positively evil. After "Who Says" stalled in the high seventies, all the momentum we had built up with the first single vanished and Chrysalis stopped working the record. They pulled our tour support and turned their backs on us. I sat down with Gene to discuss what we should do. Neither of us wanted to continue with Paul, but who hires a new singer for their second record?

As all this was happening, some exciting writing projects came along that I wanted to work on. I didn't want to jeopardize my songwriting career by ignoring these opportunities. I'd already invested too much time in the band only to have it blow up in my face. I welcomed the new distractions, and that's when I decided to cut Paul loose. We weren't going to make another record with him and I didn't have the energy to look for another singer. Maybe I would let the band idea rest for a while and rethink it when I had some distance. Maybe not. Looking back, if anyone were to ask whether I have any regrets during my career, I'd say one. I wish I had been patient and waited until the right singer had come along. Could've, would've, should've. The irony is that, with YouTube, so many people have posted Device videos and tracks from *22B3* that, thirty-two years later, we have over half a million fans.

I went back to doing what I did best, focusing on my songwriting, and signed a new publishing deal with EMI who offered me a lot more money than my last deal with Chapman, and an administration deal which meant I got to keep all my publishing from that point on. That really drove a wedge in my relationship with Mike. From day one, I had been signed to his publishing company. But there comes a time in everyone's life when you have to move on if your gut is telling you so.

A few years later I called up Freddy and invited him to lunch. To my relief, he said, "I'd love to." We met at Morton's and, when we sat down, I said, "I just wanted to apologize for the way I spoke to you and stormed out of your office a few years ago."

He was so gracious and laughingly said, "Listen, I know what creative people are like, and I forgave you the minute you left my office. I understood why you were upset." We had a great lunch, and after that I always thought of him as my friend. In a final twist of irony, many years later, Paul Engemann was hired to be the new lead singer in Animotion.

I had other things in the works and had yet to write the biggest song of my career.

CHAPTER FIFTEEN

LIVING IN A HAUNTED HOUSE
(ELVIRA, MISTRESS OF THE DARK)

Los Angeles, 1986

"That sounds so good it's scary!"
("Haunted House" performed by Elvira)

E ver since I was a little girl, I've been drawn to the macabre and mystical. On Saturday nights I would curl up in front of the television to watch *Chiller Theater*, which featured all the classic black-and-white monster movies like *Frankenstein* and *Dracula* with Lon Chaney Jr. and Bela Lugosi. My favorite shows were *The Addams Family*, *The Munsters*, *The Outer Limits*, and *Dark Shadows*. They were all pretty campy, but it was just the beginning of my attraction to all things witchy and metaphysical. This also explains my love of Elvira, Mistress of the Dark, the unconventional horror show hostess who emerged during the eighties.

One evening I attended a star-studded premiere for *9½ Weeks*, a sexually charged movie starring Mickey Rourke and Kim Basinger. MGM had licensed the Knight and Des Barres version of "Obsession" for an elaborate movie trailer, and, already, a big buzz was circulating around town. I dressed to the nines in a long, fitted Betsey Johnson dress and found my seat in the packed theater. Elvira was sitting in front of me, not as Cassandra Peterson, her real persona, but Elvira—outrageous wig, costume, and all. As captivating as her character was, one of the things I had always admired even more than her beauty was how funny she was. Her wig was about a foot higher than the top of her head, and I couldn't see the screen but I was so excited that she was sitting in front of me, I didn't care. I was more preoccupied with meeting her and trying to think of something clever to say to her after the screening. But she saved me the trouble when she turned around and said, "I'm so sorry, it must be awful sitting behind me. If I could cut a hole in the middle of my hair so you could see the screen, I would." She immediately won me over.

The next time we met was a few months later at a concert at the Palladium in West Hollywood. I was alone that night and as I took a seat up in the VIP section of the balcony, a friendly red-headed woman started chatting with me before the band came on. I thought she was hilarious, and her face and voice seemed so familiar to me that I asked her, "Have we had met before?"

The more we talked, the more we realized we had a lot in common, and our thirty-five-year friendship grew from there. I think she was as impressed with me as I was with her. Any woman who could harness her innate creative talent and energy and parlay it into a successful career was a force to be reckoned with. Like Ann and Nancy Wilson, we gravitated towards one another, appreciating what it took to rise to the top of the heap—dedication, drive, a love for what we did, and tenacity.

Cassandra had a radio show as Elvira back then where she put together her own playlist of current songs that she loved, and she started playing Device's "Hanging On A Heart Attack." She made some funny cracks on the show about me trying to copy her image in the video, and it was only then that I realized embarrassingly—she was right! I think it was more subconscious than intentional but there were definitely one too many similarities. Then again, imitation is the sincerest form of flattery. Nevertheless, I decided to tone down my image for the next video.

Leave it to a woman to hire me as a producer, something no one else had been willing to do. Cassandra asked me to write and produce a song for her second Halloween compilation, *Elvira's Monster Hits*. I cowrote a gruesomely funny song with John Paragon, one of her comedy writers, called "The Bride of Frankenstein." We recorded it on almost zero budget and it sounded surprisingly good. I programmed the drums and then recorded a gothic sounding pipe organ, as well as the bass. Gene came in and laid down some guitars. Cassandra did a great job with the vocals, bringing her comedic and zany Elvira personality to the party. We had another female backup singer come in so the three of us could do stacks of background vocals together. We were fabulous! We sounded like three bitchy cats in heat. It was surrealistic, standing next to Cassandra, who was wearing baggy jeans and sneakers that day, while Elvira's throaty voice emitted from her.

John Paragon had written some extra lines we could do as voiceovers in the middle where the scene was supposed to take place at a wedding reception. Fred Schneider of The B-52s did a hilarious voiceover in a fiendish ghoul's voice. He was so good I had him do it on every chorus. There was a lot of laughter that day, and I reveled in doing something so utterly different from the norm. I also loved being in charge. It felt as natural to me as breathing in air.

Halloween is Elvira's biggest time of year. It also happens to be my favorite holiday. Like KISS, Cassandra has managed to brilliantly monetize and parlay her name and image into an amazing collection of Elvira merchandise and memorabilia. Her Elvira costume and makeup kits are documented as the biggest-selling items of all time during the month of October. There are Elvira pinball machines—she kept the original one in her house, which I used to play all the time. And just as it was with KISS, whenever I went out to dinner with her, I relished the fact that I alone knew who she was, that my auburn-haired gal pal was the one and only Mistress of the Dark.

Because "The Bride of Frankenstein" turned out so well, a few years later Cassandra asked me to write and produce a new song for the follow-up, *Elvira's Revenge of the Monster Hits*. I wrote another ghoulishly comical song with John Paragon called "Haunted House." I think I subconsciously created an homage to the infamous "Peter Gunn" theme with lots of eighth notes. I'd always thought it was a shame that Cassandra never did a video to "The Bride of Frankenstein," but this time something wonderful happened. When the company for IMAX Theaters heard "Haunted House" they wanted to not only use the recording, but offered to make a lavish video with Elvira as the centerpiece to announce their new 3D plat-form. They shot the video in 3D, and the things that seemingly came flying out into the theater were items that mimicked the lyrical con-tent of the song. "The plates and silverware came flying through the air...." And of course, her infamous breasts bounced around in full 3D glory. I was out of town when IMAX Theaters premiered the video at a celebrity-filled gala, but Paul Stanley called me up to tell me how much he loved the song and video.

Like me, Cassandra had a taste for mischief. One day, some years later, she invited me and my second husband, Michael, over for din-ner. She'd asked both Mark, her husband at the time, and mine what they would like to eat several times over the course of a few days but they never gave her a solid answer. Finally, on the third try, they both said something to the effect of, "Any old shit is fine." Cassandra, being a gourmet cook, was not happy with their lack of interest or appre-ciation for her efforts in the kitchen. When she told me about it, we decided to play a prank on them. I stopped at a joke shop and bought some realistic looking piles of rubber shit. That night, when we all sat down to a beautifully appointed candlelit table, she brought out two plates of shit and lay them on the table. The look on their faces was priceless. They didn't say a word, just gawked at her like she had lost her mind. Finally, Mark looked like he was going to be sick, and, covering his mouth, he said, "Uh Cassandra…wanna explain this?"

"Well, you said any old shit would do."

Chapter Sixteen

SO YOU WANNA BE A COWBOY? (BON JOVI)

Los Angeles, 1986

"And when you spit you better mean it."
("Stick To Your Guns" performed by Bon Jovi)

Afterward my marriage to Jeff ended, I realized that I was too isolated, living alone in the Marina, and ever since Rod Stewart
had come over, my neighbors had become quite nosy, waiting to see if he would come back, or who would be next. For the
first time in my life, I could afford to move somewhere nice, money
was finally coming in from songs that had been doing well. Being a
true-blue New Yorker, I liked the idea of moving into a building with
security, a doorman, and an elevator. That's all I knew growing up in
Manhattan, always living above the eleventh floor. Years ago, when I
had moved to LA, I had discovered a mile-long stretch of residential luxury high-rises in an area called the Wilshire Corridor. I vowed
that, if I could afford it, one day I would move there.

I found a spectacular two-bedroom apartment in the first building I walked into, the L'Elysee, which means a place or state of perfect happiness in French. That pretty much summed it up.

Four weeks later, I was sitting on one of two new dove gray flannel couches facing each other with a large coffee table in the middle, in my spacious living room. I had donated all my old second and thirdhand furniture. This move was a symbolic one, an acknowledgement that I had arrived at this moment through my own resolve and effort. There was no sugar daddy, ex-husband, or family inheritance that got me the keys to this place, just me. I looked out of my floor-to-ceiling windows and sighed with pleasure, stretching like a content, lazy cat. It certainly was a nice view from up there. My Steinway piano glistened in the corner between two glass windows, seemingly enjoying the view as well, and there was a huge square balcony, which, because I was only on the fourth floor and had a corner unit, was surrounded by large sycamore trees with huge, prehistoric-looking leaves. My next investment was going to be some professional-quality recording equipment, so I hired Art Kem, a tech well known for setting up home studios and all-around good guy. He helped me build a recording room in the second bedroom with an Otari one-inch tape recording machine and a Trident console for mixing. I set about learning how to use it all. The last thing I needed was an engineer in the room while I wrote, waiting to do my bidding. I wanted to be as self-sufficient as possible, to be able to work in my studio at three in the morning in my underwear, and there were many times I did.

I had a large kitchen that opened to the living room, which was awesome because I loved to cook, and this way I could do it while my friends sat on the other side of the counter and hung out while I poured them some wine. I traded in my beat-up VW Rabbit car for a Biturbo Maserati, not exactly the top-of-the-line model, it always stunk of burning oil, but still, it was a Maserati. It was then that I discovered my lifelong penchant for sports cars, and from then on, I've always had one in some form or another, mostly Jaguars and Porsches.

Even the sound of a race car revving up turns me on. The band, My Life with the Thrill Kill Kult said it best: "Sex on Wheelz."

All the doormen and concierge knew me by my first name, and whenever anyone looking remotely rock 'n' roll walked in the building, they immediately buzzed me on the intercom to let me know that so-and-so was here to see me. There was a small TV behind the reception desk that always seemed to be on in the background, and late at night when things were quiet, it always seemed to be on MTV, the omnipresent zeitgeist of the eighties. And where it was, so was I, on either side of the glass, as viewer or songwriter. One night as I stood waiting in the lobby for the valet to bring my car around, "Love Is a Battlefield" came on. It wasn't lost on me that the success of that song had afforded me the means to live in this building, and the doorman, unaware that the writer was standing beside him, turned it up and started whistling along. The rush I got from seeing people enjoy my music never got old.

If single men can be admired for their infamous bachelor-pad lifestyles, then so can women: mine was the bachelorette version, and I gleefully dubbed it the Kitty Cave. When I wasn't working in the studio in the second bedroom, it became a veritable den of socializing and partying. One of the biggest plusses was that I discovered I could play really loud without annoying the neighbors. Miraculously, nobody ever complained. In fact, one day, in the elevator I met a young woman who asked me, "Are you the one making all the music?" "Yes," I admitted hesitantly, thinking she was about to complain, but, instead, she exclaimed, "Oh, I love it, it's so good, keep it up!" Then she shyly asked me what I did. It was a replay of the same conversation I'd had in the elevator of Lincoln Towers so many years ago.

For the first time, I felt like a grownup. I was thirty and had been living on my own since I was fifteen. It had taken this long to grow up.

My neighbor who lived across the hall came calling one day. "Hi, sorry to bother you," he grinned and held out his hand. "My name is Randy. Do you happen to have a MIDI cable I can borrow?" No stick of butter or cup of sugar, just a MIDI cable for his keyboard. I guess he'd heard the strains of live music emanating from my apartment. His last name was Jackson and it turned out he was Michael Jackson's younger brother, and just as soft spoken. From that moment, we became friends, music our common ground. I kept hoping Michael would come and visit him, but if he did, I never saw him.

After a while, I noticed some of the same people coming in and out of the L'Elysee. One was an adorable-looking guy whom I recognized from two well-known movies, *E.T.* and *The Outsiders.* We got in the elevator at the same time, smiled at each other, and started talking. His name was C. Thomas Howell, and soon he introduced me to his eclectic group of friends, many of whom were actors. He was fascinated with my life as a rocker and songwriter, and I was fascinated with his. Amongst his posse was Charlie Sheen and Jennifer Jason Leigh, who had starred in *Fast Times at Ridgemont High*, a screenplay that was written by Nancy Wilson's boyfriend Cameron Crowe. There was my own crew of friends as well, a boyfriend or two and music associates. All of them came through the Kitty Cave.

One evening, my friend, bassist Phil Soussan, who'd played with Ozzy Osbourne and Billy Idol, called to see if I wanted to meet him at the Rainbow. We arrived at the same time to the all too familiar stench of beer and sweat. Even for a weeknight, the place was unusually quiet as I glanced around the main room. But seated in one of the dingy red leather booths was Jon Bon Jovi.

"Oh, he's a mate of mine. I should go over and say hi." Phil said.

"Can you introduce me?" I asked. "I'd love to meet him."

"Of course. Let me go say hello to him first, and then I'll introduce you."

We sauntered over, but I stayed in the background. Sitting next to Jon were two blond women, one on either side of him. After Phil and he exchanged the proverbial bro handshake and talked for a minute, Phil motioned me over. "This is my good friend Holly Knight, she's a great songwriter and wants to meet you."

I couldn't believe what Jon did next. He put down his drink, waved the two women away, then moved over to make room for me and patted the seat next to him. I sat down. "Holly Knight," he announced cheerfully while putting his arm around me. "Why haven't we written anything together?"

Of all the things he could've said, that was the last thing I expected. "I don't know, but we should."

Bon Jovi was in the midst of enjoying mammoth success with *Slippery When Wet*, which had hit number one and remained there for eight weeks. I thought that they were just another good-looking hair band and had never been a big fan, but they had come a long way. To be honest, the only reason I wanted to write with Jon was because I knew their next record was going to be huge as well and this was a business, after all. There was no rule that said I had to love the music of every band or artist that I worked with. They weren't the first and they wouldn't be the last.

Jon continued, "I've actually been trying to get ahold of you, and here you just walk right into the Rainbow."

"I guess that's why they call it destiny, right?" I winked. "How long are you in town?"

"We have to finish up this last leg of the tour, so we're leaving the day after tomorrow, but I may have some time tomorrow if you're available. We've already started writing for the next record."

Hah, that's a good one—"if you're available," I thought. "As it so happens, I am free tomorrow!" I said. "And I have a studio setup, a decent enough room to write in, in my apartment near Westwood. I'd love to get together if you can work it out," I said enthusiastically.

"Give me your number and I'll call you first thing in the morning," he promised.

Title. Think of a title, have something to start with. Part of me thought Jon wouldn't call or would be unable to squeeze me in, that it was too good to be true. Plus, I knew how flaky musicians could be, especially successful ones. They just had too much going on all the time. I kept my fingers crossed and waited. Sure enough, Jon called early the next day, ever the consummate professional, and said, "Okay, we're doing this. How's one o'clock?"

Two hours later, the doorman buzzed and cheerfully announced, "Jon's here, can I send him up?"

I dashed to the mirror to make sure I looked okay. When Jon walked in, he seemed a little annoyed, a stark contrast to the night before.

"Is everything alright?" I asked him.

"Yeah..." He gave me a hug and looked around. "Nice place. I'm sorry, there's this girl who's been stalking me for days outside of the hotel, and now she's followed me here to your place. It's enough already. I love my fans, but I think she's a little crazy."

"Ah, the price of fame. Do you want me to call down to the doorman and see if she left or is still hanging around outside?"

"I'm sure she is and there's nothing legally I can do about it."

I called down to inquire, and sure enough she was parked in front of the building. I have to give her credit, if for nothing else, her tenacity. *Hmmm...tenaciousness, never giving up, wanting something so bad...*It made me think of a phrase my mother had said to me once, which was ironic, coming from her. I was telling her about a business dilemma, and she said, "Holly, just stick to your guns. You don't need to take BS from anybody." I had honed those skills with her, actually, but I liked the phrase, "stick to your guns" and wanted to see if it did anything for Jon. I had some other ideas, but we didn't get that far because he liked that one from the get-go.

"Listen, let's just keep checking while we're writing, and if she's still there when we're finished, I have an idea."

I hadn't had any time to come up with something musically, so this was an occasion where we jammed. He played an acoustic guitar of mine, I played keyboard, and together we came up with a chord progression. Jon started singing, "So you wanna be a cowboy..." which surprised me because I knew they had already alluded to the cowboy thing in "Wanted Dead or Alive." I was thinking of "stick to your guns" metaphorically. (What was it with men? Did they always have to be so literal?) But I didn't mind, I was digging the song and I wasn't about to shoot down his idea.

This was over thirty years ago. I don't remember who came up with, "And when you spit you better mean it," but kudos to whoever did. Jon wrote some more lyrics with cowboy allusions—"and go for the trigger, but only if you have to," or "ain't nobody riding shotgun in the world tonight." My only regret was that I wished we had stepped away from that. It would've made the song better, less cliché. It's little things like that that can make or break a tune, turn it into a hit single or reduce it to an album track. At the end of the session, we made a demo with acoustic guitar, bass, programmed drums, and Jon's vocals. As we were writing, I looked over at him. Here was a Jersey boy whose idol was Bruce Springsteen. It was almost hard to believe that he was a rock star of the magnitude he was because he was so normal. He didn't dress like a rock star or wear tons of jewelry or makeup, which actually was kind of refreshing. What you saw was what you got. His chiseled face didn't get in the way either. In the months to come, as I got to know him better, if there was anything remotely negative to be said about him, it was that he took himself and everything so damn seriously. I was born in the Chinese year of the monkey, so I have a mischievous side to me that I never saw in him. He's a tiger.

I kept checking with the doorman to see whether Jon's obsessive fan was still around. Clearly, she was going to wait this out. By the end of the afternoon, a mere five hours later, we had written everything except lyrics to the bridge. Jon said, "I'd like Ritchie to finish this with us." I wasn't thrilled to hear that because we easily could've have finished it on our own, but I didn't want to mess with band politics. For me, the fewer writers, the better, as this was my only source of income, while they could go out and make money touring and selling merchandise. This happened a lot, especially in the coming years when labels and managers would send their artists over to write with me. The singer would almost always come with their guitarist and I could never figure out if this was a just a security blanket or a deliberate move on their part to get a bigger share of the publishing.

In general, I preferred to write with one other person. I wasn't opposed to writing with two people, but there had to be a reason. These days, when I look at writing credits and see ten names on one song, a common practice, it drives me crazy. If you need that many folks to collaborate on a single song, you shouldn't be calling yourselves songwriters. I told Jon that I was planning to go to New York in two months. "Well," he said, "maybe that's when we should finish this because our tour will be over."

That being settled, we had to deal with the stalker downstairs. What happened next was so ridiculous and cliché that I can barely believe it happened. I put my idea into action: I went into my walk-in closet and emerged with a dark brunette, long-haired wig, a remnant from a Halloween party I'd gone to. Jon, who had been wearing a baseball hat the whole time he'd been there, handed the cap to me, and I put it on, tucking my hair inside it. I had him sit down so I could put the wig on his head.

"I don't wanna know where this wig's been," he said as I laughed. I was having fun with all this. "How do I look?" he asked.

"Like Cher on steroids."

We looked silly but if it worked, that's all that mattered. I didn't think I remotely resembled him, but it was worth a try. Maybe I could pass for him from a distance, especially once I put his sunglasses on and was driving his car. We traded keys, and I told him where my car was parked.

"I'll meet you at the Sunset Marquee," he said. He left first in my Maserati, heading in the opposite direction from where he'd come.

Five minutes later, I rolled out of the garage in Jon's rental. In my rearview mirror, I saw her sit up straight and start her car, then speed up to get closer. I took a lot of windy back roads through the residential streets of Beverly Hills, slowing down enough to stay within her eyesight. After ten minutes, I pulled up to a stop sign and let the car idle until she was right behind me. Putting my arm out of the window, I waved for her to pass. She pulled up beside me and looked into my window, which I'd rolled down. I will never forget the stunned look of confusion on her face when she realized it wasn't Jon. I actually felt bad for her. She looked like Violet Beauregarde from *Charlie and The Chocolate Factory* after she swallowed the purple gum. I waved hello and winked, then drove away, making sure she didn't follow me, and headed to the Sunset Marquee to exchange cars with Jon. Of course, she knew where he was staying, but at least he had some peace of mind the rest of the evening.

When I got there, he invited me to come up to his suite, and when I walked in, I saw a bunch of people in the room. I met Ritchie Sambora, and he and I sneaked off to another room to do some blow. He liked to party, but Jon didn't, so we tried to be discreet. The band was good friends with the comedian Sam Kinison, who was sitting on one of the couches doing lines off the coffee table. Being a songwriter was boring, said nobody.

"Living on a Prayer" came on MTV and all the guys started singing along. I wish I'd had a smart phone back then, because it was one of those defining moments that personified the eighties, so weird and fantastic. I felt like I was on the other side of the looking glass, where the real band was on the TV and the one in the room was some kind of doppelganger.

It had been a long day, so I said my goodbyes. There were hugs all around because I was "best friends" with everybody by the time I left. Jon called from the road a few days later and said that his stalker hadn't given up and had followed the band to the airport. She had even parked her car and followed him into the terminal. He finally walked up to her to tell her to fuck off, and she practically passed out in ecstasy.

CHAPTER SEVENTEEN

I LOVE A MAN WHO TAKES CHARGE (DON JOHNSON)

Los Angeles, 1987

"You need your love I need my mental stimulation ..."
("Space" performed by Cheap Trick)

A bout a month after my writing session with Jon Bon Jovi, Don Johnson, whose show *Miami Vice* had gone through the roof, called me. I'd never really watched the show, but I knew all about it. The show drew heavily upon MTV music and culture, and they had licensed Tina's version of "Better Be Good to Me" for one of their episodes. It ended up on the Platinum-selling *Miami Vice* soundtrack as well.

Don wasn't even on my radar as someone I wanted to write with or for, although he'd just had a hit with "Heartbeat," which reached number five on the Billboard Hot 100 chart. I knew he was good friends with Michael Des Barres, and I thought that's probably how he'd gotten my phone number, but then I remembered he was

Don Johnson and could probably get the president's number if he wanted to.

"Is this Miss Holly?" he said.

"Yes, it is, who is this?" I answered, not recognizing the voice.

"It's Don Johnson. How are you, darlin'?"

I took a breath, then answered, "Well hello there, Don Johnson, I'm doing great, how about you?" Not thirty seconds into the call and we were already flirting. What woman wouldn't have?

"Can you guess why I'm calling you?" he asked.

"Hmm, well, let me see. You would like to meet me."

"Yes, that's true, but do you know why?"

Oh, the things I wanted to say, but I told myself to behave. "You want to write with me," I answered.

"Yes! Exactly. So, when are you free?"

"Are you in LA?"

"I am," he said.

"Do you want to come over now?" I said in my best coquette voice.

"Boy, you don't waste any time."

I laughed. This was kind of fun. "I was kidding, Don. When would you like to come over?"

"Give me your address," he said. "I'm coming over right now."

Jesus, I thought looking in the mirror, *I better hop to it*. I was still in my robe and my bedhead hair was sticking straight up. I showered, put on some eye makeup, and threw on a pair of clean ripped jeans and a white T-shirt. It may be the fastest I ever got ready for anything.

Even over the phone, he was a smooth talker who oozed sexuality, and he had quite the reputation for being a ladies' man. You'd have to be blind not to see why. He was ridiculously good looking with a lazy southern drawl that sounded like it had been cured with whiskey and molasses. According to *Rolling Stone*, "No one had more swagger in the Reagan era than Don Johnson."

My hair was still wet when, half an hour later, the doorman buzzed me and cheerfully announced that Don Johnson was on his way up. By now, all the doormen loved me because of the celebrities that flowed in and out of my apartment. Once, a friend of mine, who knew Boy George, said that Boy was in town and was looking to score some pot. He asked if I could get some, and I said sure, because I wanted to meet him. An hour later, I opened the door and tried not to stare. The Brit pop star came, said hello, paid for the grass, rolled a joint, and then said he had to run. I don't even think he knew that I was a well-known songwriter and probably thought I was a drug dealer.

Don hugged me hello like we were old friends, swaying back and forth, then walked in. It *felt* like we were old friends. My nerves dwindled away within minutes, and maybe it was that grin or the languid way he talked, but at some point, I found myself practically sitting on his lap with his arms around my waist.

"You're pretty cute, you know that?" he asked.

Even though he was flirting with me, I somehow knew that we were just being silly and having fun. I didn't read anything into it. Once we started to talk about songwriting, I stood up and took over.

"Listen, I think the best way for us to do this is for me to start a track and then have you come over so we can work on the lyrics together."

I spent a day or so coming up with an idea, a dark mid-tempo minor chord progression, and a pretty catchy melody. It was the start of something worth working on. I called Don and he came over. We wrote most of the song that afternoon, but as the day went on I started thinking that the lyrics we were writing were probably more suitable for a woman than a man. The song was called "Do We Dare." I wasn't sure how much songwriting Don had done before, since "Heartbeat" had been written by other songwriters, but he seemed to like it a lot and I left it at that. I was having so much fun with him, I almost didn't care if he ended up cutting the tune.

Before he left, I invited him to the Bon Jovi show on Friday night down in Irvine as Jon had arranged tickets and VIP passes for me.

"Hell yeah, I'd love to go, but I'll have to get back to you on that, I'm supposed to fly to Washington, DC, that night. Let me see how I can make it work. It sounds fun. Can I call you tomorrow and let you know?"

Sure enough, Don called the next day. "Do you like lobster?" he asked.

"I love it, why?"

"Here's what we're going to do. I'm going to pick you up at six, drive to Santa Monica Airport, then we're going to board a helicopter and fly to Irvine, which should only take about fifteen minutes. We'll see the show, go backstage and say hello, and afterwards, fly back to LA, go have a delicious lobster dinner, and then, if you're okay with accompanying me to Burbank airport, I can grab my jet and leave, and the driver will take you home. How does that sound?"

God, I love a man who takes charge. There's no doubt about it, the man was a class act. Friday night came, and I dressed to the nines. I wasn't going to waste an opportunity like this, being in the same room backstage with Don Johnson and Jon Bon Jovi. I wanted to look wicked, so I wore a black, Betsey Johnson skintight mermaid shaped dress down to the ground. The bottom had deep purple organza that fluffed out—and the pointiest black boots with stiletto heels that I owned.

Don picked me up in a stretch limo. "Hey, pretty!" he said when I climbed in.

It feels like I'm telling someone else's Cinderella story, but it was real, and it was mine. Unfortunately, over the years I had discovered that stretch limos made me sick. Ever since I was a little girl, I've been prone to car sickness. Maybe it had something to do with all the windows; it felt so unnatural to me. By some miracle and a few tablets of Dramamine that I had taken right before we left, I was able to keep my shit together and not get sick. When we got to the small airport, I prayed that the Dramamine would continue to work. I'd been on helicopters many times before and vomited every single time, even after taking the medication. But that night, I was okay. Whatever small amount of queasiness I felt disappeared once we arrived at the airport near the venue, and my feet were back on solid ground. I didn't want to tell any of this to Don as it wasn't exactly a glamorous conversation to have.

One of the secrets to a great rock band is the dynamic between the lead singer and the guitarist. Almost every iconic front man has a secret weapon by his side, an amazing guitarist who, in tandem, fits perfectly with his or her style: Robert Plant had Jimmy Page, Mick Jagger had Keith Richards, Steven Tyler had Joe Perry, Billy Idol had Steve Stevens, Ann Wilson had Nancy Wilson…and Jon Bon Jovi had Ritchie Sambora. We went and stood in the VIP section where we had a great view of the stage. Don really enjoyed the show, he thought the band was terrific. My heart skipped a beat when I looked over at Don and saw him smiling and rocking out to the music. The whole thing felt unreal, but then again, so much of my life seemed that way.

After the show ended, we went back to the band's dressing room, and the bodyguards took one look at Don and just waved us through. Jon was in great spirits, smiling as we walked in and holding open his arms. I introduced the two men to each other, and while they talked, Ritchie and I chatted. After a few minutes I joined them and as I stood there listening to them converse, it occurred to me that I was in the enviable position of working with two of the hottest men on the planet.

We hugged and said our goodbyes. Jon promised we'd finish "Stick to Your Guns" when I came to New York. I was happy that he wanted to finish it. I knew a lot of songs had already been pitched to them, and they were starting to write with quite a few other song-writers. There was a lot of competition, with everyone wanting to get a song on their next record, but I was used to this by now. You never counted on a song making it onto a record until the disc was cut and the album cover was done. I had my fingers crossed. The limo driver took Don and I back to John Wayne Airport.

Once we were up in the air and heading back, all of a sudden, Don took over the controls.

"I've been taking lessons for a while now," he said gleefully as he nose-dived under a bridge and swooped back up. He did it each time we approached another bridge. He was having a blast and I was ready to throw up all over him. I was scared shitless. *He's been taking lessons?* I was sitting behind him and the pilot, and he couldn't see me, he didn't see the little brown paper bag I'd brought with me that I kept breathing into, something I'd learned in summer camp that helped to keep from throwing up. Thank god, it worked.

I could've kissed the solid ground when my wobbly legs stepped onto the tarmac at Santa Monica Airport.

"Are you okay?" Don said, looking at my green face.

"I'm fine," I responded weakly. I didn't want to be a party poop and ruin his plans. We got in another stretch limo (oh please god, not again) and drove to a restaurant in West Hollywood. It was an elegant place, and Don ordered champagne and a couple of Maine lobsters, something that I would've normally scarfed down in five minutes, had I not felt so ill.

In addition to all this misery, I was nervous, wondering if Don was going to plant a sexy kiss on my lips at Burbank as he was leaving. I would've been just fine with that. If he didn't, that was okay too. I didn't feel any deep intellectual connection with him, he was just irresistible, and fun to be with. Before he got out of the limo, he gave me a peck on my lips and said, "Thank you for an amazing night. I'll call you when I'm back next week." Then he winked, Sonny Crockett-style, and disappeared. The limo driver drove me home, and now that I had the limo to myself, I lay back, kicked off my pointy boots, which were killing me, and breathed in a deep breath of air for the first time all evening.

Finding a perfect match with a cowriter is rare. I've only had a handful during my career that were wired to the same frequency as me, and, truly, that was when I had the most fun cowriting. Mike Chapman and I were like that, which is why we wrote such special songs together. When I wrote with people who didn't have much experience writing, I had a hard time being assertive or honest when I didn't like something that the other writer came up with, mainly because I didn't want to hurt their feelings.

Don and I got together one more time to write the bridge lyrics, but we'd written a fairly mediocre tune. The music was great, the lyrics were…meh, as was the demo we did with him singing. I knew it and I guess eventually he knew it too because the song didn't make it on his next record. But we stayed friends, and a few months later, I flew to Miami to be with my Grandma Ethel for her eightieth birthday party. While I was in town, I called Don to say hi.

"Hey darlin', why don't you come down to the set and I'll show you around, introduce you to the crew, and you can watch them film today's scenes." It was fascinating to see Don in his element. I watched him transform himself into Sonny Crockett as he filmed his sequences. When he was done shooting, we hung out in his trailer and chatted. It was a sweet moment. Then, as is often the case with so many of the celebs I worked with over the years, we lost touch. I still think of him as a friend. Sometime, somewhere in the future, I'll probably run into him and it'll be all warm and fuzzy again.

Two months later, I flew back east for a few business meetings and to finish writing "Stick to Your Guns" with Jon and Ritchie. When I called Jon and told him I was in town, he was happy to hear from me. The band had finished touring and were in town, doing some kind of press junket. Afterwards, they were going to throw a small party in a hotel room at the United Nations Plaza Hotel, and he invited me over. That's when I met their keyboardist, David Bryan, who also had a classical piano background, and in the room was a grand piano, which we took turns playing. He was a generous and friendly guy. That's usually how it was, the band members of all the bands I worked with were always the nicest and most genuine.

Jon arranged for a town car to pick me up at the Mayflower, a hotel I often stayed at on the Upper West Side, and take me out to his home in New Jersey. "We can finish the song and then you should stick around if you can, because I have a bunch of friends coming over for a barbecue."

Barbecue with Bon Jovi, check. When the limo arrived at his home, there were about twenty fans hanging around outside his gate; I guess it came with the territory. Kudos to him. I knew I would hate it.

As soon as Ritchie showed up, we went into a tiny room and finished the lyrics, sitting on the floor. In just an hour, we were done, and Jon took off with Ritchie to help out with the barbecue. I spent some time talking to Jon's wife, Dorothea, as Jon's entourage and friends started showing up, bearing cases of beer and food. I liked her. Her energy was stronger than a lot of the celebrity wives I had met over the years.

I walked out to the pool and realized I didn't know anybody other than Jon and Ritchie, and they were off somewhere. And Dorothea was busy hosting. Somehow, I got into a meaningless conversation with one of Jon's roadies, who seemed like a total meathead, and I was disagreeing with something he said, although I can't remember what it was. The roadie said he was going to throw me in the pool if I didn't stop disagreeing with him. Maybe he was drunk, or thought he was being cute, but the next thing I knew, he picked me up like a sack of potatoes, his hands on my ass, and threw me in the pool. I was outraged. I was Jon's personal guest, a peer, and who the fuck did this asshole think he was? Would he have had the balls to do that to a man? In today's socio-climate, would someone even get away with something like that? I was embarrassed and humiliated, and no one there made an effort to offer me a hand and help me out of the pool or ask if I was okay. Even the women did nothing. It took me right back to elementary school when I had no friends. This was not my crowd. It was hard to believe we were this close to Manhattan. I was surrounded by a crowd of suburban hillbillies.

To make matters worse, I had a small packet of pharmaceutical grade blow in my pocket that was totally ruined. Dripping wet, I found Jon and told him what had happened, hoping he would straighten out his employee and defend my honor, but he was surprisingly unsympathetic. If anything, he thought it was funny.

"Well, you shouldn't be doing blow anyway. It's bad for you," was all he could muster.

I should point out that I haven't touched cocaine in thirty-two years. When I quit, I quit on my own for good. I did the same thing with cigarettes. I just decided I was done. I'm certainly not saying that it's easy to break a bad habit (with me it's always been food). You hear so many stories about people who screwed up their lives, not to mention the collapse of their septums, and had to go into rehab. I'm glad they got the help they needed and were able to recover and go back to leading healthy lives. But not everybody who snorted coke was an addict. Not everyone who enjoys wine is an alcoholic.

I didn't appreciate Jon judging me, and his indifference surprised and annoyed the hell out of me. I had just been manhandled and humiliated, and I thought for sure he would reprimand his employee, but he did nothing. I asked him to call the driver so I could leave, and while I waited for the car to show up, I sat by myself and thought about the lyric we had just written a few hours ago.

> "Stick to your guns,
> Ain't nobody gonna hurt you baby,
> And go for the trigger but only if you have to,
> Aim from the heart, some will love
> and some will curse you baby,
> And you can go to war, but only if you
> have to, it's only if you have to."

I needed to follow the wisdom of those words. I had no intention of walking out of there with my tail between my legs. When the car arrived, I walked up to Jon and said, "You know what? This is unacceptable, I'm not only hurt that you did nothing to rectify this mess, I feel disrespected by both of you. At the very least, your roadie owes me a fucking apology." I huffed off with my dignity intact.

It was such a bizarre ending to an otherwise wonderful experience. I was so bummed, and I was certain that after this incident, they would never record "Stick to Your Guns." But they did and it came out great. It didn't get released as a single, but it was on the record, and for that I was grateful. They named the album *New Jersey* and it went to number one the second week of its release. It produced five top ten hits and was certified seven times Platinum. The album was also the band's first UK number one album.

Somehow, we got past the incident at his house. Several heavy hitters had been brought in to produce Cher's new record on Geffen Records, and Jon was one of them. He produced two songs, one of which was a remake of her hit, "Bang Bang (My Baby Shot Me Down)." and he called me to come in and play the keyboards and sing background vocals on it. I guess that was his way of apologizing, and I was more than happy to move on.

CHAPTER EIGHTEEN

WE GOT A SOUL LOVE
(HALL & OATES)

New York City & Los Angeles 1987

"Typical talk in the daytime, at night, only hot desire...."
("Soul Love" performed by Hall & Oates)

Before Tommy Mottola ran Sony Records for thirteen years, he had a successful management company called Champion Entertainment, based out of New York City. While LA had its glitzy West Coast management companies like Irving Azoff's HK Management, New York had its own brand of street cred as far as management firms went. They had other clients, such as John Cougar Mellencamp, but their main act was Hall & Oates. My pal Kathy knew Tommy because at one point she and her bandmates had been talking to him about managing the Go-Gos. She introduced me to Jeb Brien, one of Tommy's associates, one night over dinner in LA. I liked the fact that he and Tommy were about as New York grit as it got. Word on the street was that Tommy was connected to the Mafia in some undefined way and everyone was always trying to guess whether it was true. People even speculated that Tommy had created the rumor to build some mystique, or create fear. Maybe it was just bullshit, but I will tell you this much, he was Italian and very soft spoken, and I found the notion credible. Maybe it was the gun he pulled out of his shoulder bag and placed on the table in front of me the first time I met him, without missing a beat in the conversation.

As I sat there wondering whether it was a real gun, I listened to him talk. I liked him immensely. I definitely got the feeling that Tommy respected songwriters and I could feel the reverence with which he treated me. "You are an amazing songwriter, no, you really are," he said unabashedly as I started to shake my head. The gun move intrigued me more than it scared me. I thought he was showing off, or trying to test me. Maybe it wasn't even real. It could've been one of those lighters that looked like a Derringer. Neither one of us said anything about it, we just carried on with the conversation.

"So, what can I do for you?" Tommy asked.

"I want to write with Daryl Hall. I think the two of us could write some great songs together. I know he doesn't need to write with anyone, he's doing just fine with John Oates and on his own, and actually I don't *need* to write with him either."

"No, you're right, you don't need him either," he smiled.

I'd wanted to write with Daryl for years. I'd loved his voice from the first time I heard "Sara Smile," and even though my wheelhouse was more rock based than blue-eyed soul, I thought the combination of his style and mine would be amazing. We both loved Todd Rundgren and we both knew how to write hit songs, so that was reason enough. I figured if Tommy could put him in the same room with me and leave us alone, we would take care of the rest.

I almost met Daryl and John when I was nineteen. I had seen the ad in *The Village Voice*, they were auditioning keyboardists for a tour. I don't know how I summoned up the nerve to call the number in the paper, but I did, and I set up a time to audition. As the date got closer, I chickened out. The more I thought about it, the less I thought it was a good idea. I had just returned to New York after being away for almost four years, and the last thing I wanted was to go out on the road again. What I really needed to do was stick to the plan I'd put together. But that was in the past.

"Don't worry," Tommy said. "We'll make it happen. I just have to catch him at the right moment."

"That would be awesome, Tommy, thank you!"

He scrutinized me for a few seconds, the wheels turning in his head. "So, what's your next move?"

"What do you mean?" I asked, confused.

"Have you thought about making a solo record?"

I laughed. "No, why would I do that?"

"Why not?" he shot back. "You sing, don't you?"

"Not really. I've sung backups on some of the songs I've written, and I sung a lot on the Device record, but I'm not a *lead* singer. Why?"

"Because you're marketable," he said. "You're a star."

"That's crazy, I've worked with some of the best singers in the business. I can't follow them, not with my voice. I'm not a *real* singer."

"Really? You sure about that? Think about it. If I managed you, I could probably get you a record deal with Columbia. Take some vocal lessons." I'd never thought about making a solo record because I knew deep down that I didn't have the chops as a singer.

True to his word, a month or so later, Tommy and Jeb found themselves in LA with Daryl and set up a dinner at the Ivy for the four of us. The Ivy was another one of those places where agents and industry people power lunched and which at night transformed into a who's-who of actors and musicians…it was a smaller, more romantic version of Le Dome. As I walked into the restaurant, I passed Barbara Streisand on my left and Don Henley on my right. Towards the back, near the table that I was headed to, was Cher.

I was wearing the same sleeveless black leather jumpsuit I used to wear on stage with Device, and a black leather jacket on top of that, along with my favorite black suede boots with Cuban heels. That was sort of my look back then. The three men were already sitting at a candlelit table in the corner and stood up when I walked in. After Tommy and Jeb hugged me, Tommy introduced Daryl to me, then offered me the seat directly opposite Daryl, two feet away from his smiling face. We spent dinner pretty much ignoring them and just grinning at each other like little kids. With the random subjects we touched upon, it was clear we were going to get along really well. He was into the mystics and metaphysics like me, and we had a lot of the same books on our shelves, weird stuff like Aleister Crowley and wiccan theology.

I invited them back to my apartment for a drink and as we waited for the valet to bring our cars around, I asked Daryl what sign he was.

"I'm a Libra, Scorpio rising," he said looking straight into my eyes.

"Hmm, that's interesting," I remarked, my legs starting to feel weak.

"How about you?" he asked.

"I'm a Libra, Scorpio rising."

Back at my apartment, I put some music on and poured everyone drinks. I took them to my studio, turned all the equipment on, and played them a track I was working on. Daryl walked up to one of my keyboards and started playing along. I turned on another keyboard and before I knew it, we were jamming. Tommy and Jeb were having a business discussion while Daryl and I got lost in the music. I'm pretty sure we played for at least an hour before we noticed that they had left. We went back in the living room to see if they were there, but they had slipped out. I poured Daryl and myself more drinks and we started to kiss. Instead of moving back into the studio, I led him into my bedroom.

A few months later, I flew to New York. Champion had set up a writing session with Daryl and John, which I was really looking forward to. I'd prepped myself for the session by coming up with a new groove and chord progression. I was staying at Morgans on Madison, another one of my favorite hotels, and, since it was a beautiful day, I decided to walk to Daryl's place in the West Village. Walking is the best way to see the city. I passed by one storefront after another, small restaurants and secret societies, dusty looking bookstores, and in the middle of them all was a Crazy Eddie store with about twenty TVs plastered against the store window, all airing the same image: a popular video on MTV. I recognized the men in togas serving drinks at a pool party immediately, it was my very own "Obsession," the Animotion version. I could hear the music coming out of some outside speakers and stopped to stare: "Like a butterfly, a wild butterfly, I will collect you and capture you…"

Daryl buzzed me up to his apartment, and of course, I was happy to see him. John put out his hand and introduced himself. After we chatted for a bit, I played them the idea I had, they liked it a lot.

Daryl started picking out the bass line and chords on a keyboard before stopping and saying, "Here. I like the feel you have on the bass. You play and I'll sing."

I was incredibly flattered. I'd always thought of him as an accomplished keyboardist, and I was struck by how gracious he was being. A lot of people didn't always have the nicest things to say about him. I'd heard that he was arrogant, narcissistic (what rock star wasn't?), moody, and even an asshole. Yet he never acted that way around me. I think, when it came down to it, Daryl was the type of person who chose who he wanted to let in, because he was an awkward character, and he had chosen to let me in, at least for the time being.

"I have a title. 'Soul Love,'" I said. "I've been thinking about how there are all kinds of love, and that the ultimate love is deep, soul-based."

"Yeah, that's cool," John said.

Daryl nodded in agreement. "I dig that. Let's play around with it."

Somehow, I had taken on the role of leader, which I was used to, except in this situation, I was writing with Hall & Oates and I didn't expect that. I guess I figured they were already working on a lot of songs for the next record, and would probably appreciate some new ideas, some fresh blood. And while we were in the same room, I had to forget that I had slept with Daryl, or at least act as if I hadn't. Men were always able to keep things separate. If I wanted this to work, I had to think like a man. This was business, and I was wearing a different hat now.

"Okay, here's how the melody goes in the chorus...." I sang them the idea, but instead of working on the lyrics, all we ended up doing was jamming on the tune for a few hours, which was fun, but not very productive. They weren't hitting any of the balls I was tossing them back to me. I knew that sometimes songwriters liked to go off on their own and work on lyrics in solitude when they aren't under pressure. Even I could be like that, so I wasn't too worried. They probably had a lot of stuff going on, and they'd mentioned earlier that they had an engagement they had to attend after this, so we stopped.

"I have to go back to LA in a few days," I said.

"Don't worry, I'll finish this on my own," Daryl said as he gave me a hug goodbye.

Meanwhile, now that Hall & Oates' manager, Tommy, was also managing me, he wanted me to leave my attorney and move over to his lawyer's firm.

"Isn't that a conflict of interests to have the same lawyer as my manager?" I asked him.

"No, not at all, Bruce Springsteen and his manager use the same attorney. Sting and his manager use the same attorney...." On and on the list went. "So, don't worry about it."

I was happy with my attorney. She had grown up with a rock 'n' roll pedigree: her father, Dee Anthony, had been a well-respected manager of many huge acts in the seventies, most notably, Peter Frampton; Emerson, Lake & Palmer; and King Crimson. "Why do you want me to change attorneys? I like mine, she's badass."

"She? Who's your attorney, what's her name?" he demanded.

"Her name is Michelle Anthony."

"Well, I never heard of her, and she's a woman. No one is going to take her seriously."

I couldn't believe what he'd just said. Still, I gave in and went with an attorney he recommended at Grubman and Indursky. It didn't take long before I realized I didn't like the guy.

I felt like he really answered to Tommy, not me, so if I had something about Tommy I wanted to discuss, there was no way I felt I could trust him. After a trial period of a few months, I left the firm and went back to Michelle. Everything was fine until a year later, when she called me up and said, "Holly, I can't be your lawyer anymore, I've been offered a job at Sony and I'm going to take it because it's a great opportunity. I have another lawyer I can recommend to you, and I'm sorry to let you down like this, especially after you came back to me."

It didn't take me long to find out that Tommy had hired her to help him run the label. Over time, she became his right hand "man," becoming the president and chief operating officer of Sony Music.

Just as I started to wonder if Daryl had gotten anywhere with "Soul Love," somebody at Champion Management sent me a copy of the finished version he'd worked on. It was going on their new album, *Ooh Yeah!*, and while I was thrilled that they liked it enough to put it on their record, I was disappointed with the lyrics Daryl had written: "Gimme that, gimme that nasty touch, I love it so much."

To me, the word "nasty" didn't belong in the same sentence as "soul love," and there was another line I'd initially sung him, "I'm like you and you're like me," to which he added, "so what, we got it—soul love." So what?

I could be wrong, but my guess is that Daryl threw most of the lyrics together in real time as he put the vocal down. And to make up for the fact that there were very few lyrics, he threw in "soul love" everywhere he could to fill in the gaps. I'd given them a great idea with a much cooler bass line that had "potential hit" written all over it and they'd turned it into an album track. I had so much awe and respect for Hall & Oates, and I was embarrassed that this was the best we had come up with after sitting in Tommy's office and making the bold statement that "Daryl and I could write some amazing songs together." I still believe that given another chance, we could have done that, but the opportunity never arose again.

Tommy never commented on the song, and I was relieved. I hoped this wasn't going to change his opinion of me, and thankfully it didn't because he was able to get me a solo deal with CBS Records. There's no doubt that his relationship with them had a lot to do with it because I hadn't even written any songs for it yet. While I loved the idea of making a new record, for the first time I felt like I was in over my head. I didn't have a muse to write for, just me, and I felt lost.

Management had set up a meeting for me with an up and coming producer/engineer by the name of Chris Lord-Alge. They thought that he might be a good coproducer for my record. He had already gained notoriety for mixing some prominent records, and so I went over to Unique Recording Studios in Manhattan to meet with him. I immediately liked him. He was a real Jersey boy, friendly, funny, and cocky. He seemed to be genuinely interested in coproducing my record, so I reported back to Tommy that I thought he and I would make a great team. We even ended up dating for a while, but decided we were better off as friends and co-workers. In the coming years Chris became one of the highest paid and most revered mixers in the music business, winning six Grammys, and to this day he remains one of my closest friends.

Around the same time that Hall & Oates were working on *Ooh Yeah!*, I played Daryl another song I had just written for myself, "Heart Don't Fail Me Now," and he fell in love with it.

"I want to record this song," he exclaimed. "It's a hit. Write something else for yourself." Under any other circumstances, I would've loved for them to cut it, but I said no, because I was starting to save songs for my own record. And it's one of my biggest regrets. When I recorded the song, Daryl graciously came down to the studio and sang all the background vocals at the end of it. Hearing him sing it, it was painfully obvious that I had made a mistake.

I was afraid to say something to Tommy since he had put so much effort into putting the deal together for me. I felt like a fake. I had left my safety net and the perfect job I already had, and my ego had bought into the myth that I could be a solo artist. Maybe, before I started recording, I believed it for a while, at least until the moment of truth when I stepped up to the mike.

The record wasn't a total disaster. Musically, it was really good, and at least I was confident in my abilities as a producer and musician. Once again, I hired Gene to do all the guitars. He did a fabulous job. For drums, I hired Kenny Aronoff and a few others, including Stewart Copeland. I was such a huge fan of the Police and felt so honored when he came over to play. But he had a hard time playing to a click track and kept speeding up. With the Police, when he sped up and down, they sped up and down with him, and it worked for them. They were one of my favorite bands, but it didn't work on my sessions. He left my house shaking his head in disbelief. "That's never happened to me before," he said, stunned. Nancy Wilson came in to play and sing backgrounds on five tracks, including "It's Only Me," a song she and Susanna Hoffs from the Bangles had cowritten with me. Nathan East played bass, and the Brecker Brothers played horns on one song. And I want to thank all of them.

The week that my record was scheduled to be released, Tommy called me in to his office.

"Take a seat," he said gravely. "I have to tell you something. You may have heard some rumors floating around." I looked at him blankly and just shook my head. "I'm moving over to Sony Records. I've been offered to head the whole US operations of their record company, which is now going to be called Sony Music Entertainment."

None of it registered, the magnitude of the situation, so I remained quiet and still as he continued. "Your record is being released next week, and I'm going to be honest with you. My promotion is either going to be a really good, or really bad thing for you: good because I can make your album go to the front of the line, and I can pull a lot of strings to help it along. But bad, because as president of the label, I'm about to get pulled in a million directions and won't have the time to focus on breaking your record. Your album could easily get lost in the shuffle."

I stared at him, stunned. This was the last thing I had expected to hear. "Does that mean you won't be my manager anymore?"

"Yes, that's correct."

"And I probably won't make a second record if this one doesn't do well?"

"Let's not jump to any conclusions just yet," he cautioned.

This was the best news he could've given me. "Does that mean you won't be managing anyone, not even Daryl and John?"

"Probably" he said. "We have a few things that need to be worked out."

I sat staring at the floor for a minute. "Well then, I guess I should say congratulations."

"Thanks," he said, beaming. "Listen, I wish I could tell you more. Your record *is* coming out, that much I can tell you."

I hated the solo record I made. If I could find every copy and burn it to the ground I would. I know my strengths and weaknesses. I'm a great songwriter and musician, but I'm a not a lead singer. If I'd been born with the gifts of a vocalist, I would've been a vocalist. I've worked with some of the best out there, which makes me even more critical of myself...I can admit that. I was relieved as hell! To me this whole ordeal had been an experiment, a reckoning with my demons, and the truth had been staring me in the face the whole time: I missed being behind the scenes and being a songwriter for as many artists as I could. I went home and slept well for the first time in a year and a half. I saw Tommy once after that, when he invited me to have lunch in his private dining room in the black tower of Sony Records. I went back to focusing on songwriting. I didn't see Tommy again for almost thirty years.

CHAPTER NINETEEN

WHY I PUT MY DRESS ON
INSIDE OUT (STEVEN TYLER)

Los Angeles & Vancouver, 1987

"I'm feeling like a bad boy..."
("Ragdoll" performed by Aerosmith)

My personal life was running shotgun with my professional life. I was almost thirty-two and waiting to close on my first home on Stone Canyon Road in Bel Air. Being a city girl and used to living in high-rise buildings, it was going to be an adjustment moving into a house on the ground floor, albeit a two story one. Since I was a single woman, the first two things I took care of had to do with security. I had an alarm system installed and bought a shotgun.

In anticipation of the move, I started packing and going through things, photos, letters, awards I'd won, and reflected on my life thus far. I used to joke with my friends and say that I was successful in spite of myself.

One day, I got a call from John Kolodner, who was A&R/president of Geffen Records. John and I had been friends since my days working with the Wilson sisters. He had this monotone way of talking that went along with his eccentric white suits and John Lennon-ish glasses. John had an uncanny eye for talent, having signed artists and bands like Phil Collins, Foreigner, and Peter Gabriel, and he had a passion for breathing new life into the careers of bands whose glory days were behind them. I loved his loyalty, his belief in the fact that they weren't ready to be put out to pasture.

John was calling because he had signed Aerosmith, who were finishing up their new record, and there was one song he thought was "really good, but wasn't quite hitting the mark in its present form." He felt it had the potential to be one of the singles. "I don't know what it would take to make this better, but would you listen to it and see if you want to work on it?"

I was barely sixteen when Aerosmith's debut record came out in 1972. I was already living on my own, barely getting by on food stamps and shitty jobs. I thought Aerosmith was the coolest hard rock band to come out of America. They were cool the way the Stones were cool, played blues-based hard rock with hints of heavy metal, and were the quintessential poster boys for sex, drugs, and rock 'n' roll. I've never met a woman who, if they were an Aerosmith fan, didn't think Steven Tyler was hot and fantasized fucking him, present company included.

But it was the music that truly drew me to the band, and by 1976, when they hit their stride with *Rocks*, I was living in Beantown. I used to put "Back in the Saddle" on and crank it as loud as my crappy stereo system would allow, just to get my mojo going in the morning and get ready to tackle the day. That song had one of the most relentlessly badass guitar lines, one so good that the lead guitar, rhythm guitar, and bass all played it in unison. The melody and lyrics showed off everything Steven was known for—range, attitude, singing, and screaming. That song alone was reason enough to love them.

People within the music business knew that heroin and alcohol addiction were the cause of Aerosmith's demise. John was determined to resurrect them, and as a result of their new clean and sober status, they had agreed to try things they would never have agreed to before, like working with outside writers. John said, "This is their comeback record, their make-or-break album." I was still in awe of Steven Tyler and Joe Perry, and even if they never sold another record, I wanted to do it. At the very least, I could say I had worked with them.

"How does Steven feel about someone outside the band coming in and changing a song he's already written? And what about Joe Perry? That's not really something I've ever done, so unless Steven tells me it's cool," I said, "it would feel too weird to get involved."

"No no no, Steven's fine with it. I told him all about you, and he knows the song isn't right yet...I've worked all this out."

I agreed to give it a try. John said he would messenger the song over and to expect Steven's call. A few hours later, I was listening to the sassy "Ragtime" for the fourth time. The music was great, and it had an infectious drum groove. But it was missing something relatable, something that put Steven back in the song, because, at that moment, it meant nothing to me.

Back in the Spider days, when Jack Douglas had shown an interest in producing us, he let us tag along as his guests to see Aerosmith play Madison Square Garden a few times. We even went backstage, although we never got to meet the band. Steven's stage presence and body language was so arrogant and sexy, and the way he used the mike stand as an extension of his body was hot. He even put it between his legs and rode it like a pony around the stage, like a little kid...all while singing his heart out. As the years went on, the original members stayed together, even when it seemed they couldn't stand each other anymore. That was saying a lot. In interviews, Steven couldn't have been any more animated. Their sense of fashion, especially Steven's, on stage and off, was part of the Aerosmith legacy. They were rock stars, and they dressed the part, always in clothing that looked like they were poured into it, black patent leather, black rubber, long coats, no coats, bare-chested, and long-haired—they had it all.

I knew I was incredibly lucky. I'd worked with the most talented rock singers out there. Now, here was an opportunity to work with Steven Tyler, which, once again, had seemingly fallen into my lap.

I was curious whether Steven was going to be a nice guy or not. He had this reputation as a womanizer, but then again, what male rocker didn't? Either way, I was a big girl, and I was confident enough in my abilities as a musician and songwriter to hold my own and win him over. Sure, I had one or two insecurities and anxieties in other areas to contend with, but songwriting wasn't one of them. I hoped that by working on this song, in the future, we could write the way I was used to writing, from the beginning.

The following morning, my phone rang at 7:00 a.m., and it was Steven. He was like an excited kid, flirtatious, goofy, and corny. We talked about everything but the song, eventually getting around to it. "I just want to make sure you're good with this and I'm not being shoved down your throat," I said. Naturally, that provoked a sexual response. Ba da boom! Then on a more serious note Steven went into great detail about his and the band's commitment to sobriety and what it meant to them. He said, "You would've hated my guts when I was that person. I was a demon." Hating his guts was the exact opposite of what I was feeling at that moment.

Over the next two weeks, Steven called every morning like clockwork and we would talk anywhere from two to four hours. One time, my answering machine picked up in the other room as I reached for the phone. As a result, it recorded a good part of the conversation. I won't go into details, but suffice it to say he told me had had a dream about me and that I had shaved a certain part of my body, which was now "bald as an eagle." He was such a nut, he made me laugh a lot. I still crack up every time I hear that message which I saved. It was all in good fun.

I listened to him. I listened to the song. He listened to me. Tightening a screw can be a delicate thing. I told him that in my opinion, there was no reason to change the music, that the weakness lay in the title, and that we needed to change some of the lyrics to work with the new song title. Most of the time, I could hardly tell what the lyrics in Aerosmith's songs meant anyway. To me, they were usually a vague set of rhythmic razzamatazz Tylerized lingo that only he spoke. It always sounded good though, and nobody seemed to care what the lyrics meant.

Talking so much on the phone wasn't a planned thing, it just sort of happened, and I think that Steven needed someone to talk to. I guess I did too. I fell in love with him during that period. He was so damn adorable and nice, sometimes when we'd be hanging on the telephone, I'd forget he was a rock star. He was just an interesting and sweet guy. If I started to think about who he was to the outside world, I couldn't handle it, I'd start to get nervous and self-conscious, so I tried not to. In fact, it was that way with pretty much all the famous people I worked with. If I really thought about who they were, I found it debilitating. I had to pretend that it was no big deal, even though it was. As a result, I was always shy about asking them to take a photo with me. They had to do enough of that with their fans.

If the record did well, I probably would never have the luxury of his time again, and as it turned out, I was right. I had to be careful with this one because I had genuine feelings for Steven. When it came to my personal life, most of the time, I preferred to keep things platonic, yet still friendly with the people I worked with. And then, yes, there were the few occasions where I went for it. I worked with some incredibly charismatic and unusual men, they were creative and different...and fun. Who wouldn't find that intriguing? And they were always flirtatious, which was the kind of rapport I was used to myself, even with my own friends.

Opportunities would come along all the time, and I'd ask myself, "Are we being unprofessional by sleeping together? Will a few moments of salacious pleasure be worth it? Will I be reduced to merely a woman in their eyes, instead of the equal cowriting partner I've worked so hard to establish?" That would've been terrible, and that did happen once or twice. I wanted to be on equal footing with any male collaborators and it seemed to be more effective if I was unattainable and stuck to business. As a songwriter, if I kept some level of decorum and sex was off the table, it kept things simple, and men treated me with more respect. It was that classic Madonna/whore thing: men usually can't think of a woman as both.

I didn't have a lot of time to meet and hang out with people outside of the music business. Most guys I went out with were either in bands or did something in the music business, like engineering records, mixing records, producing records, and directing videos. So it was inevitable, over the years, that I dated a few of them long-term, even married one or two.

Toward the end of our two-week-long phone conversation, Steven finally said, "We need to be in the same room if we're going to finish this tune. I bet we can bang out the changes in a few hours, and then I can put down the vocal while you're there. Besides, I want to meet you."

"Yes, we need to meet," I agreed, my heart fluttering.

Then he said, "I just spoke to John and the label is going to book you a flight up to Vancouver. Can you come up tomorrow?"

"Of course!" I said.

The band was cutting *Permanent Vacation* at Little Mountain in Vancouver, the legendary studio where Bon Jovi had recorded *Slippery When Wet* and *New Jersey*. After *Permanent Vacation*, it was dubbed the "Betty Ford Clinic" for musicians.

We were finally going to meet. It was my first time in Vancouver, and I was excited to be there. The town had always held an allure for me. When I first ran away from home, it was the place my finger had landed on when I was trying to figure out where to run to, although I never actually made it that far.

I worried that it might not be as natural with Steven and I in person as it had been on the phone, but I worried for nothing. We hugged like old friends. He was tinier in person than I had expected and his features were almost effeminate, even though his libido was masculine. Most rockers I knew had this same androgynous quality.

"You're pretty," Steven said.

"No, you're pretty," I said back.

We talked for a bit and it was even better in person. Loverboy was recording in the next room and a couple of the members came into the lounge. Steven introduced me to Mike Reno, the lead singer, and their guitarist, Paul Dean. Canadians are some of the nicest people and they were no exception.

Steven and I went into a small empty studio to get started and sat on the floor. I got right into it and suggested we change the name from "Ragtime" to "Ragdoll," because I sort of saw him that way with all his scarves and his wild outfits. He liked the change. I told him a funny joke. "What did Mae West say to John Wayne when they met? 'Is that a rocket in your pocket or are you just glad to see me?'" then moved on to her most famous quote, "Come on up and see me," which Steven sang on the second half of every chorus.

I wanted to focus on making the chorus more personable, more about him. I thought that by doing that, his fans would connect to the song more. "Ragtime" just left you with nothing to hold on to. For the most part, the fact that the verses were vague didn't bother me much, that was typical Steven vernacular, but we came up with lines such as, "I'm ripping up a ragdoll, like throwing away an old toy..." to tie it all together. Same thing with "Hot tramp, daddy's little cutie." We changed a few of the lyrics in other parts of the song to tie in with "Ragdoll" and that was it. I could've rewritten more of the lyrics, but why? My logic always remained the same—whatever served the song.

Steven grabbed the lyrics and went to tell their producer, Bruce Fairburn, that he was ready to do the vocal. "We got it," he said, grinning. His delivery was flawless. He sung it straight through twice.

That was it. I'll always remember him that way, looking at me through the glass, sitting on a stool while he sang his ass off.

Joe Perry barely said a word to me. I should've been used to this by now, this underlying feeling that I wasn't welcome. It brought back those uncomfortable times working with Rod Stewart's band, and just like with Rod, I had no problems with Steven (quite the opposite), but some of the other guys seemed to be giving me the stink eye.

It could've ended right there. I could have said goodbye to everyone and gone back to my hotel room since I had an early flight back to LA in the morning, but Steven asked me, "Hey, how would you like to go get some sushi with me at my favorite restaurant when I'm done?"

"I love sushi, that would be awesome."

"Great. There's just one track left to do before we're done with 'Ragdoll.'"

"Can I sit in the control room and watch?" I asked.

He pulled me aside and said, "Listen, you need to leave for about an hour and when you come back, we should be finished and then we can go to dinner. We're waiting for a couple of strippers to stop by," he said, grinning a little sheepishly.

"Yeah, so?"

He had invited them to come in and pull their panties down so he could play bongos on their bare asses on "Ragdoll." If you find a CD or vinyl copy of *Permanent Vacation*, you'll notice a "thanks to the Flesh Bongos" in the liner notes. What Steven didn't realize was that this wasn't my first rodeo. I had seen this kind of juvenile behavior with so many bands I'd worked with at this point, and they always asked me to leave. I never felt jealous; it was more like I wanted to take the girls aside and feed them a warm bowl of soup. But who was I kidding? I knew they loved the attention. It probably felt empowering to them to turn men into drooling idiots. There was no way I was going to sleep with him.

I left and went shopping in the Gaslight district to kill time, then returned an hour later, and as promised, Steven and I went out to dinner. It was very cute sitting in our own little tatami room. I melted all over again, letting go of the annoyance I'd felt earlier. He walked me back to my hotel, and we were both behaving ourselves.

"Goodnight Steven," I said and hugged him.

"Goodnight," he answered.

I started to close the door as he turned to leave, but then he changed his mind, spun around, grabbed me, and kissed me—a big fat juicy kiss with those big fat juicy lips. Whee! And then I pushed him away and slammed the door. That was way too close.

I was sitting in the lobby the next morning waiting for my ride to the airport, scribbling some lyrics in a notebook when Steven walked through the lobby on his way to the studio. My heart pounded.

"Hey what are you writing in there?" he said smiling at me.

"I'm writing a song about you," I said.

"Really? What's it called?"

"Palace of Pleasure."

He smiled. "That sounds promising. Hey, I'll see you in LA."

One more hug and he was gone. Be still my beating heart.

Mission accomplished, I'd tightened a screw, albeit an important one, the one that got them back on the radio when the record came out. Kolodner was happy, the band was happy. Steven asked me what I thought was a fair share of compensation for my contribution. I had already pondered the issue and really didn't want very much, so I told him 10 percent, and he sounded relieved. "That's exactly what I was thinking." So, Steven was happy too. That's the smallest percentage I've ever taken in my career. I really didn't give a shit about the money, it's not why I did it.

A few weeks later, the band came to town, and Steven invited me to dine with them and Kolodner at the Ivy, the same place I had met

Daryl. Steven offered me the seat to his left, and Tom Hamilton sat to my right. What a gentle soul Tom was: he complimented me on my scarlet red dress and said his wife wore a lot of Betsey Johnson dresses too. No one drank any alcohol.

By now the house was mine. It was a lovely stone French villa; even the walls on the inside were made of the same stone, giving it a medieval feel. It was perfect for me. It was still completely devoid of any furniture, except for my studio gear, which I'd already moved in. I wanted to set up my studio first because the equipment was so expensive and I didn't trust the movers to transport it without damaging any of it. I'd had my studio tech, Art, set it all up for me. The rest of my belongings were being moved in the following day.

I'd hired an alarm company to install a new system, and they'd left a bunch of things for me in a box, which was in the trunk of my car...gate openers, booklets, keypad instructions. I had stopped by the house before dinner to pick up the box so I would have everything I needed for the next day's big move. I'd even gone to the Bel Air Patrol guardhouse at the Bel Air main entrance and asked them how I should go about procuring a gun legally for protection. They hooked me up with a gentleman who was a retired cop. "Listen," he said, "you're better off getting a shotgun. That's going to be a better weapon for someone like you—" (that is, inexperienced) "—than a handgun. With a shotgun, all you have to do is point it in the direction of an intruder and one shot will take out the entire wall." He also pointed out that I needed to find a place to practice shooting so I would actually know how to use the damn thing if the need ever arose. Once I moved into my new house, I started to trap shoot every few weeks with an instructor and was surprised to discover that I liked it a lot. There was something very zen about the sport. You had to raise your gun and aim it at a point in the sky, timing it so that the clay disc met with the bullet in a synchronistic moment, shattering in mid-air. It was a thing of beauty to behold, and while, on the one hand, it felt strange to own a weapon, it allowed me to sleep safely at night.

I even started to take fencing lessons because I'd always loved swords and knives. I bought and collected beautiful pearl-handled switchblades whenever I went to Germany (long before airports had such tight security). They were works of art. Some of my friends loved them and were so fascinated by them, they asked me if they could have one, and soon my collection dwindled. (They liked to cut cocaine lines with them.) I'm not a violent person, and I don't condone the use of weaponry by any means when it's used to hurt or kill people, but as a sport I think fencing can be fun and a good way to improve your awareness and hand-eye coordination. Anything that sharpens your senses is a good thing. I'm still a tomboy in many ways, and there's always been this warrior spirit that I carry inside me. When it comes to my personal safety, anything that involves taking care of myself instead of relying on a man to do it, is not only satisfying, but necessary.

As the Aerosmith dinner at the Ivy came to an end, Steven asked me, "Where are you going after this?"

"I'm celebrating. I just bought my first house and was going to go check on it. I'm moving in tomorrow. Would you like to see it? I'll drive you back to your hotel afterwards." Damn if he didn't say yes.

It was only a fifteen-minute drive from the Ivy. When we got there, I fumbled in the dark with the box of gate openers and keys until I finally got the front door opened. Once we were in the house, I turned off the alarm, switched on some lights, and showed him around the first floor.

I was proud of my new home. I opened the door to my studio, which was just a converted bedroom filled with my Trident console and an Otari one-inch tape machine, lots of keyboards and guitars, my Fairlight, all kinds of toys, and a bunch of Gold and Platinum plaques piled on the floor in a corner. When Steven entered the room, he couldn't help but start to sing and before we knew what was happening, we began writing a good song. Now I was happy! Now he could see I really was a bona fide musician and songwriter, and not just a screw tightener. Ever the professional, I taped it on my cassette player so neither of us would forget it.

"Hey Steven, I haven't shown you the upstairs part of the house. Would you like to see it?"

"Of course, I would." he said.

I led him upstairs, tripping over the box with the gate opener and alarm instructions I had left at the foot of the staircase. I ignored it and kept going up the stairs. All conscience and any sense of propriety went right out the window. The truth is that at some point when we were making music in my studio, I knew we would end up on my bedroom floor. It was inevitable, given our intense like for one another. Steven is a delicious kisser. As for the rest, you'll have to use your imagination. I lost track of time until suddenly, through my opened bedroom door, I saw beams of flashlights through the downstairs windows bouncing on my walls and high ceilings. Who the hell was on my property? Robbers? How did they even get past my front gate? It scared the hell out of me to think there were robbers in my backyard. I hadn't even moved in yet. And naturally, the shotgun was stashed away in a box in my old apartment.

When Steven saw the beams, he sat bolt upright and started freaking out. "This is not good, this is not good at all," he groaned. As we scrambled in the dark, trying to find our clothes, which had been flung everywhere with reckless abandon, I could hear walkie talkies crackling outside. I peered out onto the street through the window, and that's when I realized it was the Bel Air Patrol. I ran downstairs and went outside to talk to them. I had put my dress on inside out, and it probably would've been really funny if the whole thing hadn't felt so bizarre. They asked me for the alarm code and password to verify that I was the homeowner. It was hard to focus on their questions, especially with flashlights glaring in my face. Steven thankfully stayed upstairs, poor guy—I'm sure he didn't want any photographs or questions.

The romantic spell had broken. I was annoyed with the patrol men and wanted to know why the hell they were walking around my backyard flashing lights everywhere and cross-examining me like I was a suspect. All my indignation and righteous anger evaporated when I learned what had happened.

I had set off the panic button when I tripped over the box on the stairs, and which had silently been sending the security company a distress signal for the last forty-five minutes. I felt so stupid, so utterly embarrassed. I just wanted them to leave, and when they finally did, I went back upstairs to tell Steven what had happened. It took him a while to calm down, so we just lay on the floor, staring at the ceiling and talking.

I took him back to his hotel, and for the first time, the two of us had little to say to each other. Just as I dropped him off, he looked at me, and I looked at him...and we both burst into uncontrollable fits of laughter. In stereo. Finally, we said goodnight, and hugged goodbye.

The label hired Marty Callner, who had directed just about every video that Aerosmith ever made, to direct the "Ragdoll" video. I knew Marty from the "Never" video shoot he had directed for Heart, as well as "Invincible," so our paths had crossed enough that we were well acquainted. Also, his wife and sister-in-law ran a successful hair salon in Beverly Hills where I had my hair cut and styled for years.

"Ragdoll" was filmed on location in Tennessee and New Orleans. There was what became the famous scene of Steven driving a Shelby Cobra through a college campus, and at every house, he blew a kiss to yet another sexy woman who had come out to wave goodbye to him, one after the other. It was annoying in a way, but it also portrayed Steven in a realistic light, and he would probably be the first to admit it. The video went straight into heavy rotation on MTV and parked its ass there for a long time. *Permanent Vacation* became the band's greatest success in a decade. They were very generous and sent me quite a few plaques to hang on my wall, every time it sold another million copies, so I have five of them. For a while we still talked on the phone until he got married, and twenty-six years went by before I saw Steven again. I really miss him. He is one of a kind.

CHAPTER TWENTY

SLOW BURN (OZZY OSBOURNE)

Los Angeles, 1988

"And I never got to say...goodbye."
("Slow Burn" performed by Ozzy Osborne)

I don't really like to write about the songs I wrote that *almost* made it onto records, but in this case I think it's worth mentioning because both my cowriter and I loved this song, and I can't tell you the reason why it never ended up on his record, even though he'd captured a beautiful recording of it.

Yet another cold call out of the blue: this time it was a British woman. "Hello, is this Holly?" I told her it was, and she said, "It's Sharon Osbourne, how are you, darling?"

I was relieved she'd said "darling" because Mike had once told me they couldn't stand each other. I'm not sure what had happened between the two of them. I only knew she managed Lita Ford, and Mike had produced Lita's record *Stiletto*, for which Lita and I had written the title track together. He had also produced a stellar duet between Lita and Ozzy called "Close My Eyes Forever." Rumor had it that Sharon had sent Mike a box of excrement.

This was the first time I'd ever talked to Sharon, and from that first phone call on, she was always kind and a straight shooter. We shared a mutual respect, but I'd heard enough stories to know that I didn't want to be on the receiving end of her wrath. Personally, I thought it was badass that people feared her. I admired her, knowing how hard it was to be assertive as a woman in a business dominated by men. She founded Ozzfest, which was a highly successful yearly music festival from 1996 to 2018. You'd have to have been sleeping under a rock to not have heard of the infamous Osbourne reality show, which led the brigade in family reality shows that followed.

She came from a music background, working for her father, Don Arden, a successful manager to stars like Little Richard, Small Faces, Electric Light Orchestra, and Black Sabbath.

I had read somewhere that Sharon met Ozzy while her father was managing him, and when her father decided to sack him from Black Sabbath, she took over, which made her father livid. Reportedly, the next time Sharon visited Don, his vicious pet dogs attacked her, and because she was pregnant at the time, she lost the baby. She eventually married Ozzy and had no contact with her father for twenty years. What I loved about her was that she was a survivor.

She said to me, "I want you and Ozzy to get together and write." I was a fan from the first Black Sabbath record, which came out in 1970 when I was fourteen. I loved all the dark chords and gothic lyrics. I'd read in Ozzy's autobiography that he wasn't at all into witchcraft or black magic, but it seemed like a cool subject matter to perpetuate for the band. I was mesmerized by the witch on the cover and felt oddly connected, not so much because she was evil looking, but because she was a witch.

Sharon wanted to meet me before setting up the session, so she invited me over to a house they were renting in West Hollywood. She had a bunch of cute little dogs running around the place yapping their heads off. You could tell she was a dog lover; even the pillows on the couches had needlepoint of dogs on them. She was very warm towards me. "Holly, it's lovely to meet you, come in, darling, and have a seat." She wasn't the glamour-puss she is now, she was chubby and nice to hug, like an aunt you wanted to sit and have tea with. I liked her and never asked her about the box of shit as I didn't want to say anything that would ruin my chances of writing with Ozzy, but I thought, if it was true, I loved the idea that she had stood up to Mike. She was my kind of woman. I didn't meet Ozzy that day, but she talked a lot about Jack and Kelly, who were toddlers. It was obvious she adored them.

Soon after our meeting, Ozzy's road manager drove him to my house. I loved him the minute he walked through my front door bumbling and mumbling, "Hello, Holly," in his British accent. After listening to his music for so many years, he seemed larger than life standing in my studio, hidden behind a pair of stark blue spectacles. He was so self-deprecating that it was disarming, and I couldn't help but laugh along with him as he jokingly talked about liposuction with a straight face.

"So, Ozzy, what kind of song would you like to write with me. What do you like to listen to these days?"

"I love the Beatles, man. I think 'The Long and Winding Road' is a fucking masterpiece."

"Are you saying you want to write a song like that? That's a bit of a departure for you, but we could do that if you want." I said.

"Hah, that's an understatement, bit of a departure. Yeah, I'd love to write something slow and musical like that. I love that kind of music."

For some reason, I hadn't prepared anything for this session. I thought Ozzy had enough spandex-clad rock guitarists in his own camp, that he didn't need me to write anything metal. I'd decided that in his case, it might be better to wait until we were together to see where his interests lay. "Long and Winding Road" was almost classical-based, and that, I could do in my sleep. I started to play a moody chord progression that we both liked immediately.

"What do think of the title 'Slow Burn'?"

"Yeah, that's beautiful."

The chorus we came up with had a really smooth melody and lyrics:

> "It was a slow burn but you finally fell into the fire,
> You took a bad turn, you were living the life of a lie
> and I never got to say…goodbye."

We wrote the entire song that day, even recorded a finished demo. It was beautiful and melancholy. We doubled all his vocals as he said, "I like to sing all the vocals doubled. It's my trademark." I already knew that from listening to his records. I think he doubled them out of insecurity because he thought it made his vocals sound better. In my opinion, he was more accomplished than he thought he was. His pitch was dead on and he had his own unique style, kind of an anti-style. I played piano and put cellos and strings on it. He was in great spirits when he left, and I wasn't sure what the outcome would be. Would he or wouldn't he put the song on his record. It was definitely something different from what his fans were used to hearing. I could certainly imagine John Lennon or Paul McCartney singing it.

Ozzy called about a month later. "Hello is that, Holly?" he asked.

I knew it was him right away. "Hey, Ozzy! How are you?"

"I'm fucking great. Listen darling, I'm in the recording studio. I want to play you something. Hang on, hang on." And then he played me an epic rendition of "Slow Burn." When the song finished, he said, "So, what do you think? Do you like it? I think it sounds bloody brilliant."

"It's beautiful, I love it, well done. Does this mean it's going on the record?"

He laughed and said, "Is it going to be on the record? It's probably going to be the first single."

I was so happy to hear that. I guess stepping outside the box had been a good idea after all.

"Do you think I could get a copy of it? I promise I won't play it to anybody, I'd just like to be able to listen to it at home."

"No, Sharon won't let me do that, I'm afraid. Sorry about that, but as soon as the record is mastered, I'll send it to you."

Every now and then a recording artist would be cagey, afraid of bootleg advance copies cropping up or leaking, and with good reason, as it happened all the time.

Unfortunately, the record came out, and "Slow Burn" wasn't on it. Something had happened between our conversation and the release. Maybe the label thought it was too different from his other recordings. I thought it showed a more sophisticated side of Ozzy, if there is such a thing. I also thought that maybe it was Sharon who didn't want it to go on the record because it was too pretty. I loved working with him, and I liked them both so much, I was grateful we had met and become friends and had written a song like that anyway. We stayed in touch much longer than the usual "friends" I encountered through my work. My friend Paul Chavarria, (the one who had introduced me to David Bowie) was the head of production on many of Ozzy's tours and told me, "Ozzy and Sharon love you, they talk about you all the time and Ozzy always says how rotten he feels that he didn't cut the song the two of you wrote together."

Soon after that, I met and married my second husband, Michael, and they sent me a wedding present, two beautiful silver goblets. And I received a Christmas card from them for many years.

Several years later, after I had given birth to my second son and was living in Connecticut, I went to see Ozzy perform, and he and Sharon invited me to say hello before the show. When I walked in, they cleared the entire room and Sharon patted the seat next to her on the sofa. "Sit, tell us everything that's going on your life," she said. I could never figure out why they liked me so much, but I lapped it up like a love-starved kitten.

"I'm so sorry we didn't record our song, truly I am," Ozzy said.

I couldn't believe he was apologizing again, no one had ever done that before or since then. "It's fine, Ozzy. It's a beautiful song, but it happens. You really don't need to apologize."

Twenty years later, I saw Ozzy and Sharon at a show in London and they were just as gracious and loving as they'd always been. We haven't seen or talked to each other since, but I have only great memories with the two of them. They are two of the most unique and lovely people I have ever met.

Can I tell you how many demos I have with rock stars singing on them, demos that will probably never see the light of day? Besides Ozzy, there's Bryan Adams, Heart, Rod Stewart, Robin Zander, the lead singer of Cheap Trick, Katy Perry, and a whole bunch more.

I've always been a fan of Cheap Trick since their first record in 1977. The first time I met their guitarist, Rick Nielsen, it was kind of surreal. He had called me the day before and said, "We should jam." so I invited him over. After loving the band for so long, to see him playing guitar in my studio was crazy! Growing up in New York, I used to watch a black-and-white TV show called *The Bowery Boys*. There was one character called Sach, and I often wondered if that's where Rick had gotten his image.

We recorded an upbeat rock instrumental track together, and the following day Robin came over without him to write the lyrics and melody with me. Oh god, it was a total flirt fest with Robin, and the lyrics to "My Girl Can't Help It" reflected it.

We got together to write some more, and one evening, after we finished, I called Kathy Valentine and told her to meet me for dinner at El Coyote, an old Hollywood haunt. I said that Robin and Tom Peterson, the bass player, whom I'd yet to meet, would be with me. There was more flirting, those two were so darn cute. We all went back to my house afterwards, and by then, we were like the four musketeers. They were two of the happiest and sweetest guys I'd met in all the bands I worked with.

Paul Chavarria and his wife, Patricia were the lead production team for Prince, and one night I invited Robin to go see him perform with me. We had seats at the monitor console. It was one of those "I love my life" moments.

Cheap Trick ended up recording a tune I'd written with Mike Chapman called "Space" for their record, *Lap of Luxury*. It had originally been recorded by a talented young Texan, Charlie Sexton, but both his version and Cheap Trick's were a little disappointing from a production standpoint. I felt the song was better than the recordings. It's still one of my favorite tunes, and I recently recut it with a woman singing it. It's much more empowering and badass coming from a woman as you'll see in the lyrics.

"You push hard, you stop my circulation,
I know you really need a physical relation,
We may not be the perfect combination,
You need your love, I need my mental stimulation."

A short time later, Robin began writing songs for a solo record and he came over to my studio. Together, we wrote a whole bunch of tunes over a two-week period, but for some reason, in the end he didn't record the album, not at that time anyway. Some of the demos we did with his vocals sound like records to me. Two tunes in particular, "End of the Road" and "Girls on Parade," were the most memorable ones—they sounded like classic Cheap Trick, but they never saw the light of day. When Robin and I did the demos, I marveled at his expertise. He recorded countless background vocals, perfect takes one after the other. We probably put twenty tracks of stacked background vocals on everything.

It happens when you're a songwriter. Not everything you write gets cut. Not by a long shot. I was starting to build up a vault of unreleased songs, ones with big stars singing on them.

We lost touch for about twenty years and then saw each other again. It was like no time had passed, sure, they looked a little older, we all did, but they were still the happy, sweet midwestern guys that I remember.

CHAPTER TWENTY-ONE

SIMPLY THE BEST (TINA TURNER)

Los Angeles, 1987–1990

"You speak the language of love like you know what it means."
("The Best" performed by Tina Turner)

"The Best" was not written for Tina Turner, but it was meant for her.

I'll never forget the first time I saw Paul Young's video for "Everytime You Go Away" on MTV. *Holy shit!* I thought. *Who is this guy?* I was so transfixed that I forgot all about the dinner I was cooking for a friend. Everything was ruined and I nearly burnt down the house in the process. After that, whenever the video came on, I would stop whatever I was doing to watch it. I thought Paul was sexy, and I loved his husky voice and stage presence, even the old-school way he used the mike stand as a prop. The song, which had that retro Philly sound I loved so much, was fantastic, and for some reason, it reminded me of Hall & Oates and Todd Rundgren, some of my earliest influences. When I found out that it was a cover of a Hall & Oates song, I thought, *Of course! No wonder I love it so much.* Todd had produced Hall & Oates. Okay, so that explained even more. All this led up to one of three things: I was either going to try and work with Paul Young or sleep with him—or both.

A few months later, Paul's tour brought him to Los Angeles, and I took my friend Jill with me to see him open for Genesis at Dodger Stadium. It would've been easy to be swallowed up on a stage that large, especially as the opening act, but Paul delivered a performance that was just as exciting live as he'd been in the video. Sure, I knew that a lot of people dismissed him as being a teen idol, but I thought he was too talented to be boxed into a category reserved for poseurs. He was the real thing. No doubt his label was responsible for packaging him as a teen idol and I bet he hated it.

I'd also managed to score backstage passes through my publishers. Once Paul's set ended, Jill and I weaved through the rowdy crowd of Genesis fans. I asked around until I found Paul's trailer and his manager, who was standing in front of it talking to some people. The usual suspects were standing around, decked out groupies waiting to meet Paul, record company execs, and photographers. For a week, I'd been rehearsing what I would say to him to get a personal introduction to Paul. When I saw him finish talking to some other people, I moved in before someone else could and, offering my hand, said, "Hello, I'm Holly Knight," before going on to tell him I was a successful songwriter, dropping the names of a few of my biggest hits, especially the ones with Tina, and watched his face change from indifference to genuine interest. Shocker. Then I said, "I would love to write a song for Paul, I think he's great, and oh—would it be possible to say hello to him for just a minute?" He was very accommodating and offered to take me in the trailer himself to make the introductions.

It was quiet inside, and if there were other people there, I didn't notice. Paul was soft-spoken and polite, quite a contrast from the singer I'd just seen go through his paces on stage. I'm not usually shy, but here I was, trying to maintain some kind of professional acumen. It was hard. All I'd hoped to accomplish that night was to meet face to face and plant a seed in the hopes that he'd remember me when I sent him a song. As he was speaking, I momentarily drifted away, imagining him taking hold of me and ravishing me. Embarrassed, I answered, "I'm sorry, what did you say?" To my delight, he was inviting me to meet him at the after-party.

I dropped Jill off at her boyfriend's apartment and headed over to the party. Paul and his entourage arrived at the same time as me. He was being led to a table and invited me to join them, even offering me the seat next to him. This was going better than I'd expected. Everyone wanted to meet and talk to him, so we barely said more than a few words to each other. When he did talk to me, he leaned in close so we could hear each other because it was quite noisy. That was enough for me. I was smitten.

The next day I got together with Mike and asked him if he would be interested in writing a song with me for Paul. There was no reason to divulge that I had a "thing" for the singer, and of course, I knew that had I told Mike the truth, he probably would've told me to go write it myself. But whatever the reason, if an infatuation was what it took to write a great love song, so be it. I mean, isn't desire the fount from whence all great love songs are derived anyway?

Not long after, Mike stopped by for a drink, and after a few glasses of wine, we ended up at my Steinway Grand. That night, I felt like playing, he felt like singing. Coincidentally, Mike had been thinking about writing the ultimate love song for his own reasons, and already had the title, "The Best." Between our individual motives, the beginning strains of something special found its way into my living room.

I started to play some chords that sounded like an intro and a verse, we were just stumbling our way through, not knowing what it was yet. The chords moved, while the bass line pedaled on the same note creating tension, the building up of "something." Years later, it dawned on me that that was sort of a signature of mine. Mike started phonetically mumbling things that had a definitive melody and rhythm to them. Often, I would literally try to decipher what the hell he was saying, catching them like fireflies in a mason jar, and turn them into lyrics later. I threw in the line, "You come to me…" and he finished it with, "wild and wired." "Hey, you should repeat that!" "You come to me, come to me, wild and wired." "Yeah repeat it again." "You come to me, give me something, something, something…." Then we moved on to the chorus. Mike started singing, "You're the best." I mumbled back something similar to "blah-blah-blah, all the rest…." "Rest" just seemed like a natural choice, since it rhymed with "best." Once we had the three-chord intro to the chorus, we worked on the vocal entry. We started singing the first line, "You're simply the best" acapella, so when the chorus came in, so did the music. Often, a transition from a verse into a chorus like this can sound cheesy or pompous, but in this case we just went for it. It lent itself well to a big chorus entry and celebratory vibe.

We wrote most of the song that night, at least musically. Whatever lyrics we didn't come up with, Mike finished a lot of them on his own over the next few days. They were passionate and romantic. I especially loved the lines,

> "In your heart I see the start of every night
> and every day,
> In your eyes I get lost, I get washed away."

We got together one more time and finessed the lyrics some more, and by the end of the week, we had a tight demo with drums, bass. guitar, keyboards, Mike's vocals, and the two of us singing the background vocals. By this point, we knew it was a very, very good song, but we had no way of knowing it would become the biggest song either one of us would ever write, a feel-good love anthem for the eighties that only got bigger with each passing decade.

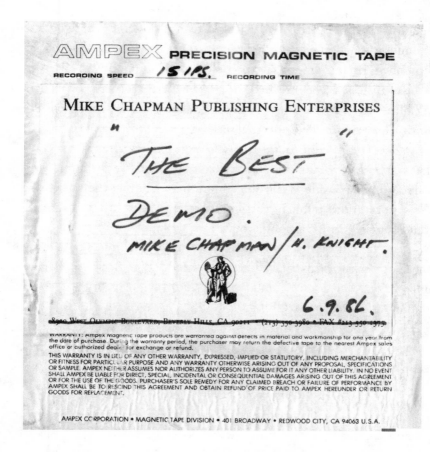

We sent the demo to Paul's manager and waited. I concocted all kinds of wonderful scenarios in my head—Paul falling in love with the song, me visiting him in the studio, watching him shoot the video, going out to dinner, running away to the Amalfi coast. For the next week, every time the phone rang, I jumped. I couldn't wait for him to tell me how much he loved it. Finally, his manager called. First, he thanked us for sending it, and then he said they were passing. *Wait…what?*

Part of being a songwriter is developing a thick skin when it comes to rejection, so I should've been used to it by now. But this was different. I had invested my heart into this song, and it was so good,

I couldn't comprehend why he would turn it down. I even wondered, after all that, whether Paul had even listened to it, because sometimes someone in management says no before passing it along.

Regardless, I was crushed. So much for my fantasy of impressing him with a musical love letter. The whole dream collapsed like a sandcastle being pulled into the sea.

Mike didn't seem too miffed about it. I don't think he'd been all that impressed by Paul in the first place. He knew we'd written a great song and felt confident it would find a better home, the right home. We sent it to our publishing administrators and told them that they could start sending the song around.

Not long after that, Bonnie Tyler, the Welsh singer best known for "Total Eclipse of the Heart" recorded "The Best" on her new album, *Hide Your Heart*, named after a song I had cowritten with Paul Stanley and Desmond Child for KISS. I'm not even sure if it was released in the US, but it came out in Europe and achieved only mild success. Back to the drawing board, the search for the right artist to record "The Best" continued.

———

By now Kathy Valentine and I were closer than ever. She'd been in a long term relationship with Clem Burke, the drummer in Blondie for years, she had first met him when she was in the Go-Gos, and they were like a superstar couple in the beginning. Clem was a cool, quiet guy, who always dressed in black suits and Ray-Bans (like Johnny Cash).

I introduced Kathy to Mike Chapman at a birthday party he had thrown for me at his house, and she woke up in his bed the next morning. She was pretty smitten and started seeing him, eventually falling in love with him. Clem was out on the road touring with Eurythmics and she wanted to be honest and tell him what was going on. I worried that Mike was going to end up hurting her, but she was so into him, I stayed clear of the whole thing. She called me one evening to tell me she was going to Europe to break up with Clem.

"Do you want to come with me? It could be fun!" Her timing couldn't have been better. A rock 'n' roll adventure in Europe sounded great to me.

"Why not?" I said.

We met up with the Eurythmics tour in Rome and found ourselves sitting in a limo with Siobhan Fahey of Bananarama, who'd recently married Dave Stewart, and two girlfriends of hers. One of them was telling us what was going on that week in the city, places to go and people to see. "Oh, and yeah, Paul Young's in town, he's performing a concert tonight." My ears pricked up. Although he'd passed on "The Best," I still felt annoyingly attracted to him.

The following day, Kathy, who hadn't gotten around to breaking up with Clem, and was staying with him, called my room. "I want to go see the Vatican and the Sistine Chapel. You should come with me."

"I'll meet you downstairs in half an hour," I said, "I'm looking forward to seeing all the Michelangelo paintings on the ceilings that I've read about my whole life."

When we arrived at the Vatican City, we walked around for hours, marveling at the Roman, Baroque, and Gothic architecture, the exquisite masonry and the artwork within its walls. In the process, we accidentally split off in two directions. I wandered into the Sistine Chapel and spent the next hour staring at the ceilings. It was unfathomable to me that one man painted all that exquisite art. At one point, I accidentally backed into someone. "I'm so sorry," I said as I turned around to apologize, only to find myself staring into Paul Young's face. Surely this was a hallucination. He looked as surprised as me, but pleasantly so. "Hello," we blurted out at the same time.

"Holly, right?" he said.

I nodded, probably red in the face. "Paul! I heard you performed a show in town last night, otherwise I would be much more surprised to find you here. I'm sorry I missed it."

"What are you doing here in Rome?"

"I'm sort of on vacation. I came with Kathy Valentine," I said, smiling.

"Well, I'm here with this very nice VIP guide who was about to take me on a private tour of the Sistine Chapel," he said. "He's going to show me parts of the building that most people don't get to see."

Right on cue, the tour guide gently motioned to him that they had to get started. "Why don't you come with us?" he said. "It should be interesting."

It was. The ceiling was forty-four feet above the main floor of the chapel, and we walked around its secret turrets and walkways up near the roof as our guide described the origins and history. I feel lucky to have seen the Sistine Chapel this way. Experiencing it with Paul made it all the more thrilling. Before we said goodbye, Paul said, "Listen, I have the night off and was planning to take my band and some of my crew to a special restaurant. Would you like to join us?" Of course, I said yes.

On the way back to the hotel, I found a fantastic shoe store near the Spanish Steps and bought a pair of Italian high-heeled pumps, aka fuck-me pumps. When I found Kathy, I apologized for disappearing on her, and explained what had happened. She thought it was fantastic.

"What do you think I should do if he asks me up to his room or makes any innuendos?" I asked, knowing well enough what she would say. She was as wild as I was.

"I would go for it, have fun," she said, grinning.

There's an empowering feeling a woman gets when she chooses to be physically intimate with someone, when it's 100 percent consensual and she's acting on her own volition, her own desire. It's her prerogative, and she's no different from a man in this way. I worked in the music business, I was single, and a lot of the men I worked with were single or lied and said they were. Why the hell wouldn't I go for it? Plus, I happened to be in one of the most romantic cities on earth.

I put on a brand new Alaïa maxi coat that I'd bought in London on Bond Street. After Tina had introduced me to her designer-friend in Paris, I'd become obsessed with his clothing. The cut made me feel curvy, and I slipped the new black patent leather heels on. I could hear an opera singer's voice, an alto, echoing from the street below. I arrived at the restaurant and was led to a table of about twelve colorfully dressed men and women. Paul greeted me with a kiss on each cheek, then introduced me to everybody, throwing in the fact that I was a "talented and famous songwriter." That surprised me. He offered me the seat next to him that he'd been saving for me. The women were Paul's backup singers and they were entertaining and bawdy. Everyone at the table was in a festive mood as family-style plates and bottles of wine were brought one after the other. Paul seemed a lot more relaxed and talkative that night. I liked this version of him.

After dinner, several of us went back to his hotel and sat down to drinks in a cozy spot in the lobby. Even though he had turned down "The Best," I'd decided to let that go. Shit happens, and he was entitled to his opinion…it was his loss. It didn't stop me from liking him, nor should it have. Little by little everyone drifted off to their rooms, happily yawning and drunk, until it was just Paul and I alone in the corner by a fireplace. I was wondering if maybe I should leave too. I've always believed that it's better to leave the party while it's still good. But Paul looked me in the eyes and quietly said, "You're a very sexy woman." That was it: if he didn't take me up to his hotel room, I was dragging him up there.

Kathy and I took a train to Florence the next day where the next Eurythmics concert was, and she didn't have to ask. She knew by the cat-that-ate-the-canary grin on my face, and messy hair that I'd had a memorable evening.

Back to "The Best." I can't even take credit for getting the song to Tina Turner. It never occurred to me to send it to her because it had already been cut and released by Bonnie Tyler. I should've known from personal experience that that never stopped Tina from cutting a song if she wanted to do it. She was old school—in the days of Motown and Stax, songs would get cut over and over until someone had a hit with it.

As far as I know, a kid at EMI Publishing, Ron Handler, was the one who sent it to Tina's record company, and they sent it to Roger Davies for Tina. She called me up after hearing it and said, "Holly, I love this song and I want to cut it, but I need you to write me a bridge, and after the bridge, I want the key to go up a step when the chorus comes in. You know what I'm talkin' about?"

"Yes!" I said. I was so excited. This was the best news I could have gotten. "I'm sure Mike and I will come up with something terrific. Your suggestions are spot on." I asked her to give us a few days, so we could write the bridge and demo it.

"Fantastic. I'm excited, I can't wait to hear it," she said.

This is the first and only time I'd been asked to rewrite a song that had already been recorded and released. I hadn't talked to Mike in quite a while as things were still tense between us. After being signed to his publishing company for so long, I had chosen to move on and sign with EMI Publishing. He wasn't very happy about it. This would be a good opportunity to reconnect with him in the best way possible—creatively. I called him for the first time in months, and he seemed glad to hear from me, especially once I told him the good news. We made arrangements to meet in the morning at my house. When he walked through the door, we were so happy to see each other, which was always the way with us: we created, wrote hit songs, fought, flung insulting remarks at each other, things that in the end were petty and ego-driven on both sides. But we always managed to make up and carry on. That much was real. And we put all that passion into our songs.

We wrote a beautiful bridge and didn't bother redoing the whole demo. We just matched the tempo and sound and inserted it—no small feat at a time when digital recording didn't exist: you couldn't easily cut and paste a section in. Tina knew exactly what she was talking about. The song was much better and sounded like a hit now, even with the demo we'd made.

So, you might be wondering what it means to say, "It sounded like a hit now." What makes a hit anyway? I shy away from analyzing and dissecting my own songs. I think that demystifies them, but let me take a shot at it just this once: "The Best" has memorable music and a strong melody, the verses have romantic, well-written lyrics that set up the chorus beautifully, and the chorus itself is an anthem. The words convey a positive and loving message and are easy to sing along with. It has drama: "Tear us apart, baby I would rather be dead." It has passion: "I call you when I need you and my heart's on fire." And the bridge lifts the listener up to a higher plateau, setting up the emotional release of the final chorus with its key change. The whole end section sounds victorious and celebratory. "Ooh, you're the best!!"

It's a pretty simple song, but I've often found that the simplest tunes can be the hardest to write. "The Best" was a song that very much fit the times we were living in, and timing played an essential role in the trajectory of this song. It was the end of the eighties when we wrote it, the last of the feel-good times on many levels, the last of excess and partying, the last of blind innocence and a certain level of escapism and freedom. It was the decade where some of us went dancing and rollerblading in discos night after night, hung out in rock clubs, and went to concerts, head-banging to our favorite bands, when we all got away with sleeping with whomever we pleased if it pleased us, with some of us ingesting copious amount of drugs. The consequences have finally caught up with us, with the whole planet.

"The Best" had one other secret weapon that would push it over the edge. Tina. Turner. The Universe had been saving "The Best" for her.

First, Rick Nowels, an LA based songwriter and producer took a shot at producing "The Best" with Tina, but I never had a chance to hear that version, it disappeared that quickly. Then they brought in Dan Hartman, a very talented producer and songwriter with whom I had recently written "Time Waits for No One" for Dusty Springfield. I really enjoyed writing with him—he had such a genuine and kind personality. Dan was a great songwriter, having written "Free Ride" for Edgar Winter, as well as another fantastic song, "I Can Dream About You," which he performed himself.

Roger hired him to coproduce "The Best" with Tina. Suddenly, everything was coming together. Sadly, he died five years later from an AIDS-related brain tumor at the age of forty-four. He never got to see how successful "The Best" would become.

I was in New York when Tina recorded the master for "The Best" at The Hit Factory. It's probably one of the fondest memories I have of her. On that day she was feeling her oats, just one of the guys, a mere mortal instead of the elevated rock star that the rest of the world identified her as. Like Ann Wilson, there were other times when she put up a fortress that you couldn't penetrate, I'm sure in the interest of self-preservation. Tina was dressed down in faded jeans and a T-shirt. She ate some greasy French fries along with the rest of us. It was one of those rare moments when she let her guard down. I knew a bit about Tina's past, but it was only later, when her book, *I, Tina*, came out that I learned about the brutality she'd gone through with Ike Turner. While she had moved on, partly in thanks to her devout following of Buddhism, I knew from my own physical abuse at the hands of my mother, that the pain never completely leaves you.

What it does do is it helps you to become a survivor. And survivors always have the best stories to tell.

In addition to Dan, I knew several other people in the control room really well. Chris Lord-Alge was the recording engineer and Gene Black was the guitarist. I took pride in knowing I had discovered him. He is truly one of the best musicians I've ever worked with. Apparently, a lot of people thought so too because every time I introduced him to a recording artist I was writing for, they ended up hiring him to play on their record. Roger Davies was there too.

As I stood there watching Tina sing, I thought back to the beginning, to the first hit we'd had together on *Private Dancer*. That record sold twenty million copies. Twenty million. What Tina has done for me as a songwriter, not to mention as a woman trying to carve a place for herself in this world of ours, can't really be put into words. Out of the many artists I've written for, Tina is the one I feel most proud of. She is the best and the most inspiring, a phoenix who has risen from the ashes.

That day, she sang with the same passion and fire that I felt when I cowrote the song with Mike. In the back of the control room I noticed a midsized TV showing MTV with the sound turned down. MTV, the ever-present catalyst that bookended the eighties. This wasn't the last song I wrote for Tina, but it felt like a fitting close to that decade. Tina left a message on my phone once—"I want you to write me something like, 'Addicted To Love.' You're my little rocker, you write my rock songs." She recorded some more tunes of mine moving forward, but "The Best" was, and remains, the crown jewel in my catalogue, and I'd like to think that maybe it was in hers as well. Somehow, the things I wrote about and the music I created must have spoken to Tina, because she kept coming back for more. She could have recorded any number of songs by other songwriters, and she did—God knows everyone was vying to get a cut on her records—but she recorded nine songs of mine. She chose me.

I stood transfixed, watching her sing her heart out. It didn't take more than a few takes to nail it. Roger didn't waste any time. Once the record was mixed and mastered, Tina flew out to Los Angeles and filmed the video. Roger invited me to watch them film it and I drove into the valley to the massive hangar they had booked. I had no idea what the concept was going to be, but I was fascinated when I saw an elegantly dressed equestrian trainer walk in leading a beautiful stallion. For years I couldn't connect the dots—why was there a horse, beautiful as it was?—I didn't get it until years later when I saw an interview with Tina who said, "'The Best' is a special song…it could be about anything, a car, a person…a horse." Then I understood. I feel that way about my beautiful Siberian husky, Elektra.

Now, all the stars were aligned. The same song that had previously been released with another artist and barely made a blip on the radar was about to become the biggest hit of my career. I have to thank Tina for believing in the song, pushing us to make it better, and making it her personal anthem.

In addition to "The Best," I cowrote three other songs for *Foreign Affair* with Albert Hammond, the soulful "Be Tender with Me Baby," "Ask Me How I Feel," and "You Can't Stop Me Loving You."

I don't think I quite realized how universal "The Best" had become until one day, years later, a Russian plumber came to my house to fix a leaky pipe and saw the plaques on my studio wall.

"What are all these records for?" he asked suspiciously.

"I'm a songwriter."

"Are they real gold?" He was probably calculating what they would sell for on the black market.

"No, they're not."

He peered at some of the shiny Platinum records and said, "You wrote for Tina Turner?" Then he stared at me. "What did you write?"

I told him that I'd written "The Best." He gave me a blank look. Then, I remembered that many people think the title of the song is "Simply the Best," so I sang, "You're simply the best, better than all the rest..." and his lined face lit up as he broke into a big goofy grin and started singing along in his heavy Russian accent.

When *Foreign Affair* came out and "The Best" was released as the first single, it didn't do that well on the American charts. It stalled at number fourteen on Billboard, and while it did much better in the rest of the world, for all the impact it's made over the years, and all the success and accolades that it's received, you'd think it would have had reached number one. In this case, slow and steady wins the race.

Here it is, more than three decades later, and "The Best" just keeps on going. My guess is that maybe it gives us a chance to reflect on the beautiful things in our lives, to acknowledge the good that is always there if you look for it, even in the worst of times. Music has a way of transporting us, catapulting us into the future or taking us back to a time long past, back to what was happening the first time we heard someone sing something that profoundly changed our lives forever. For me, "The Best" poses a succinct and perfect ending to the eighties and everything I struggled so hard to achieve; it made the bad times tolerable and, as a result, forced me to become a stronger, better, and more resilient woman.

Pretty soon things would change, rock would morph into grunge and bizarre strains of music that had come before would still exist, only watered down and redundant. It became the antithesis of glamour and rock stardom. Platform boots and designer duds were traded for plaid shirts and negative attitudes, and a new term, "alternative rock," was concocted to describe the new breed of bands like Nirvana and Soundgarden. After Kurt Cobain died, they called it post-grunge, and so on and so on. House, techno, and industrial music emerged as times got more sinister and MTV changed, featuring more reality and game shows than music videos. The "M" didn't stand for music anymore. The pace of the world changed and started to move at lightning speed. There were extreme advances in technology as we entered a new age, the digital age, and a new millennium. Terrorism was on the rise as the Cold War ended...but before all that happened, there was MTV and there was The Eighties. And yes. I am the warrior. xx

AFTERWORD

New York City, 2013

The ballroom was dark but for the stage at the front of the room whose backdrop was decorated in a kind of caveman motif. How ironic that the producers for the annual Songwriters Hall of Fame gala had chosen this as their theme. Forty years earlier, I walked into the man cave of the music business without a clue or expectation—only a dream.

Strutting across the stage, Patty Smyth, along with a live band, performed "The Warrior" before an elite crowd of roughly one thousand industry people, an impressive turnout. The yearly event is the only one of its kind where the songwriters are the superstars, honored for their bodies of work. On this particularly balmy summer night, the audience was rowdier than usual. This year, the majority of the seven inductees being honored were rock royalty, and that alone was reason enough for the party atmosphere permeating the large ballroom.

"Well I am the warrior and heart to heart you win if you survive the warrior," she sung.

Among the two categories, Performing Songwriters, and Non-Performing Songwriters, the class of 2013 consisted of Steve Tyler and Joe Perry (Aerosmith), Mick Jones and Lou Gramm (Foreigner), and three non-performing songwriters, Tony Hatch, J. D. Souther, and yours truly.

Patty belted out the last line, "Victory is mine!"

By now, every attendee was on their feet, singing with fists raised. Even the piano man, Billy Joel, was up and singing his heart out. As the song ended, the crowd hollered and applauded. Previous inductees had included Burt Bacharach and Hal David, Bob Dylan, Mick Jagger and Keith Richards, David Bowie, Joni Mitchell, and the four members of Queen, all my idols.

Later that evening, during his acceptance speech, Steven Tyler summed it up succinctly—of all the awards he'd been given, including induction into the Rock & Roll Hall of Fame, this one was very special to him. Sting, a previous inductee who was there to perform, pretty much said the same thing in a speech he made that evening. To many artists, the Songwriters Hall of Fame is the holy grail. It honors the writers of timeless songs that touch people at the core of their being. In the best and worst of times, music is a touchstone that gets us through it all. And the songwriters that are able to do it, not just once, but over and over again, let's just say, they know what they're doing.

Patty Smyth, who had made "The Warrior" a classic, finished singing and shimmied over to the podium as the audience erupted into applause and whoops. As she began an empowering speech to induct me, my mind wandered back to when my legs didn't reach the floor as I climbed onto the piano bench and happily picked out my first notes on the piano. I was too young to have ambition; all I knew was the pure happiness it brought me.

Until that moment, the Hall had inducted a total of four hundred men and sixteen women. Of those sixteen women, only a few were songwriters for other artists; most were singer/songwriters like Joni Mitchell. Of the few that were just songwriters, I was the one woman who'd written rock songs for and with rock bands and solo artists. The audience cheered as Patty announced, "Ladies and gentlemen, tonight I'm honored to induct Holly Knight into the Songwriters Hall of Fame." All I could focus on was making it to the podium without tripping in my five-inch heels and long black gown. With the exception of two of the inductees that night, I'd written hits with all of them. I hadn't seen much of them in twenty years, yet there we were, together again, the class of 2013 Rock 'n' Roll High School. Everyone looked a little older and wiser.

I would be lying if I said it wasn't validating. While the success of my songs is all the proof I need to know that I've made my mark, the fact that my name stands alongside my idols who've been my inspiration—well, that's pretty thrilling.

By now, you've read a part of the wild ride that is my life. I've been married and divorced three times. I bore two incredible sons, Dylan and Tristan, from my second marriage, which lasted for ten years. They were born four years apart, almost to the day, on October tenth and eleventh.

In 1994, I sold my home in Bel Air and moved back east with my family to Fairfield, Connecticut, to give New England one last try, but after four dreadful years of cabin fever and winter weather, we admitted we'd made a mistake and moved back to Los Angeles, specifically to Pacific Palisades. We missed the ideal weather too much. After my second divorce, I found myself raising my children completely on my own, and I loved every single moment of it, although balancing full-time parenting with a substantial career wasn't without its challenges. Anyone who's a parent will understand what I mean.

I never stopped writing songs. New songs of mine still find their way onto artists' records, but it's not the exciting and fast pace I enjoyed back then. I am constantly finding ways to reinvent myself. I produce more records now with artists as varied as The Donnas and Otep. I teach master songwriting classes from time to time, which I enjoy. I have songs in two successful musicals, *Tina, The Tina Turner Musical* and *Moulin Rouge*, with another two on the way.

More than ever before, my songs are continually licensed for popular TV shows and movies, such as *G.L.O.W*, *Glee*, *South Park*, *Stranger Things*, *Schitt's Creek*, *Saturday Night Live*, the HBO Tina Turner documentary, and many more. In 2021, the same year that Tina released her doc, she was inducted into the Rock & Roll Hall of

Fame. Her record company asked me to write a two-thousand-word liner note for a special boxed set of *Foreign Affair*.

I hope that reading my memoirs has given you a glimpse not only of my life as a songwriter, but also of what was so fantastic about a very special time in history, the MTV eighties era. If you were there, maybe my memoir has made you smile or laugh out loud, reminiscing where you were when you heard this song or that one—or even "Love Is a Battlefield." If you weren't alive yet and hadn't lived through that period, maybe, for the time you were inside these stories, you'll wish you had.

Sure, times are different now. It takes a committee of people to write a song. Some of the biggest stars have been born out of TV competitions or shows on Nickelodeon, and hard rock has been relegated to an otherworldly universe of its own, for those loyal fans that still live and breathe it. Of course, I'm one of them.

I have the best job in the world. I want to say thank you to all the fans and music lovers because without you, all my efforts would be for naught. Thank you for sharing your love with me. To all my collaborators, cowriters, the bands, solo artists, engineers, producers, and artists, I love you all, and I hope you had as much fun as I did.

Tibetan monks have been practicing a ritual for centuries during which they create beautiful mandalas on the floors of their temples. They spend months pouring vivid colors of sand together into an intricate design, chanting and meditating as they do, creating a work of art together. When the design is complete, they stand back and admire it, saying a final prayer of gratitude, then open the doors of the temple and let the wind blow it all away. The mandala is dismantled to illustrate impermanence.

It was always about the doing, not the final destination. It was always about the journey, and this has been mine. So far...

With love,
Holly Knight

SONGS I WISH I HAD WRITTEN

How many times have I heard a song that moved me to the point of tears or deep emotion, a song so deep that it hit me in the heart or made me feel blissful and happy to be alive? Or maybe it was just the coolest song ever in its simplicity. I want to take a moment to name some of them and explain why I wish I could lay claim to writing them. What started out as a top ten list quickly became a top thirteen (in no particular order). I just couldn't stop at ten.

1. WALK ON THE WILD SIDE
Written and performed by Lou Reed

This is a song I have used over and over again as inspiration, consciously and unconsciously. "Better Be Good to Me" and "Obsession" are two examples. "Walk on the Wild Side" only has two main chords, leaving a lot of space for the lyrics and melody to breathe. The aforementioned two songs of mine are the same in that they rely only on two chords. Most of all, I love the lyrics, a narrative of the street culture at the time, reminding me that with rock 'n' roll, attitude is everything and simplicity is golden. "Hey babe, take a walk on the wild side."

2. CAN WE STILL BE FRIENDS
Written and performed by Todd Rundgren

Todd's music always lifts my spirits and makes me feel happy. There's something about the structure of his chords in all his songs that is uniquely Todd. For all you musos, I once stumbled upon what it was that gives him his unique musical imprint and came up with this: if you play, say, an F chord on a piano, the most obvious note to play on the bass would be the root note of the chord, which, in this case, would be an F. But Todd would play one note higher than the root on the bass and play a G. Try it in any key and you'll hear his musical imprint. That alone makes his songs great. And then there's his melodies and lyrics which can be sublime and quirky or beautifully simple.

"Memories linger on…it's like a sweet sad song."

It was a hard toss-up between this song and "Love is the Answer" or "Real Man." Over the years, I have been greatly inspired and influenced by Todd Rundgren.

3. SATISFACTION
Written by Mick Jagger and Keith Richards
Performed by the Rolling Stones

I can't put together a list like this and not mention any Stones songs. But which to choose? There are so many. I'll just have to be decisive and pick this one. "Satisfaction" is the epitome of a perfect rock song, starting with the iconic guitar riff, and the lyrics are all attitude-driven with such swagger.

"I can't get no satisfaction…'cause I try and I try and I try and I try…."

Even today the lyrics are as relevant as they were when the song was written. The perfect nymphomaniac song.

4. HOUSE OF THE RISING SUN
Writers: Unknown
Performed by the Animals

Because of the Animals' recording of this song in 1964, I've always thought of it as a rock song. For a while, I even thought that they wrote it, but it was a folk song written in the early 1900s in Appalachia that got passed from one artist to another, taking on several incarnations, sort of like a chain letter.

"It's been the ruin of many a poor boy…and god I know I'm one." "Poor boy" or not, it's been argued that the narrator was a woman, which wouldn't surprise me. It's been covered by so many artists including Bob Dylan, Woody Guthrie, and Lead Belly and is what is thought of as an "evergreen"—a classic well known song that will always stand the test of time and never die. Any song in a minor key with this much soulful howling and melody wins my heart. Like "Satisfaction," it is a musical oracle from whose well I often go back to take a drink of inspiration.

5. LIL' RED RIDING HOOD
Written by Ronald Blackwell
Performed by Sam the Sham and the Pharaohs

Musically, this song is similar to "House of the Rising Sun": it's written in a minor key, something I often like to write in. I love how the song-writer took the well-known fairy tale of "Little Red Riding Hood" and wrote a song playing with the original words, and turning it into an adult stalker tune.

"You're everything that a big bad wolf could want."

I'm always surprised by how few people know this song. It just missed hitting the number one spot in 1966, knocked out by "Wild Thing," another classic. I often use this one as inspiration when I want to write a darkly playful song. I have never tired of listening to it. There's even some wolf howling on the record, which always wins me over.

6. FRAGILE
Written and performed by Sting

From the beginning bars of the guitar intro, I was hooked the first time I heard this song. It has such grace, and, lyrically, it taps into the frailty of humans. The lyrics are gorgeous. Sting consistently writes intelligent and thought-provoking lyrics, but this one really touches my heart in a deep place. I've listened to this song so many times and cried.

> "On and on the rain will say how fragile we are, how fragile we are."

I used to hold my son Dylan when he was a baby, stare into his innocent eyes, and listen to this. It's one of those songs that really makes me feel vulnerable.

7. ONE OF US
Written by Eric Bazilian
Performed by Joan Osborne

I love how the lead guitar line and vocal melody on the chorus are the same. What a melody! The lyrics are so clever in the way they humanize the idea of God.

> "What if god was one of us, just a slob like one of us, just a stranger on the bus trying to find his way home."

Every component of this song is perfect. The first time I met Eric Bazilian, I told him that I wished I had written this song, and I bowed down to him. We became friends and eventually wrote a great song together, but it wasn't nearly as powerful as this.

8. I CAN'T MAKE YOU LOVE ME
Written by Mike Reid and Allen Shamblin
Performed by Bonnie Raitt

Great songs evoke emotions that touch people because they are so relatable. Who hasn't been in love with someone at some point in their life where it wasn't mutual? I certainly have, and it hurt like hell. The first time I heard this song, I felt the pain all over again. That's what a good song is supposed to do.

"I can't make you love me if you don't—
You can't make your heart feel something it won't."

Happy or sad, great songs are musical photographs that take you right back to that place like PTSD. It's as perfect a song as there is.

9. A CASE OF YOU
Written and performed by Joni Mitchell

It's so hard to narrow Joni Mitchell's body of work down to one song, but if I had to pick one, it would be this one. Such a simple chord progression and recording, but the lyrics are soul deep and so romantic.

"Oh, I could drink a case of you, darling...and I would
still be on my feet."

When I was about twelve, I taught myself how to play guitar with a Joni Mitchell songbook. Her lyrics are awe-inspiring. I also have to mention "Ladies of the Canyon" too. Each verse is a different archetype of a woman, which I've always found relatable.

10. HALLELUJAH
Written by Leonard Cohen
Performed Jeff Buckley

Leonard Cohen wrote vignettes on humanity and relationships, and put words together like pure poetry. While I love to listen to his voice, when I heard Jeff Buckley sing it, it brought me to my knees. I've heard this song in so many movies, with different plot lines, and "Hallelujah" works in all of them. I interpret the lyrics to mean: embrace everything and trust the process good or bad. The hallelujah is like an amen. I wish I wrote this song, but I don't even know if I'm capable of writing a lyric this good. I bow down to Leonard on this one.

11. THESE BOOTS ARE MADE FOR WALKING
Written by Lee Hazlewood
Performed by Nancy Sinatra

I think this is one of the best pop songs ever to come out of the sixties, and it still has a life of its own. Simple and catchy, with clever lyrics that slang all over the place with messin' and talkin.'

> "These boots are made for walkin' and that's
> just what they'll do,
> One of these days these boots are gonna
> walk all over you."

What a line! For its time, it was a pretty empowering song for a woman to sing and it's interesting that a man wrote it. I love the descending guitar line at the end of the chorus, and at the end of the song when Nancy says, "Start walking." I start strutting around the room. Classic.

12. JAMES BOND THEME
Written by John Barry

This song is part of the soundtrack to my life. Even without lyrics it has influenced me greatly. There is a huge controversy as to who the writer of this song is. I read that a writer named Monty Norman was hired to write the theme for the first James Bond movie, *Dr. No*. He claims to have written the theme and John Barry was brought in to arrange it. But John Barry said that he wrote the theme and I believe him. When I listen to the thirteen theme songs he wrote for subsequent James Bond movies following the first movie, and the eleven James Bond scores, there is such an obvious connection to the signature theme of the James Bond franchise. As a songwriter, I hear Barry's musical imprint on every song and every movie cue. I hear it in the movies, *Out of Africa* and *Dances with Wolves*. It's undeniable. I haven't heard anything of Monty Norman that sounds even remotely like this classic and instantly recognizable piece of music. Barry is a composer who won five Academy Awards and numerous Grammys, yet was denied a writer's credit for probably the most recognizable movie theme ever written. If this is true, not only was he robbed of the writer's credit, but millions and millions of dollars. Sadly, John Barry passed away in 2011.

I love to drive around in my Porsche listening to Bond music and pretending I'm a Bond girl.

13. THE LOOK OF LOVE
Written by Hal David and Burt Bacharach
Performed by Dusty Springfield

I can't possibly have a list of favorite songs without adding at least one song by this amazing songwriting team. This song was written in 1967, an era that profoundly affected my musical sensibility. I could just have easily named "Close to You," "This Guy's in Love with You," or "Raindrops Keep Fallin' on My Head." Hal and Burt were the kings of romantic pop songs.

> "The look of love…it's saying so much more than words could ever say."

Simple, yet deep at the same time. And the melody is downright sexy.

DISCOGRAPHY

SONG	ARTIST	ALBUM	YEAR
A			
"Alive"	Meatloaf	*Bat Out of Hell III: The Monster Is Loose*	2006
"All Eyes"	Heart	*Heart*	1985
"Angel Tonight"	Leigh Nash (Sixpence None The Richer)	*Blue on Blue*	2006
"Ask Me How I Feel"	Tina Turner	*Foreign Affair*	1989
B			
"Baby Me"	Chaka Khan	*CK*	1988
"The Best"	Tina Turner	*Foreign Affair* *Simply the Best* *All the Best* *Platinum Collection* *Tina: The Musical* cast recording	1989 1991 2005 2009 2019
"The Best"	Bonnie Tyler	*Hide Your Heart*	1988
"The Best"	Jimmy Barnes Anthology	*Jimmy Barnes Anthology*	1996
"The Best"	Wynonna Judd	*Her Story: Scenes From a Lifetime*	2005
"Babies"	Real Life	*Down Comes The Hammer*	1986
"Be Tender with Me Baby"	Tina Turner	*Foreign Affair*	1989
"Better Be Good to Me"	Tina Turner	*Private Dancer* *Miami Vice* soundtrack	1984 1991
"Between Two Fires"	Jimmy Barnes	*Two Fires*	1990

C			
"Change"	John Waite	*Ignition* *Visionquest* soundtrack *Anchorman II* soundtrack	1982 1985 2013
D			
"Do Something"	Tina Turner	*On Silent Wings*	1996
"Don't Look Back"	Grayson Hugh	*Road to Freedom* *Thelma and Louise* soundtrack	1992 1991
F			
"Fear of the Unknown"	Suzi Quatro	*Fear of the Unknown*	1993
"Force to Be Reckoned With"	Cherie Currie (the Runaways)	*Blvds of Splendor*	2020
G			
"Girl"	Pat Benatar	*Go*	2003
H			
"Hands Tied"	Patty Smyth (Scandal)	*The Warrior*	1984
"Here's Comes the Bride"	Elvira Mistress Of the Dark	*Haunted Hits*	1994
"Heart Don't Fail Me Now"	Holly Knight	*Holly Knight*	1988
"Here for the Party"	The Donnas	*Bitchin'*	2007
"Hide Your Heart"	KISS	*Hot in the Shade*	1988
"Hide Your Heart"	Ace Frehley	*Trouble Walkin'*	1989
"Hide Your Heart"	Bonnie Tyler	*Hide Your Heart*	1988
"Hide Your Heart"	Molly Hatchett	*Lightning Strikes Twice*	1989
"Hold on to the Good Things"	Shawn Colvin	*Stuart Little II* soundtrack	2002
I			
"I Burn for You"	Nancy Shanks/ Danny Peck	*The Secret of My Success* soundtrack	1987
"I Burn for You"	Chris Max	*Christopher Max*	1989

"I Can't Untie You from Me"	Grayson Hugh	*Road to Freedom* *Thelma and Louise* soundtrack	1992 1991
"I Engineer"	Animotion	*Strange Behavior*	1986
"I Love You"	Heart	*Brigade*	1990
"I Pledge Allegiance (to the State of Rock & Roll)"	KISS	*Psycho Circus*	1998
"Invincible"	Pat Benatar	*Seven the Hard Way* *The Legend of Billie Jean* soundtrack	1985 1985
"It's Over when the Phone Stops Ringing"	Eighth Wonder of The World	*Fearless*	1988
J			
"Just Between You and Me"	Lou Gramm (Foreigner)	*Long Hard Look*	1989
L			
"Little Darlin'"	Rachel Sweet	*And Then He Kissed Me*	1981
"Little Darlin'"	Sheila B Devotion	*Little Darlin'*	1981
"Looking Daggers"	Smokie	*Strangers in Paradise*	1982
"Love Is a Battlefield"	Pat Benatar	*Live from Earth* *13 Going on 30* soundtrack	1983 2004
"Love Is a Battlefield"	Queen Latifah/ Pat Benatar	*Small Soldiers* soundtrack	1998
"Love Is a Battlefield"	Cee Lo Green	*The Voice*	2011
"Love Is a Battlefield"	Luke Evans	*At Last*	2018
"Love Is a Battlefield"	Raining Jane	*The Other Woman* soundtrack	2014
"Love Thing"	Tina Turner	*Simply The Best*	1991
"Love Touch"	Rod Stewart	*Every Beat of My Heart* *Legal Eagles* soundtrack	1986 1986
M			
"My Heart Is Failing Me"	Riff	*Riff*	1991

"Monstro"	Meatloaf	*Bat Out of Hell III: The Monster Is Loose*	2006
N			
"Never"	Heart	*Heart*	1985
"New Romance"	Spider	*Spider*	1980
"Not the Same"	Hawk Nelson	*Hawk Nelson Is My Friend*	2008
O			
"The One"	Rev Theory	*Light It Up*	2008
"Obsession"	Animotion	*Animotion* *Hot Tub Time Machine* *What The Bleep* *Do We Know* *Nip Tuck* *The Following* *Dirty John* *The Hitman's Wife's Bodyguard* *Fresh*	1983 2004 2004 2006 2013 2018 2018 2022
"Obsession"	The Yeah Yeahs	*Flesh & Bone* soundtrack	2015
"One of the Living"	Tina Turner	*Mad Max Beyond Thunderdome* soundtrack	1985
"Overrated"	Less Than Jake	*In with the Out Crowd*	2006
P			
"Perfectly Flawed"	Otep	*Ascension*	2007
"Pleasure and Pain"	Divinyls	*Oh What a Life!*	1985
R			
"Ragdoll"	Aerosmith	*Permanent Vacation*	1987
"Raise Your Glasses"	KISS	*Psycho Circus*	1998
"Rendezvous"	Hunter Valentine	*Lessons From Late Night*	2010
"Road to Freedom"	Grayson Hugh	*Road to Freedom*	1992
S			
"The Sanctuary" (Full Version)	Darling Violetta	*Angel: Live Fast, Die Never* soundtrack	2005
"Sometimes the Good Guys Finish First"	Pat Benatar	*The Secret to My Success* soundtrack	1987

"Soul Love"	Hall & Oates	*Ooh Yeah*	1988
"Space"	Cheap Trick	*Lap of Luxury*	1988
"Space"	Charlie Sexton	*Pictures for Pleasure*	1985
"Stick to Your Guns"	Bon Jovi	*New Jersey*	1988
"Stiletto"	Lita Ford	*Stiletto*	1994
T			
"Tall Dark Handsome Stranger"	Heart	*Brigade*	1985
"Temptation"	Zander	*Zander*	2012
"There's the Girl"	Heart	*Bad Animals*	1987
"Time Waits for No One"	Dusty Springfield	*Reputation*	1989
"Try a Little Harder"	Aaron Neville	*Tattooed Heart*	1995
"Turn It On"	Marilyn Martin	*Marilyn Martin*	1986
"Turn It On"	Kim Wilde	*Weird Science* soundtrack	1985
"The Warrior"	Patty Smyth featuring Scandal	*The Warrior*	1984
"Wasted"	The Donnas	*Bitchin'*	2007
"Wildest Dreams"	Tina Turner	*Silent Wings*	1996
"Whatever Love Is"	Suzi Quatro	*In the Spotlight*	2011
"Where Were You"	Bonnie Tyler	*Bitter Blue*	1992
"Wrap Your Arms Around Me"	Agnetha Fältskog (ABBA)	*Wrap Your Arms Around Me*	1983
Y			
"You Can't Stop Me Loving You"	Tina Turner	*Foreign Affair*	1989
"You Make Me Happy"	Will Hoge	*Still Standing* soundtrack	2002
"You're a Woman Now"	Otep	*Smash the Control Machine*	2001
Personal Discography			
"New Romance"	Spider	*Spider*	1980
"Everything Is Alright"	Spider	*Spider*	1980

"Little Darlin'"	Spider	*Spider*	1980
"Burning Love"	Spider	*Spider*	1980
"Don't Waste Your Time"	Spider	*Spider*	1980
"Better Be Good to Me"	Spider	*Between the Lines*	1981
"Change"	Spider	*Between the Lines*	1981
"Can't Live This Way Anymore"	Spider	*Between the Lines*	1981
"Go and Run"	Spider	*Between the Lines*	1981
"It Didn't Take Long"	Spider	*Between the Lines*	1981
"Obsession"	Knight & Des Barres	*A Night in Heaven*	1983
"Hanging on a Heart Attack"	Device	*22B3*	1986
"Who Says"	Device	*22B3*	1986
"When Love Is Good"	Device	*22B3*	1986
"Sand, Stone, Cobwebs, and Dust"	Device	*22B3*	1986
"Who's on the Line"	Device	*22B3*	1986
"Pieces on the Ground"	Device	*22B3*	1986
"Fall Apart Golden Heart"	Device	*22B3*	1986
"I've Got No Room 4 Your Love"	Device	*22B3*	1986
"Tough and Tender"	Device	*22B3*	1986
"Didn't I Read You Right"	Device	*22B3*	1986
"Heart Don't Fail Me Now"	Holly Knight	*Holly Knight*	1988
"Sexy Boy"	Holly Knight	*Holly Knight*	1988
"Every Man's Fear"	Holly Knight	*Holly Knight*	1988
"Palace of Pleasure"	Holly Knight	*Holly Knight*	1988
"It's Only Me"	Holly Knight	*Holly Knight*	1988

"Nature of the Beast"	Holly Knight	*Holly Knight*	1988
"Howling at the Moon"	Holly Knight	*Holly Knight*	1988
"Love Is a Battlefield"	Holly Knight	*Holly Knight*	1988
"Baby Me"	Holly Knight	*Holly Knight*	1988
"Why Don't You Love Me Like You Used To"	Holly Knight	*Holly Knight*	1988

SONG PERMISSIONS

"Love Is A Battlefield"
Words and Music by **Holly Knight** and Michael Donald Chapman
© **1983 Primary Wave Anthems (ASCAP) / Knighty Knight Music (ASCAP)**
All Rights for BMG Rights Management (US) LLC
Used by Permission. All Rights Reserved.

BMG Gold Songs (ASCAP) administers **50.00%** for the **United States** obo **Holly Knight / Primary Wave Anthems (ASCAP) / Knighty Knight Music (ASCAP)**.

"Invincible"
Words and Music by **Holly Knight and Simon Climie**
© **1985 BMG Rights Management (UK) Limited (PRS)/ Primary Wave Anthems (ASCAP) / Knighty Knight Music (ASCAP)**
All Rights for BMG Rights Management (US) LLC
Used by Permission. All Rights Reserved.

BMG Monarch (ASCAP) subpublishes **50.00%** obo **BMG Rights Management (UK) Limited (PRS)** for the **WORLD** obo **Simon Crispin Climie**
BMG Gold Songs (ASCAP) administers **50.00%** for the **United States** obo **Holly Knight / Primary Wave Anthems (ASCAP) / Knighty Knight Music (ASCAP)**.

"The Warrior"
Words and Music by **Holly Knight and Nick Gilder**
© **1984 BMG Blue (BMI) / Primary Wave Anthems (ASCAP) / Knighty Knight Music (ASCAP)**
All Rights for BMG Rights Management (US) LLC
Used by Permission. All Rights Reserved.

BMG Blue (ASCAP) claims **50.00%** for the **WORLD** obo **Nick Gilder**
BMG Gold Songs (ASCAP) administers **50.00%** for the **United States** obo **Holly Knight / Primary Wave Anthems (ASCAP) / Knighty Knight Music (ASCAP)**.

"Obsession"
Words and Music by **Holly Knight** and Michael Philip Desbarres
© **1984 Primary Wave Anthems (ASCAP) / Knighty Knight Music (ASCAP)**
All Rights for BMG Rights Management (US) LLC
Used by Permission. All Rights Reserved.

BMG Gold Songs (ASCAP) administers **50.00%** for the **United States** obo **Holly Knight / Primary Wave Anthems (ASCAP) / Knighty Knight Music (ASCAP)**.

"Better Be Good To Me"
Words and Music by **Holly Knight**, Nicky Chinn and Michael Donald Chapman
© **1984 Primary Wave Anthems (ASCAP) / Knighty Knight Music (ASCAP)**
All Rights for BMG Rights Management (US) LLC
Used by Permission. All Rights Reserved.

BMG Gold Songs (ASCAP) administers **33.34%** for the **United States** obo **Holly Knight / Primary Wave Anthems (ASCAP) / Knighty Knight Music (ASCAP)**.

"The Best"
Words and Music by **Holly Knight** and Michael Donald Chapman
© **1989 BMG Rights Management (UK) Limited (PRS)/Knighty Knight Music (ASCAP)**
All Rights for BMG Rights Management (US) LLC
Used by Permission. All Rights Reserved.

BMG Gold Songs (ASCAP) subpublishes **37.50%** obo **BMG Rights Management (UK) Limited (PRS)** for the **WORLD** obo **Holly Knight / Knighty Knight Music (ASCAP)**.

"Love Touch"
Words and Music by **Holly Knight**, Michael Donald Chapman and Walter Eugene Bloch
© **1986 Primary Wave Anthems (ASCAP) / Knighty Knight Music (ASCAP)**
All Rights for BMG Rights Management (US) LLC
Used by Permission. All Rights Reserved.

BMG Gold Songs (ASCAP) administers **40.00%** for the **United States** obo **Holly Knight / Primary Wave Anthems (ASCAP) / Knighty Knight Music (ASCAP)**.

"Hanging On A Heart Attack"
Words and Music by **Holly Knight** and Michael Donald Chapman
© **1986 Primary Wave Anthems (ASCAP) / Knighty Knight Music (ASCAP)**
All Rights for BMG Rights Management (US) LLC
Used by Permission. All Rights Reserved.

BMG Gold Songs (ASCAP) administers **50.00%** for the **United States** obo **Holly Knight / Primary Wave Anthems (ASCAP) / Knighty Knight Music (ASCAP)**.

"Hide Your Heart"
Words and Music by **Holly Knight**, Paul Stanley and Desmond Child
© **1989 Primary Wave Anthems (ASCAP) / Knighty Knight Music (ASCAP)**
All Rights for BMG Rights Management (US) LLC
Used by Permission. All Rights Reserved.

BMG Gold Songs (ASCAP) administers **25.00%** for the **WORLD** obo **Holly Knight / Knighty Knight Music (ASCAP)**.

"Pleasure And Pain"
Words and Music by **Holly Knight** and Michael Donald Chapman
© **1985 Primary Wave Anthems (ASCAP) / Knighty Knight Music (ASCAP)**
All Rights for BMG Rights Management (US) LLC
Used by Permission. All Rights Reserved.

"Never"
Words and Music by **Holly Knight**, Walter Eugene Bloch, Nancy Wilson and Ann Wilson
© **1985 Primary Wave Anthems (ASCAP) / Knighty Knight Music (ASCAP)**
All Rights for BMG Rights Management (US) LLC
Used by Permission. All Rights Reserved.

"Soul Love"
Words and Music by **Holly Knight** and Daryl Hall
© **1988 BMG Rights Management (UK) Limited (PRS)/Knighty Knight Music (ASCAP)**
All Rights for BMG Rights Management (US) LLC
Used by Permission. All Rights Reserved.

"Stick To Your Guns"
Words and Music by **Holly Knight**, Richard Sambora and Jon Bon Jovi
© **1989 Primary Wave Anthems (ASCAP) / Knighty Knight Music (ASCAP)**
All Rights for BMG Rights Management (US) LLC
Used by Permission. All Rights Reserved.

"One Of The Living"
Words and Music by **Holly Knight**, Richard Sambora and Jon Bon Jovi
© **1985 Primary Wave Anthems (ASCAP) / Knighty Knight Music (ASCAP)**
All Rights for BMG Rights Management (US) LLC
Used by Permission. All Rights Reserved.

"Slow Burn"
Words and Music by **Holly Knight** and James Michael Reyne
© **1989 Knighty Knight Music (ASCAP)**
All Rights for BMG Rights Management (US) LLC
Used by Permission. All Rights Reserved.

ACKNOWLEDGMENTS

Special thanks to: John Silberstack, my literary agent; Permuted Press and my editor Jacob Hoye; my copy editor Devan Murphy; my managing editor Heather King; Tina Fasbender, my business manager and dear friend for thirty-six years of support and friendship, thank you for understanding the nut that I am, hard on the outside and soft on the inside; Chris Epting, the Larry to my Richard and my literary coach; my little men, Dylan and Tristan, you're my best and proudest accomplishment; my beautiful wolf Elektra; MTV and the original five VJs: Mark Goodman, Nina Blackwood, Alan Hunter, Martha Quinn, and J.J. Jackson. And all the VJs over the years; Lissa Forehan, my bestie; Cassandra Peterson, my not-as-dark-as-everyone-thinks-bestie; Mike Chapman, my creative soulmate; Tina Turner, my greatest muse, you are better than all the rest; Chris Lord-Alge, my Jersey boy with the magic ears; Larry Mestel and the Primary Wave family; Lita Singer, my spiritual guide, you are sorely missed; Morticia Addams; Kathy Valentine; Bill Aucoin; Gary Gilbert; Conrad Rippy; Eric Custer; Jeremy Rosen; Paul Young for not recording "The Best"; James Bond; Roger Davies; Gordana Lazarevich; Dayna Steele, for getting women played on the radio; Bill Pfordresher, for always helping to plug my songs; Ken Nahoum; my bro Robert Erlanger; Erica, Sidonie, and Alex; and my little faery queen, Sasha.

Heartfelt thanks and deepest appreciation to all the people I worked and created with, and to all the coolest of musicians that I met along the way, whom I'm proud to call my friends: Steven Tyler, Steve Vai, Nancy Wilson, Ann Wilson, Patty Smyth, Pat Benatar, Robin Zander, Daryl Hall, Rod Stewart, Nick Gilder, Paul Stanley,

Gene Simmons, Ace Frehley, Ozzy and Sharon Osbourne, Matt Beard, Bon Jovi, Lena Hall, Peter Frampton, Albert Hammond, Keith Lentin, Anton Fig, Jimmy Lowell, Phil Lewis, Chrissy Amphlett, Rita Wilson, Lou Gramm, Gene Black, Phil X, Matt Laug, Billy Steinberg, Charlie Midnight, Andrea Remanda, Antonia Bennett, Ridley Scott, Jace Everett, Billy Idol, Mike Porcaro, JJ Farris, Keith Emerson, Rudy Sarzo, Otep, Mike Plotnikoff, the Donnas, Sasha Krivtsov, Benise, Simon Climie, Animotion, Chaka Khan, Elvira, Michael Des Barres, Gray Russell, John Waite, Robert Plant, and James McCaffrey.

And finally, a heartfelt thank you and big hug to all the fans and lovers of music, without you, where would I be?

ABOUT THE AUTHOR

Photo by Matt Beard Photography / mattbeard.com

Throughout the 1980s, Holly Knight didn't just compose anthems that became the soundtrack for millions of people's lives, she also created and crafted empowering odes to independence, liberation and equality—and her work helped define the MTV 1980s. These universal themes have never been more relevant than they are today, which is why we still hear her music every day. On television, films, and commercials, Knight's work has become not just ubiquitous, but also generation-defining.

Her songs have appeared in movies as varied as *Mad Max Beyond Thunderdome*, *Thelma and Louise*, *Thirteen Going On Thirty*, *Anchorman ll*, *Dallas Buyers Club*, *The Other Woman*, and have featured on TV shows including *Schitt's Creek*, *GLOW*, *Stranger Things*, *The Masked Singer*, *Saturday Night Live*, *The Tonight Show Starring Jimmy Fallon*, *American Idol*, *The Voice*, *The Simpsons*, *South Park*, and *Family Guy*.

In 2013, Knight was inducted into the Songwriters Hall of Fame.